Hate Crim

Since the ... ... of *Hate Crime* in 2005, interest in this subj... ... ... political domain has grown considerably both in Brita... ... North America, but significantly also in many other parts of the world. As such, this second edition fully revises and updates the content of the first, but within a broader international context.

Building on the success of the first edition, this accessible, cross-disciplinary text also includes a wider range of international issues, and addresses new and emerging areas of concern within the field. The book will be of particular interest to academics, undergraduate and postgraduate students, criminal justice practitioners, and policymakers working within the area of hate crime and related fields of crime, social justice and diversity. It will also be of value to others who may hold a more general interest in what is undoubtedly a rapidly evolving and increasingly important area of contemporary and global social concern.

Nathan Hall is a Principal Lecturer in Criminology and Policing at the Institute of Criminal Justice Studies at the University of Portsmouth. He is a member of the Cross-Government Hate Crime Independent Advisory Group and the Association of Chief Police Officers Hate Crime Working Group. Nathan has also acted as an independent member of the UK government hate crime delegation to the Organization for Security and Co-operation in Europe, and is a member of the Crown Prosecution Service (Wessex) Independent Strategic Scrutiny and Involvement Panel.

Hate Crime
Second edition

Nathan Hall

Routledge
Taylor & Francis Group

LONDON AND NEW YORK

First published 2005
This edition published 2013
by Routledge
2 Park Square, Milton Park, Abingdon, Oxon, OX14 4RN

Simultaneously published in the USA and Canada
by Routledge
711 Third Avenue, New York, NY 10017

Routledge is an imprint of the Taylor & Francis Group, an informa business

British Library Cataloguing in Publication Data
A catalogue record for this book is available from the British Library

Library of Congress Cataloging in Publication Data
A catalog record has been requested for this book

ISBN: 978-0-415-54026-1 (hbk)
ISBN: 978-0-415-54027-8 (pbk)
ISBN: 978-0-203-10742-3 (ebk)

Typeset in Times New Roman
by Cenveo Publisher Services

Printed and bound in Great Britain by
CPI Group (UK) Ltd, Croydon, CR0 4YY

We shall not cease from exploration
And the end of all our exploring
Will be to arrive where we started
And know the place for the first time.
T. S. Eliot
Four Quartets

Contents

Illustrations

Figures

Tables

Acknowledgements

Writing a second edition is an interesting experience. If you have read the first edition then you will notice that this book is quite different. Contrary to the helpful views of some of my friends expressed at the outset, the process did involve slightly more than just 'digging out the first edition and changing a few dates'. Indeed, such are the changes to this edition that it has been like writing a completely new book. So in addition to an opportunity to thank those who have contributed to the development of this second edition who perhaps weren't around for the first, I also now have the chance to thank, and apologise to, those to whom I faithfully promised never to put through this again. So to everyone, be they friends, family or colleagues, who have found themselves having to be a bit (or a lot) more patient with me than normal in recent months, I offer both my sincere thanks and my apologies. I won't do it again. Ok, I probably will, but for now let's just pretend I won't.

One always writes a book by oneself, but one is never alone in the process. As such I am indebted to a great many people who have variously offered support and guidance, shared ideas and conversations, provided insights and opportunities, and delivered encouragement and inspiration. In particular, as ever, I owe a huge debt of gratitude to John Grieve, without whom I wouldn't be writing this. I am also grateful to Paul Giannasi, Kathryn Stone, Abbee Corb, Michael Whine, Mike Ainsworth, Iqbal Bhana, Sylvia Lancaster, Doreen Lawrence, Neville Lawrence, Ruth Barnett and to all of my colleagues on the Cross-Government Hate Crime Independent Advisory Group. The passion that you all share for this subject is a continual source of inspiration.

I am also very grateful to all of my friends for providing encouragement and welcome distraction in (mostly) equal measure. In particular, Andy Williams, with whom sharing a decent bottle of red continues to be a great pleasure, and a vital part of the process of thinking and writing; Frank Dwyer, with whom I am often fortunate enough to share many a pleasant evening discussing all manner of things whilst taking in the Manhattan skyline; and Neil Turitz, whose inspired writing of a different kind is taking us to some pretty exciting new places – loving working with you buddy!

Particular thanks also to Nathan Bishop, Oliver Windsor and Sharon Cicco, who have all been there throughout. Thanks also to Russell Glass, especially for the games of Words with Friends, which provided a frequent welcome distraction (but also probably delayed the production of this book a bit!). A special mention too for Clive Douglas. Thank you for inspiring a passion for learning and teaching all those years ago.

I am also grateful to my friends and colleagues at the University of Portsmouth, and to my student classes of 2012/13, who, by a majority verdict, are responsible for the choice of cover on the paperback edition of this book. Thanks also to Tom and Nicola at Routledge, and to Maire Harris for being a very patient and understanding copy editor! It has been a pleasure working with you.

The biggest thanks of all though go to those closest to me, who have been a continual source of support and encouragement throughout – my parents, my grandfather and Sarah, who has had to redefine the meaning of 'patience'. I am more grateful than you know.

And finally, a special thank you to Lilly-Rose and Mason for the daily smiles and waves on the way to school. When one spends their time immersed in a subject such as hate crime there is something very refreshing in the reminder that there can be a point in life when your biggest source of anxiety is where your next finger painting is coming from, and when you can have a completely unshakeable belief that all the world's problems can be solved by Batman (or Spiderman, depending on your superhero leanings that day). If only.

Foreword to the second edition

In 1993, at about the time of Stephen Lawrence's racist murder, the Metro-politan Police Service was renovating its London-wide system of local intelligence cells. One of the models we were using was drawn from the intelligence system used during the Battle of the Atlantic by the Royal Navy and Royal Canadian Navy as they fought against the Nazi U-boats during the Second World War. One of the elements we uncovered, and one that was of considerable interest to us, was the use of academics as analysts at different points in the process. If it was good enough for Churchill, it was good enough for us. Would that we had moved faster, then the kind of thinking that emerges from this book could have figured in our tactical doctrine, investigations and prevention campaigns.

Despite some initial internal police administrative difficulties, the academic, in the role of analyst and researcher, appeared in the intelligence cells and was given added impetus by advisory groups in counter-terrorism, and by the findings of the Stephen Lawrence Public Inquiry in 1999 and the resulting evidence of, inter alia, intelligence failure. Nathan Hall was one of the first of those early academics who made the perilous descent into the fetid gutters of anti-racist policing. As a result, the material gathered here is of significance to any assessment of progress in the 'hate crime' agenda since the murder of Stephen Lawrence.

Nathan now sits on the Cross-Government Hate Crime Independent Advisory Group (whose membership contains many of the activists who have driven innovations for nearly a decade and a half) providing some useful continuity between academia and research and policy and practice that has challenged thinking, held people to account, exported UK thinking across the world and developed practical responses to the problems of hate crime not just for policing, but also for other agencies and organisations. He has pulled many of these elements together in this useful new volume. It is extraordinarily reassuring that the publishers have decided to produce this second edition, and it is a measure of the continuing importance of Nathan's work.

It is a great pleasure to write this foreword to an important contribution to what has been called 'public impact criminology', with immediate outcomes both in terms of academic knowledge and learning, and for policy and practice. For practitioners it is another contribution to their toolbox. It will prevent some crimes and lead to the arrest and conviction of offenders – what more could the intelligence–academic nexus wish for?

Prof. John G. D. Grieve CBE QPM
Independent Chair of the Cross-Government Hate
Crime Independent Advisory Group
June 2013

Preface

Since the publication of the first edition of this book in 2005, interest in hate crime as both a scholarly and political domain has increased considerably. Moreover, this surge in interest has not just been confined to the UK and the US, where the focus has predominantly been located over the past thirty years or so – these domains have also been growing, albeit at different rates and with different emphases, in many other countries around the world. This second edition seeks to reflect these developments.

Arguably, criminology is about seeking answers to seven basic questions – *What is the problem? When is it occurring? Where is it occurring? How much of it is there? Who is involved or affected? Why is it occurring? And what should we do to make the problem better?* – and although there is often some overlap, it is within a framework of these seven questions that this book is written.

Chapter One seeks to address the first question – *what is hate crime?* Before we can begin to examine any of the other issues relating to the subject, it is, of course, crucial that we have a clear understanding of what it is we are talking about. The question 'what is hate crime?' may seem straightforward, but providing an accurate answer is fraught with difficulties. Like any other crime, hate crime is a social construct, but there is little consensus amongst academics, policymakers or practitioners about what hate crime actually is. Chapter one therefore examines the social construction of hate crime through a consideration of the various attempts that have been made to define it. The chapter also examines the inherent difficulties associated with defining hate crime and discusses the considerable implications of the various attempts to do so.

The second question – *when is it occurring?* – is the subject of *Chapter Two*. Societal concern with hate crime is a relatively recent development, but given that 'hate', in its contemporary meaning at least, is a normal and natural part of being human, it seems reasonable to suggest that discriminatory acts motivated by prejudicial attitudes will have a lengthy history. This is indeed what we find in chapter two, where it is argued that whilst societal interest may only be contemporary, in fact examples of behaviours, some of them very violent indeed, that we would now label as hate crimes are littered throughout history. The juxtaposition of a 'relatively old problem' and 'relatively new concern about it' presents us with an interesting supplementary question – *why is it that we have only relatively recently taken an interest in hate crime as a problem in need of comprehension and of resolution?* In this chapter, then, we also chart the emergence of hate crime as a contemporary socio-legal problem in the US and England and Wales, and in doing so identify a number of key historical, and not so historical, milestones that have played important roles in shaping scholarly and political interest today. We also discuss the outcomes of this process in the form of the various legislative provisions that have emerged in an attempt to combat the hate crime problem.

Our third question – *where is it occurring?* – and aspects of our fourth question – *how much of it is there?* – are the focus of *Chapter Three*. Searching for the answers to these questions is far from straightforward though, not least because of the complexities associated with the various ways in which hate crime is defined and conceptualised in different parts of the world. Our journey across *The international geography* of hate reveals a very mixed picture, from countries where hate crimes seemingly occur with worrying regularity, to others where, officially at least, none occur at all. Of course this picture serves to highlight many of the issues relating to the social construction of hate crime that we highlight as being of critical importance in chapter one. So beyond simply examining what is officially happening (or in some cases isn't happening) in different countries across the world, chapter three also considers the evidence presented by those seeking to expose the 'realities' behind the various official accounts of the hate crime problem. As far as is possible, then, chapter three concerns itself with *what*, and *how much* of what, is happening *where*.

Our fifth question – *who is involved or affected?* – relates predominantly to *Chapter Four*, where we consider victims and victimisation, but also overlaps with *Chapter Six*, where our focus is on offenders and offending. Whilst the latter is for the most part best left for our penultimate question, below, the former concentrates our attention on those who are on the receiving end of expressions of negative prejudice. Once again, the expansive nature of hate crime, itself a product of the issues discussed in chapter one, means that identifying who the victims of hate crime are, or might be, is not as straightforward as one might think. In this chapter, then, we discuss the extent, nature and impact of hate crime on those who might be regarded as the 'traditional' targets of hate, but also on those who 'stretch the boundaries' of contemporary conceptualisations of hate crime.

Our penultimate question – *Why is it occurring?* – is the subject of *Chapters Five* and *Six*. One thing that will quickly become clear is that this tiny, four-letter word 'hate' masks a number of complexities that profoundly affect our understanding of why people commit hate crimes. This is in part because when we talk about 'hate' in the context of 'hate crime', we often find that what we really mean is *prejudice*. But prejudice is a far more expansive concept than hate, covering a far wider range of human emotions, and this rather complicates our understanding of hate crimes and why they occur. Chapter five therefore examines the origins of prejudice and hatred, and asks where they come from, how they develop and how they lead to expressions of violent behaviour. The chapter also dispels the common myth that hatred is an abnormal trait that 'bad people' have by arguing that the very foundations for hateful expression are entirely normal to the human condition.

Frustratingly though, as we shall also see in chapter five, despite being one of the most researched aspects of social psychology, none of the vast available literature on prejudice and hatred provides us with a causal link between prejudice and its physical expression in the form of violent behaviour. Consequently, our search for answers to the *'why?'* question necessarily spill over into *Chapter Six* where we extend our search for explanations of causation to other branches of the social sciences. In this chapter, then, we consider a range of explanatory frameworks from across the disciplines and examine what they have to offer in terms of furthering our understanding of hate crime offending and perpetrator behaviour.

Of course, finding answers to the *'why?'* question is crucial if we are to satisfactorily address the challenges presented by our final question – *what should we do to make the problem better?* As we shall see, however, our inability to provide concrete answers to the former has considerably hindered our ability to provide effective solutions to the problem of hate crime. Consequently, a range of different intervention possibilities exist, and these form the basis of *Chapter Seven*, where we discuss law and law enforcement responses, and *Chapter Eight*, where we consider and evaluate other approaches to intervention and prevention. The message from both of these chapters is, in essence, that there is a great deal of uncertainty concerning which approaches work most effectively and under what circumstances, and ultimately this is a product of similar uncertainties in the answering of the six preceding questions.

The absence of clear and concise answers to each of these seven questions, and the inherent complexities involved in trying to find those answers, has, perhaps unsurprisingly, made the field of hate crime rather fertile for those who question its very existence on moral, theoretical, philosophical and practical grounds. As such, *Chapter Nine* is dedicated to exploring both sides of the argument for and against the existence of hate crime as a distinct category of crime. Here I have attempted to present a balanced account of the issues from both perspectives, although I confess to taking on the role of devil's advocate a little in places. I make no apology for doing so though. It is my belief that the very real concerns of critics have not been challenged in their entirety and still need to be taken seriously, and should serve as something of an inspiration to everyone seeking to find better answers to the questions that remain unsatisfactorily answered.

For me, addressing the concerns of critics therefore represents a critical issue in our subject area. After all, if the critics are correct, and our subject is fatally flawed in any or all of the moral, theoretical, philosophical and practical dilemmas that cause such intellectual debate and consternation, then there really isn't too much left to say. As such, in *Chapter Ten* we shall consider some of the rebuffs made by proponents in response to the challenges thrown down by opponents. Ultimately, I take the view that hate crime *should* be viewed as a distinct category of crime, which then necessarily leaves us with much to do in order to address the gaps that exist in our knowledge and understanding. It also leaves us with a number of other critical issues to attend to, and we shall identify and discuss some of these in chapter ten as well.

Finally, in the *Conclusions* we shall revisit each of the seven questions posed here at the outset and attempt to take stock of what we know, what we think we know, what we don't know, and in what direction(s) we perhaps ought to be heading. It is in this spirit that I have included the quote from T. S. Eliot at the start of this book. So, let's begin our exploring, and having searched for answers to these seven important questions, at the end of the pages that follow we shall find out the extent to which we can return to where we started and, as T. S. Eliot so eloquently put it, know this place for the first time.

1 Defining and conceptualising hate crime

Offences that we now recognise as hate crimes have a long history, as we shall see in chapter two, but until relatively recently they were not officially labelled as such. Today politicians, criminal justice agencies, the media and the public use the term fairly liberally. Society's concern with this 'new' type of crime is therefore a relatively recent development. But what is it exactly that we mean when we talk about 'hate crime'? Before we can explore any of the issues associated with the concept it is crucial that we have an understanding of exactly what it is that we are talking about. As we shall see, much depends upon the strength and depth of this understanding. As such, this opening chapter will seek to define and conceptualise hate crime, and will examine the inherent difficulties and complexities associated with doing so. The wide implications associated with the use of various definitions will also be explored.

Defining hate crime

Barbara Perry (2001) suggests that, as is the case with crime in general, it is very difficult to construct an exhaustive definition of 'hate crime' that is able to take account of all of its facets. Crime is of course socially constructed and means different things to different people, different things at different times, and what constitutes a crime in one place may not in another. As Perry suggests, crime is therefore relative and historically and culturally contingent, and as we shall see this is particularly true of hate crime. Indeed, as will become clear, 'hate crime' is a notoriously difficult concept to define accurately and effectively. Given this inescapable complexity it should not come as any surprise that numerous academic and professional definitions exist around the world. In a statement that still resonates today, Boeckmann and Turpin-Petrosino (2002: 208) set the scene by stating that:

> There is no consensus among social scientists or lawmakers on definitional elements that would constitute a global description of hate crime. Part of the reason for this lies in the fact that cultural differences, social norms, and political interests play a large role in defining crime in general, and hate crime in particular.

In attempting to explain the phenomenon of 'hate crime' a number of definitions have been put forward by academics. In addition to simply defining hate crime, a consideration of these various definitions is important because it will allow us to deconstruct this phenomenon of 'hate crime' and present a deeper understanding of the complexities of the concept.

At the most simplistic level hate crimes are criminal offences that are motivated by hate, but this simplicity masks a number of important issues that are central to a true understanding of hate crime. Gerstenfeld (2004: 9) suggests that:

> The simplest definition of a hate crime is this: a criminal act which is motivated, at least in part, by the group affiliation of the victim.

Similarly, Craig (2002: 86) defines hate crime as:

> an illegal act involving intentional selection of a victim based on a perpetrator's bias or prejudice against the actual or perceived status of the victim.

Gerstenfeld acknowledges that her simple definition is not as precise as we might want, and hides a number of important complexities. The same might also be said for Craig's definition. Some of these complexities are noted by Wolfe and Copeland (1994: 201), who define the phenomenon of hate crime as:

> violence directed towards groups of people who generally are not valued by the majority society, who suffer discrimination in other arenas, and who do not have full access to remedy social, political and economic injustice.

Clearly, for Craig a hate crime involves an illegal act motivated by the offender's prejudice towards an individual victim, whilst for Wolfe and Copeland the act committed is specifically one that is violent in nature, aimed at a specific group and based upon the prejudices evident in wider society to which the offender presumably also subscribes. The latter definition also assumes that victims of hate crime are already marginalised in a number of other ways, implying that hate crime is somehow simply an extension of the existing oppression experienced by minority groups in society (Perry, 2001).

This oppressive view of hate crime is shared by Sheffield (1995: 438), who states that:

> Hate violence is motivated by social and political factors and is bolstered by belief systems which (attempt to) legitimate such violence ... It reveals that the personal is political; that such violence is not a series of

isolated incidents but rather the consequence of a political culture which allocates rights, privileges and prestige according to biological or social characteristics.

Perry (2001) suggests that Sheffield's definition is useful not only because it highlights the political and social context in which hate crime develops but also because it notes the significance of existing and deep-rooted social hierarchies of identity that underpin hate crime. Thus Sheffield is suggesting that society is organised hierarchically along notions of 'difference' where people are afforded a position based on identifiable characteristics such as race, gender, sexuality and so on. Simply, society is organised on perceptions of power, and hate crime is one way to express that power.

Perry suggests, however, that the definition is somewhat incomplete because it fails to take full account of the effect of hate crime on those involved. Instead, Perry argues that an adequate definition of hate crime essentially needs to consist of certain elements of the definitions put forward by Wolfe and Copeland and Sheffield. In doing this Perry (2001: 10) argues that:

> Hate crime involves acts of violence and intimidation, usually directed toward already stigmatised and marginalised groups. As such, it is a mechanism of power and oppression, intended to reaffirm the precarious hierarchies that characterise a given social order. It attempts to re-create simultaneously the threatened (real or imagined) hegemony of the perpetrator's group and the 'appropriate' subordinate identity of the victim's group.

Deconstructing 'hate crime'

So what then do academic definitions tell us about hate crime? The first point to note is that there is nothing new about the crime element of hate crime. The actual offences themselves already exist and are outlawed by other existing criminal legislation. In this sense then it is society's interest in the motivation that lies behind the commission of the crime that is new. That motivation is, of course, an offender's hatred of, or more accurately, prejudice against, a particular identifiable group or member of a particular identifiable group, usually already marginalised within society, whom the offender intentionally selects on the basis of that prejudice.

Whilst we shall examine many of these issues further in the chapters on victimisation and perpetrators respectively, this brief consideration of a small number of academic definitions of hate crime serves to demonstrate some of the complexities and the range of issues that we face when we try to define hate crime. But the problem of defining hate crime is further exacerbated by the fact that academic definitions, whilst useful in sociological terms are far too broad and complex to be of much value in practical terms to criminal justice practitioners and legislators. As Chakraborti (2010) rightly points out, despite recent and ongoing academic attempts to provide conceptual clarity, divisions still exist concerning the real meaning and value of the term 'hate crime'. Furthermore, these divisions have often hindered efforts to develop working definitions that might be of more value in practical and policy terms. Indeed, this sentiment was recently expressed to me by a policymaker working within the British government, who lamented that even if you could lock academics in a room for six months with the task of producing a single definition of hate crime, they would most likely emerge with more definitions than they had when they went in, which makes for interesting scholarly debate, but is utterly useless for those tasked with actually responding to the problem of hate crime 'in the real world'. Because of these issues, when considering official interpretations of hate crime, we necessarily face a host of different definitions.

Just as academic definitions of hate crime vary in their content, so it is for official definitions that in many cases not only vary between countries, but also within them. We shall examine in more detail what hate crime 'means' in different parts of the world in chapter three, but for now a few illustrative examples will suffice.

The United States

The situation in the US is particularly interesting here. The first official federal definition of hate crime emerged when the US Hate Crime Statistics Bill was proposed in 1985 and enacted in 1990. This stated that hate crimes are:

> Crimes that manifest evidence of prejudice based on race, religion, sexual orientation or ethnicity, including where appropriate the crimes of murder, non-negligent manslaughter, forcible rape, aggravated assault, simple assault, intimidation, arson, and destruction, damage or vandalism of property.
>
> (Public Law: 101–275)

Since the original Act, the types of offences have been broadened (see chapter three), disability was included in 2004, and in 2009 the Act was amended to include gender and gender identity (see chapter two). In this definition, then, both the categories of prejudice and specific types of offences are delineated. However, to illustrate the complexity and diversity surrounding official definitions of hate crime, in addition to those prejudices stated in the Federal Act (and subsequent Federal legislation), many individual US States have since added significant numbers of categories to their own state legislation to include discrimination based on, for example, nationality, disability (both mental and physical), age, marital status, gender, political affiliation or beliefs and economic or social status. As a consequence almost every US state has a different legal definition of hate crime, and the waters are often muddied further by the differing operational definitions of hate crime employed by individual police forces. This is an issue that we will explore further in chapter two.

Clearly, then, the situation in the US is complicated. The definitions, and the elements that would constitute a hate crime, vary greatly both between and within federal, state and local agencies. Although consistent themes can be identified, for example the presence of prejudice and the offender's intentional selection of victims on the basis of certain identifiable characteristics, the specifics vary. This in turn can have huge implications for accurately measuring the size of the hate crime problem, as we shall see shortly.

England and Wales

In England and Wales the situation is different to the US. Between 1986 and 1999, each of the 43 police forces of England and Wales collected information on racist incidents only under the Association of Chief Police Officers' (ACPO) definition, which referred to:

> Any incident in which it appears to the reporting or investigating officer that the complaint involves an element of racial motivation; or any incident which includes an allegation of racial motivation made by any person.
>
> (ACPO, 1985)

Following the Stephen Lawrence Inquiry, the police service adopted the definition recommended by Sir William Macpherson which stated that:

> A racist incident is any incident which is perceived to be racist by the victim or any other person.
>
> (Macpherson, 1999)

This definition was held to be clearer and simpler than the original (Home Office, 2002) and purposefully removed the discretionary element from the police in determining what is and what is not a racist incident – a situation that contributed to the failure of the investigation into the murder of Stephen Lawrence. However, as we shall see in the next chapter, since the publication of the Stephen Lawrence Inquiry the debate has widened beyond just issues of race to encompass the much broader concepts of 'diversity' and 'hate'. This is reflected in the current definitions employed by ACPO that are shared across criminal justice agencies in England and Wales, illustrated in Table 1.1. These definitions are notable because they allow for anyone to be a victim of hate crime, and for any offence or incident to be recorded and investigated by the police as a hate crime. Furthermore, they acknowledge that hate crimes are not always about hate, but about prejudice and hostility. This is a point to which I shall return later in this chapter.

Table 1.1 Operational definitions of hate crime employed in England and Wales

Title	Definition	Included subjects
Hate motivation	Hate crimes and incidents are taken to mean any crime or incident where the perpetrator's hostility or prejudice against an identifiable group of people is a factor in determining who is victimised.	This is a broad and inclusive definition. A victim does not have to be a member of the group. In fact, anyone could be a victim of a hate crime.
Hate incident	Any non-crime incident which is perceived by the victim or any other person, to be motivated by a hostility or prejudice based on a person's race or perceived race.	Any racial group or ethnic background including countries within the United Kingdom and 'Gypsy and Traveller groups'.
	Or;	
	Any non-crime incident which is perceived, by the victim or any other person, to be motivated by a hostility or prejudice based on a person's religion or perceived religion.	Any religious group including those who have no faith.
	Or;	
	Any non-crime incident which is perceived, by the victim or any other person, to be motivated by a hostility or prejudice based on a person's sexual orientation or perceived sexual orientation.	Any person's sexual orientation.
	Or;	
	Any non-crime incident which is perceived, by the victim or any other person, to be motivated by a hostility or prejudice based on a person's disability or perceived disability.	Any disability including physical disability, learning disability and mental health.
	Or;	
	Any non-crime incident which is perceived by the victim or any other person, to be motivated by a hostility or prejudice against a person who is transgender or perceived to be transgender.	Including people who are transsexual, transgender, transvestite and those who hold a Gender Recognition Certificate under the Gender Recognition Act 2004.

(Continued)

Table 1.1 (continued)

Title	Definition	Included subjects
Hate crimes	A hate crime is any criminal offence which is perceived, by the victim or any other person, to be motivated by a hostility or prejudice based on a person's race or perceived race.	Any racial group or ethnic background including countries within the United Kingdom and 'Gypsy and Traveller groups'.
	Or;	
	Any criminal offence which is perceived, by the victim or any other person, to be motivated by a hostility or prejudice based on a person's religion or perceived religion.	Any religious group including those who have no faith.
	Or;	
	Any criminal offence which is perceived, by the victim or any other person, to be motivated by a hostility or prejudice based on a person's sexual orientation or perceived sexual orientation.	Any person's sexual orientation.
	Or;	
	Any criminal offence which is perceived, by the victim or any other person, to be motivated by a hostility or prejudice based on a person's disability or perceived disability.	Any disability including physical disability, learning disability and mental health.
	Or;	
	Any criminal offence which is perceived, by the victim or any other person, to be motivated by a hostility or prejudice against a person who is transgender or perceived to be transgender.	Including people who are transsexual, transgender, transvestite and those who hold a Gender Recognition Certificate under the Gender Recognition Act 2004.
Hate crime prosecution	A hate crime prosecution is any hate crime which has been charged in the aggravated form or where the prosecutor has assessed that there is sufficient evidence of the hostility element to be put before the court when the offender is sentenced.	

Source: ACPO, 2013b.

It is important to note, however, that these definitions are those used operationally by the police and wider criminal justice system to recognise hate crimes, yet they differ markedly from legislative definitions. Indeed, hate crime as a distinct category of offence does not officially exist in legislation in England and Wales. Instead, the key pieces of legislation in this regard recognise only offences motivated or aggravated by racial and religious prejudice (the Crime and Disorder Act 1998 as amended by the Anti-terrorism, Crime and Security Act 2001), and those related to homophobia and disability bias (the Criminal Justice Act 2003).

Under the Crime and Disorder Act (1998: p2, s28) an offence is racially aggravated if:

(a) at the time of committing the offence, or immediately before or after doing so, the offender demonstrates towards the victim of the offence hostility based on the victim's membership (or presumed membership) of a racial group; or

(b) the offence is motivated (wholly or partly) by hostility towards members of a racial group based on their membership of that group.

Here a 'racial group' refers to persons defined by reference to their race, colour, nationality or ethnic or national origins and in section 28(3a) includes membership of any religious group. Again, we shall explore the implication of the definition shortly, but note here the narrow nature of the definition in terms of the prejudices included (race and religion) as compared to the ACPO definitions above (any prejudice).

Other countries

Whilst hate crimes in jurisdictions other than the US and England and Wales will be the focus of chapter three, it is worth noting here that the issues outlined thus far in this chapter are at least equally as prevalent in different countries around the world. As we shall see in due course, different countries define hate crime in a multitude of different ways, recognising different identifiable groups, different categories of offending and so on, and in numerous cases not recognising anything at all. Effectively, then, when we talk about hate crime, we could be talking about a number of very different things depending on where we happen to be, and when we happen to be there.

The complexities and implications of defining hate crime

Earlier in this chapter it was suggested that whilst defining crime in general is difficult enough, defining hate crime is a particularly complex task. The various definitions presented here, which themselves represent just a small sample of those that currently exist, are testament to that difficulty. But why is it that hate crime is so uniquely difficult to define and conceptualise? And why is it significant? We have already noted the importance of relative, historical and cultural issues in defining crime, but where hate crime is concerned, a number of other crucial points also bear heavily on this process. Here we shall consider some of these issues, and where relevant we shall do so with specific reference to the implications for the definitions of hate crime used officially in England and Wales. As we shall see in chapter three however, the principles applied here are applicable to many other jurisdictions around the world.

What is hate?

The first problem relates to the word 'hate' and what, exactly, we mean by it. Despite the frequency with which the term is used, for the purpose of furthering our understanding of hate crime, the word *hate* is distinctly unhelpful. As Andrew Sullivan (1999) points out, for all our zeal to attack hate we still have a remarkably vague idea of what hate actually is, and despite the powerful and emotional images that it invokes it is still far less nuanced an idea than prejudice, bias, bigotry, hostility, anger or just a mere aversion to others. When we talk about 'hate', do we mean all of these things or just the extremes of them?

If we look at the definitions presented in this chapter then we can see that none of them speak of 'hate' as a causal factor. Rather, the definitions refer to prejudice, hostility or bias, or *-isms*. Clearly, then, hate crime thus defined isn't really about *hate*, but about criminal behaviour motivated by *prejudice*, of which hate is just one small and extreme part. This is significant because prejudice is a far more expansive concept than hate, covering many varieties of human emotion. What we might think of as 'pure' hate in layman's terms is just a small part of this spectrum. The expansive nature of hate crime is a point to which I will return later in this chapter, and the complexities of prejudice will be the subject of chapter five, but it is important to understand at this juncture that for the most part it is prejudice and not hate that we refer to when we talk about hate crime. This crucial distinction, as will become clear, has many important implications for understanding and in particular for responding to hate crimes.

The concept of 'hate' becomes increasingly muddied and confused when we try to make the distinction between those prejudices that are acceptable and those that are not, how strong those prejudices must be in order to become unacceptable, how they must be expressed, whether someone is prejudiced or whether they are not or indeed how we can ever know for certain. Let us apply this to the operational (ACPO) definitions of hate crimes and hate incidents currently used in England and Wales (see Table 1.1). These state that a hate crime (or incident) is any crime (or incident) where the perpetrator's *hostility* or *prejudice* against any identifiable group of people is a factor in determining who is victimised. In the absence of a precise legal definition of 'hostility' the Crown Prosecution Service (2012) advises prosecutors that consideration should be given to ordinary dictionary definitions, which include ill-will, ill-feeling, spite, contempt, prejudice, unfriendliness, antagonism, resentment and dislike. However, the word 'prejudice' is not defined or explained.

What prejudices are unacceptable?

Furthermore, which prejudices are to be included? Which, if any, are to be excluded? And against whom must they be directed? Some clarification is provided because the police are required to record incidents based on race, religion, sexual orientation, disability and transgender. But as we shall see, creating lists of 'acceptable' prejudices is itself problematic. Nevertheless, this issue of defining prejudice is important because, as Jacobs and Potter (1998) suggest, if everyone holds some form of prejudice then potentially every crime committed by one group against another could be labelled as a hate crime. It is not unreasonable to suggest, they argue, that some form of prejudice on the part of the offender motivates *all* crime, but clearly not every crime is a hate crime otherwise the concept would just be coterminous with crime in general. This indicates then that some prejudices must necessarily be socially and officially less acceptable than others. This unavoidable situation leads us to our next problematic and contentious issue, namely, which prejudices turn ordinary crimes into hate crimes?

The ACPO definitions imply that any prejudice on the part of the offender can constitute a hate crime. But as Jacobs and Potter have suggested, offenders probably have many prejudices, both conscious and subconscious, against people who are for example, rich, poor, successful, unsuccessful and so on. If we start looking for prejudice in offending behaviour, they argue, then the closer we look the more we will find. Simply, because of its pervasiveness, prejudice of one kind or another is present in most forms of offending. Therefore, to allow a distinction to be made between *crime* and *hate crime*, we necessarily have to identify and select the prejudices we wish to challenge. In other words, the 'boundaries' of hate crime have to be established. The question is, then, what prejudices are we going to take action against? Or put another way, what characteristics are we going to protect? As will have been apparent from the definitions outlined above, answering this question is a far from simple task.

Whilst defining and stating specific categories might be seen as a helpful step in clarifying what is and what is not a hate crime, other elements of the ACPO definitions serve to complicate things considerably. For example, by adopting deliberately broad and inclusive definitions that include the phrases 'any identifiable group' and 'perceived by the victim or any other person', ACPO's definitions, adapted from the recommendations of the Stephen Lawrence Inquiry (Macpherson, 1999), unquestionably accept that anyone can be a victim of hate crime if they believe themselves to be so. But if anyone can be a victim of hate crime, and if any crime can be a hate crime, there is a danger that the very concept will effectively lose its meaning.

Of course the very notion of recognising and listing categories of prejudice is in itself problematic. Creating such a list is fraught with difficulties. The exclusion of some groups may give the impression that their victimisation is of less importance than others, whilst including every conceivable minority group will ultimately cause the original intention of the focus on hate crime to at best be watered down and at worst lost altogether. Critics would also argue that all victims should be protected from crime, so the question then becomes why should we seek to protect some more than others (Jacobs and Potter, 1998)? This is a question that we shall consider further in chapter nine.

If we are to protect certain groups more than others, then this necessarily raises difficult questions of *how* we decide what groups to protect. For example, how did we get to the position in England and Wales whereby crimes based on race and religion are specific offences, yet crimes based on other prejudices against other characteristics are not? Under the ACPO definitions this issue does not require much attention. The need to make these decisions is avoided by allowing for members of any identifiable group to be recognised as victims of hate crime if they perceive themselves to be so. Under the law, however, we can ask searching questions as to why only prejudices based on race and religion, and to a lesser extent homophobia and disability bias, are specifically singled out for additional protection whilst other identifiable groups (for example, alternative lifestyles, the elderly, the young, tall people, short people, obese people, left-handed people and so on) are not.

Writing of a similar situation in the US, Gerstenfeld (2004) suggests that legislative decisions regarding which prejudices to outlaw and thus which groups to protect are affected by a number of factors. Such factors might include economic, political and socio-demographic conditions within a jurisdiction, but they also might be influenced by media attention and the lobbying activities of advocacy groups and social movements. To this we might also add various historical conditions relating to certain minority groups. These issues will be examined further in the next chapter.

Crimes and causal links

Jacobs and Potter (1998) suggest that there are two further issues that serve to complicate our understanding of hate crime. First, we need to consider what types of behaviours are included in our definition. As we shall see in chapter five, prejudice can be expressed in a multitude of different ways, and decisions have to be made about where to draw the line between the acceptable and the unacceptable expression of negative attitudes. In other words we have to decide how strong an offender's 'hate' must be before it becomes unacceptable.

Second, we have to establish just how strong the causal relationship between the offence and the officially designated prejudice must be before we can call a crime a hate crime. In England and Wales, the definitions are particularly susceptible to the implications of both these issues. If we return to the ACPO (2013b) definitions, two phrases that have particular implications for our understanding of the problem in this regard are 'any incident' and 'a factor in determining'. We shall examine these in turn.

The first issue centres on the use of the word *incident*. Here hate crime is not just about crimes, but about incidents too. This is an important distinction to make because the two are very different things. An incident does not need to be a recordable crime. In England and Wales a hate incident may occur and be recorded by the police in the official statistics but not have the necessary elements to be classified as a notifiable offence at a later stage in the criminal justice process.

Put simply, an incident may be something that occurs that is perceived by the victim or any other person as being motivated or aggravated by some form of prejudice, but may not actually be a crime in the strictest legal sense. In England and Wales, at the reporting and recording stage of the policing process there is no evidential test that the hate incident has to pass. The definition is simply concerned with the prima facie test, rather than an evidential one (i.e. 'does this appear on the surface to be a hate crime?' rather than 'is there sufficient legal evidence for this to be classified as a notifiable offence?').

In practical policing terms, then, at the initial reporting and recording stage of the process the difference between a hate incident and a hate crime is irrelevant. Both are recorded. This lack of distinction between the two is significant primarily because if we add hate incidents to hate crimes, then the number of hate 'occurrences' that come to official attention will be vastly greater than if we were to just concentrate our attention on legally defined crimes – a situation that has important implications for effectively responding to the problem.

The second issue relates to the strength of the causal link between the incident or crime and the officially designated prejudice. Clearly, for an ordinary crime to be transformed into a hate crime there has to be a causal connection between the offence and the offender's prejudice. As Jacobs and Potter (1998) suggest, if in our definition we require hate crime to be motivated solely by prejudice to the exclusion of all other factors, then we will not experience much hate crime. Conversely, if we are happy for prejudice to be only loosely related to the offence then a great many more offences will be defined as hate crimes.

Accordingly, the ACPO definitions state that the offender's prejudice must be *a factor* in determining who is victimised, but it doesn't tell us just *how much* of a factor the offender's prejudice must be. The implication is that the slightest hint of prejudice will suffice, in which case a great many incidents can potentially be, and indeed are, officially labelled as hate crimes.

The definitions, however, suggest that the prejudice must be a *motivating* factor. But again, the question remains as to how much of a motivating factor the offender's prejudice must be.

This is an issue that also extends to legal definitions in the UK. The Crime and Disorder Act 1998, as we have seen, refers not only to racially and religiously *aggravated* offences, but also to offences that are *motivated in whole or in part* by racial and religious hostility. Whilst the categories of prejudice are narrow, the scope for labelling a great many offences as hate crimes within those categories is also, in theory at least, wide. Here, the word 'motivated' refers to offences where the offender's prejudice is the sole or *primary* cause of the offence. On the other hand, aggravation refers not to the motivation behind the offence, but to some demonstration of hostility towards the victim around the time of the offence. Aggravating factors, such as racial slurs for example, are not the primary cause of the offence, but nevertheless represent an expression of prejudice that contributes as a subsidiary element to the crime. Both contribute to differing degrees to the transformation of crime into hate crime under definitions constructed in England and Wales.

The social construction of hate crime

Let us take a moment at this juncture to summarise some of the key points raised in this chapter. Western democracies in particular have 'created' a relatively 'new' offence that we call 'hate crime', but there is little consensus either nationally or internationally, academically or professionally, about what exactly hate crime is. At its most basic level hate crimes are offences motivated by prejudice; pre-existing criminal incidents or offences in which the offender's prejudice against the victim or the victim's group plays some part in their victimisation. But of course it is not that simple, and this basic definition masks a number of crucial issues that cannot easily be ignored or cast aside.

Because of this, in attempting to adequately conceptualise 'hate crime', we must consider a number of key questions: what prejudices when transformed into action are we going to criminalise? How will we know if these actions truly constitute a hate crime? What crimes are we going to include in our definition? Which groups will be acceptable to us as victims? How strong must the relationship between the prejudice and the offence be? Must that link be wholly or just partially causal? Who will decide? How will we decide? How can we guard against hatred without impinging upon people's basic democratic freedoms? And, of course, why is it important to consider these questions? The answer to this last question is crucial. As Jacobs and Potter (1998: 27) suggest:

> how much hate crime there is and what the appropriate response should be depends upon how hate crime is conceptualised and defined.

Consider the following theoretical model proposed by Jacobs and Potter. They suggest that hate crime is a potentially expansive concept that covers a great many offenders and situations, and they illustrate this through the use of the model shown in Figure 1.1.

The horizontal axis shows the degree of the offender's prejudice (high or low, or in other words, prejudiced or not very prejudiced), and the vertical axis shows the strength of the causal relationship between the criminal behaviour and the officially designated prejudice (high or low, or strongly related or not strongly related). Both of these factors, and combinations of them, have important implications for understanding hate crimes.

As far as defining hate crime is concerned, cell *one* (high prejudice/high causation) is relatively unproblematic. Here we have offenders who are highly prejudiced, and whose prejudice is a strong causal factor in their offending behaviour. These offenders are the ones that we probably associate most when we think of the word 'hate' in its most extreme form. As such this cell represents clear-cut hate crimes where there is little doubt that the offender hates his or her victim in the truest sense of the word. To illustrate this, Jacobs and Potter present a number of examples including some of the historical activities of the Ku Klux Klan, or of members of neo-Nazi groups. We might also include the perpetrators of two of America's most infamous hate crimes in this category. In Texas in 1997 John William King was one of three men who, as part of a bonding activity for a new white supremacist group, beat up James Byrd Jr, an African American, and chained his feet to the back of a truck and dragged him for three miles until his body hit a culvert and was decapitated. In Wyoming in October 1998, Matthew Shepard was beaten to death in a homophobic attack and his body left hanging from a fence as a 'warning' to others.

In a UK context we might reasonably include here David Copeland, the racist and homophobic neo-Nazi convicted of nail bomb attacks in Brixton, Brick Lane and Soho in April 1999 where he deliberately targeted, killed

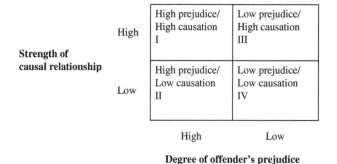

Figure 1.1 Labelling hate crime: the prejudice and causal components (Jacobs and Potter, 1998: 23).

and injured members of London's ethnic minority and gay and lesbian communities. We might also include Robert Stewart, a violent racist who murdered fellow inmate Zahid Mubarek at Feltham Young Offenders Institute in London in March 2000. We might also consider the killers of black teenager Stephen Lawrence in south-east London in April 1993. In more extreme terms, this cell might also include the Nazi persecution of the Jews that culminated in the Holocaust. Jacobs and Potter (1998) argue, therefore, that if hate crimes included only cases like these, the concept would not be ambiguous, difficult to understand, or controversial and nor would there be many hate crimes occurring because cases like these, generally, are rare.

However, it is when we consider the other three cells that things become more complicated. Cell two (high prejudice/low causation) refers to highly prejudiced offenders, such as those included in cell one, but whose offending is not strongly or solely motivated by prejudice. The hypothetical example Jacobs and Potter use to illustrate this is that of a neo-Nazi figure who shoplifts from a shop owed by a Jew, where the primary motive is to acquire the stolen goods, and not to target Jews. But is this a hate crime? Clearly, the offender will be prejudiced against Jews, but it is wrong, Jacobs and Potter argue, to assume that all offences committed by prejudiced offenders against minority groups are primarily motivated by that prejudice. In the strictest sense, such offences would not, and indeed should not, be considered hate crimes because they are not motivated by prejudice, but by some other motive, for example economics, or hunger.

Cells three and four present particular challenges for defining and understanding hate crime. Cell three (low prejudice/high causation) contains offenders who are not particularly prejudiced, or whose prejudices may be largely subconscious, but which nevertheless have a strong causal link to the offence. Jacobs and Potter use the example of Dontay Carter, an African-American man who always targeted white men as his robbery victims. In this case, however, Carter targeted white men because he believed them to be rich and not because he had any other particular prejudice against their skin colour. Therefore, his prejudice was based upon his perception of white men's financial status, and not their ethnic group *per se*. Thus the causal link between his prejudice and his offending behaviour was strong, but his prejudice in terms of 'hating' his victims was not. Nevertheless, for Jacobs and Potter it is this group of offenders and this type of offence that dominate the US hate crime statistics. In other words, the strength of the motivation is often overlooked at the expense of the perceived causal relationship; a crime is committed by a member of one group against a member of another group and a hate crime is assumed to have occurred.

Cell four (low prejudice/low causation) represents many incidents or offences that are described by Jacobs and Potter as being 'situational' in that they arise from ad hoc disputes or short tempers, but are neither products of strong prejudicial attitudes nor are they strongly causally related to the incident in question. Consider two examples. The first was recounted to the author during ethnographic research with the Philadelphia Police Department in 2003. The case centred on a long-running neighbour dispute between a black family and a white family over the persistent playing of loud music. As the dispute came to a head the arguments became increasingly volatile during which racial epithets were exchanged. Did these constitute hate crimes? Ultimately not because the cause of the incident was determined by the police to be the playing of loud music, and not differences in ethnic origin.

The second case cited as an example by Jacobs and Potter, also from the US, similarly involved a long-running dispute between two neighbours, one homosexual and one heterosexual, over the spilling of grass clippings by the gay man onto his neighbour's lawn when he cut the grass. As the dispute escalated the straight man responded on one occasion by shouting anti-gay epithets. As the argument developed the gay man sprayed his neighbour's son with water from the garden hose, and in response the son kicked and punched the gay man whilst yelling anti-gay comments. Ultimately, the son was convicted of a hate motivated assault. But again we can question the motive of the assault. As Sullivan (1999) queries, what exactly was the nature of this hate? Homophobia or, as he puts it, 'suburban property-owner madness'? The point is that under some definitions and interpretations these are hate crimes, and under others they are not. The number of hate crimes in society is therefore entirely determined by how hate crime is defined, conceptualised and interpreted. The problem is that the definitions currently in use ensure that the majority of officially labelled hate crimes are not motivated by hate at all, but by prejudice, which is often an entirely different thing.

Applying Jacobs and Potter's model

When we consider Jacobs and Potter's model it becomes clear that hate crime, like any other crime, is ultimately a social construct. Hate crime, however, is more susceptible to this process than other forms of crime because of the additional elements that have to be considered. As Jacobs and Potter suggest, when constructing a definition of hate crime, choices have to be made about the meaning of prejudice, the nature and strength of the causal link between the prejudice and the offence as well as the types of crimes to be included. Decisions in these choices will ultimately determine what is and what is not 'hate crime', and will naturally affect the size of the hate crime problem we will face, which will subsequently impact upon our response to it.

Consider the following illustration of this point. In 2010 the population of the US officially stood at 308,745,538 (US Census, 2010). In that year 1,949 law enforcement agencies recorded 6,628 hate crime incidents involving 7,699 offences. Of these, 3,725 offences were racially motivated,

1,409 were religiously motivated, 1,470 were based upon sexual orientation, 1,040 were based upon ethnicity or national origin and 46 were motivated by disability bias (FBI, 2011). In the same year the population of England and Wales stood at 55,200,000 (Office for National Statistics, 2011) and the 44 police forces of England and Wales and Northern Ireland recorded 48,127 hate crimes, of which 39,311 were racially motivated, 2,007 were anti-faith, 4,883 were based on sexual orientation, 357 against transgender, and 1,569 based on disability bias (ACPO, 2011). Statistically, then, in 2010 England and Wales and Northern Ireland recorded more than six times as many hate crimes as the US, despite the population of the US being just over five and a half times greater. Does this mean that England and Wales and Northern Ireland are vastly more hateful places than the US? Of course not. The most probable explanation for this enormous disparity lies in the construction and application of the definition(s) adopted on both sides of the Atlantic, and, as we shall see in chapter three, these issues make meaningful comparisons of the extent of hate crimes between different countries very hard to make.

So, the broad definitions adopted by ACPO mean that, superficially at least, any incident or crime could be a hate crime, and that anyone could be a victim of hate crime if they perceive themselves to be so. If we apply Jacobs and Potter's model to this then effectively the ACPO definitions cover all four cells. In other words, any incident or crime can be a hate crime, any victim can be a hate crime victim and any offender can be a hate offender. The distinction between crime and hate crime can therefore become very blurred.

Crucially, though, the application of a narrow legal definition under the Crime and Disorder Act, and the legal requirements for a successful prosecution, mean that decisions do have to be made at various stages of the legal process. In this respect, the distinction between a crime and a hate crime naturally becomes clearer as legal requirements have to be met if the hate element is to withstand legal scrutiny and a successful prosecution be achieved. In other words, prejudice as a motivating or aggravating factor has to be proved in court, but it doesn't have to be proved for a 'hate crime' to appear as such in the official statistics. The narrower legal definition therefore has a 'culling' effect in determining the number of hate crimes, evidenced in part by the lower numbers of successful prosecutions generally seen in most countries.

In the US, in law enforcement terms more selective decisions are generally made regarding the strength of prejudice and causality before a crime is officially labelled as a hate crime. Where these issues are weak, the hate label is generally withheld and the crime remains exactly that, just a crime. Moreover, the focus is more concerned with crime rather than with incidents (Hall, 2009) and this can have serious implications for policing practice, and for the picture of intergroup relations that the official statistics paint. These are issues to which we shall return in due course.

Concluding comments

In this chapter we have briefly examined a small number of academic and official attempts to define hate crime. Whilst some obvious themes emerge throughout, it is clear that there is no consensus on exactly what is and what is not a hate crime. But does this really matter? Undoubtedly, it does. It matters considerably. Effectively, everything that we associate with hate crime depends upon how we define and conceptualise it. The significance of accurately and effectively defining this phenomenon is therefore crucial. If in our definition we insist that hate crimes must be wholly motivated by prejudice to the exclusion of all other factors then society will not experience many such offences. Few offences can be said to be motivated exclusively and solely by hate. Conversely, if we are happy for our definition to require just the slightest hint of prejudice for an offence to be classified as a hate crime then the number of crimes could become astronomical. At present in England and Wales, we find ourselves both at the latter end of this spectrum, and also somewhere in the middle. We have adopted the widest possible operational definition in policing terms, but a narrower one in terms of the law. Clearly, defining, conceptualising and understanding hate crime is a complex task that is fraught with difficulties.

2 The emergence of hate crime as a contemporary socio-legal problem

You will have no doubt noticed from the previous chapter that the various attempts to define 'hate crime' have been made relatively recently. Yet, human history is littered with examples of events and actions that we would now call 'hate crimes', often leaving legacies that have shaped, and continue to shape, the modern history and collective viewpoints of many countries and cultures around the world. Whilst we shall refer to a few illustrative examples in this chapter, there is not the space here to discuss the countless historical examples of persecution along racial, religious, ethnic and other lines, but try this simple exercise: revisit the definitions of hate crime from the previous chapter, and then open up any history book. Plentiful examples are generally not too hard to find.

For our purposes now, however, we are left with a rather interesting question that we need to consider: given the lengthy history of 'identity'-motivated persecution (much of it often state sanctioned – slavery springs immediately to mind here), why is it only relatively recently that *some* countries have come to regard 'hate' crime as a social problem requiring a formal response from the state, the legislature and the various criminal justice agencies? In this chapter, then, we shall examine the emergence of hate crime as a contemporary socio-legal problem in the two jurisdictions that have arguably led the way in developing sanctions for this 'new' form of criminal behaviour – the US and England and Wales. To do this, perhaps the best way to chart the rise of any social problem is through the process by which it achieves legal recognition, which represents the ultimate official acceptance of the need to respond. It is through this lens that I shall examine the rise of hate crime as a contemporary social issue, starting with the US, before briefly considering the respective legislative provisions to have emerged from this historical evolution.

The United States

Accounts of the historical origins of hate crime laws differ. Some authors suggest that such legislation has its strongest roots in the post-Second World War period in America and can be directly attributed to the success of the civil rights movement and the resulting 'identity politics' (Jacobs and Potter, 1998). Whilst this is undoubtedly a significant area of interest for us, other authors have suggested that the origins of hate crime legislation can be traced back much further to the post-Civil War period and the creation of the US Constitution, and in some cases, even further back than that. Indeed, the earliest legislation to bear any resemblance to modern hate crime laws was passed as far back as 1649 when the predominantly Catholic colony of Maryland enacted the Act of Tolerance which extended religious freedom to all who believed in Jesus Christ and the Trinity, and included provisions for the execution of those that did not (Streissguth, 2003).

However, the most significant historical period for our purposes is the time from the end of the US Civil War onwards and as such it is here that we shall begin, in particular with an examination of the detailed historical accounts provided by Brian Levin (2002), Tom Streissguth (2003) and others, followed by Jacobs and Potter's (1998) consideration of the significance of the post-Second World War civil rights movement.

Brian Levin (2002) traces the birth of hate crime legislation to the time of the US Civil War and the drafting of the Constitution. He asserts that:

> The recent emergence of a hate crime category on the legal landscape came about only after other foundational issues relating to free expression, federalism, and the role of status characteristics were addressed ... the seeds for recognising and eventually protecting on the basis of status are found in a history that often, and conversely, used status as a pretext for unfair treatment and the deprivation of rights.
>
> (2002: 227–8)

The 'unfair treatment' to which Levin refers relates to the fact that despite the Declaration of Independence stating that *'all men are created equal'*, early America was in all reality a society based on status with various rights not extended to poor white males, blacks, Native Americans and women. Of particular significance to Levin's historical analysis of hate crime legislation is the concept of slavery. Whilst the original Constitution legitimised slavery, for Levin the subsequent effort to abolish it and thereby extend equal rights and status protection to hitherto unprotected groups represents a critical period that can be directly related to the development of the hate crime laws we see today.

Whilst the practical worth of early challenges to slavery and other repressive acts was limited by the lack of willingness of both federal and local courts to recognise status-based equality, Levin points to three crucial Constitutional amendments that would ultimately have a profound effect on the plight of those persecuted for being 'inferior':

> New, sweeping Constitutional and statutory reforms cut off the traditional legal and political methods Whites relied upon to deprive Blacks

of their rights. Although their initial success was fleeting, these new, egalitarian postwar reforms laid the foundation for changes that extended into the latter half of the next century, including the emergence of hate crime laws. They represented a newfound validation of federal authority in the area of criminal law and supremacy of national power over that of the states to protect minorities from the harms of race-based violence and discrimination.

(2002: 231)

This federal authority of which Levin speaks refers particularly to the Thirteenth, Fourteenth and Fifteenth Amendments to the US Constitution. The Thirteenth Amendment, ratified on 6 December 1865, officially abolished slavery. The Fourteenth Amendment, ratified on 9 July 1868, conveyed citizenship on 'all persons born or nationalised in the US' thereby affording equal status, equal protection and civil rights to hitherto unprotected groups. Finally, the Fifteenth Amendment, ratified on 3 February 1870, extended the right to vote to citizens previously denied because of their race, colour or because of their status as slaves. Crucially, each of the Amendments contained provision for Congress to enforce them through legislation. In theory then, the traditional relative autonomy of individual states to deprive minority groups of various rights and sustain discriminatory practices was undone.

Further to this, Levin highlights the significance of this 'enforcing' legislation and illustrates in particular the Force Act of 1871 which allowed for the imposition of criminal penalties for those who interfered with the Fifteenth Amendment, the Ku Klux Klan Act, also of 1871, which allowed for the criminal punishment of government officials who interfered with protected civil rights or deprived citizens of the equal protection afforded to them under the Constitution, and the Civil Rights Act of 1875 that allowed equal access to public places and amenities regardless of colour, race or status.

Such legislation was significant because many southern states in particular were keen to hang on to the status-based society that existed prior to the Fourteenth Amendment, and consequently were refusing to recognise the Constitutional rights of traditionally disadvantaged groups. Moreover, the laws were an attempt to enforce a 'colour-blind' justice system, combat the vigilante actions of the Klan and end the viciously discriminatory practices of local criminal justice systems and public officials, most notably in the south (Streissguth, 2003). In essence then, these Amendments and supplementary laws laid the theoretical and practical foundations for modern hate crime legislation, but more than that, the debate that raged over the extent of state and federal control at this time would continue to characterise the progress of civil rights and hate crime legislation into the modern era.

Of course, legislating against a set of behaviours is no guarantee that such actions will automatically cease and this was the case following the

Amendments to the Constitution. In practice, little changed for a considerable period of time and the dominant prejudices and status-based social hierarchies of American society prevailed. Indeed, these hierarchies were in effect upheld by the decisions of both federal and local courts throughout America, with only a handful of notable exceptions. This situation, according to Levin, had the rather curious effect of both increasing hatred and increasing the desire to respond to it:

> Neither the Supreme Court nor the majority of the White American public was ready for the exercise of equality that many Reconstruction-era laws promised ... The fact of the matter is that the law and judicial decisions of the times reflected the prevailing supremacist social and political attitudes of much of the White American populace. These attitudes in turn led to a new wave of hatred and violence that continued into the next century. The continued violence prompted new attempts to curtail not only the brutality, but also the groups and messages that promoted it.
>
> (2002: 232–3)

In seeming stark contrast to the spirit of the Constitution, many southern states responded by introducing so-called 'Jim Crow' laws in the late 1870s. These laws had the effect of separating the black from the white population, thereby ostracising blacks in almost every area of public life. However, the laws survived constitutional challenges (and prevailed in many southern states until the 1960s) on the grounds that the facilities provided for blacks were 'separate but equal' to those available to whites (Streissguth, 2003). Nevertheless, such actions represented the continuing power of whites over blacks in a way that resembled the pre-Constitutional era, and effectively presented blacks as 'inferior' to whites.

The new wave of brutality to which Levin also refers accompanied the enactment of 'Jim Crow' laws and relates in particular to the lynching of Black Americans, increasingly common from the 1870s onwards, and later the emergence of race riots directed against the same, most notably in southern states as the Klan in particular sought to return to the 'old days' through the use of violence. Again, state legislation aimed at curtailing lynching was rarely enforced in the sixteen states in which it was introduced between the 1890s and the 1930s, and federal legislation in respect of this failed to make the statute books at all owing to Senate opposition on three separate occasions between 1922 and 1940 (Foner and Garraty, 1991b cited in Levin, 2002).

Although still fairly limited, greater success was achieved following a resurgence in the violent activities of the Ku Klux Klan from around 1915, with numerous states across the country enacting anti-Klan laws to meet this rising and spreading threat, and crucially, with the Supreme Court striking down a number of challenges to these laws. So abhorrent were some of these violent acts which characterised the 'hate landscape' well into the 1960s that:

> The national media coverage given to Klan violence and police brutality against innocent African Americans decisively turned the social and political leanings of the nation toward heightened civil rights enforcement and legislative reform.
>
> (Levin, 2002: 235)

Thus, the process that had begun with the US Constitution and had survived initial resistance and opposition in public and political circles had with the aid of extreme hate violence laid the foundations for the hate crime laws we find today.

Whilst the issues identified by Levin and described briefly above clearly laid the foundations for hate crime legislation in the US, a significant factor in the process was the emergence and success of the civil rights movement in the 1960s and the resulting 'identity politics'. Jacobs and Potter (1998: 5–6) state that:

> the term 'identity politics' refers to a politics whereby individuals relate to one another as members of competing groups based upon characteristics like race, gender, religion, and sexual orientation. According to the logic of identity politics, it is strategically advantageous to be recognised as disadvantaged and victimised. The greater a group's victimisation, the stronger its moral claim on the larger society ... The current anti-hate crime movement is generated not by an epidemic of unprecedented bigotry but by heightened sensitivity to prejudice and, more important, by our society's emphasis on identity politics.

The civil rights movement, they suggest, forced a shift in thinking in relation to the treatment of certain minority groups. Indeed Jacobs and Potter (1998) argue that the resulting Civil Rights Act of 1968 can be considered a precursor to modern hate crime laws. They suggest that section 245 of the Act marked the beginning of the modern civil rights movement by specifically enumerating federal, state and local activities and protecting participants involved in those activities from victimisation and discrimination on the grounds of certain prejudices and bigotry.

Simply, then, Jacobs and Potter argue that by raising the issues of disadvantage and discrimination based on certain prejudices held in American society, the civil rights movement played a central role in the emergence of identity politics (the fight for recognition as a disadvantaged minority group) that characterise American, and now also to a lesser extent British society and politics today.

Of course the civil rights movement focused on the plight of ethnic minority groups. However, the resulting identity politics can be seen as a catalyst for the emergence of claims by other disadvantaged minority groups to be officially recognised as such and afforded equal rights, status and protection. This in turn has the effect of fuelling the attention paid to the situation and victimisation of minority groups thereby maintaining discrimination as a social and political issue in need of national attention. This increased official recognition of minority groups, and the resulting political lobbying and subsequent symbolic legislation, can be viewed as a key motivating factor in the rise of hate crime as a social and political issue, as can the political appeal of championing a disadvantaged group (MacNamara, 2003).

In relation to these issues, Jacobs and Potter (1998) also note something of a domino effect characterised by a general shift in social attitudes relating to prejudice and a greater tolerance and understanding of diversity in society amongst the majority population. Conversely, however, this rise in public awareness has, according to Jacobs and Potter, also resulted in an apparent escalation of 'hate' attacks, thereby reinforcing the need for strong legislation, although the extent to which this apparent escalation can be verified is debateable.

In essence, then, the emergence of hate crime as a contemporary socio-legal issue in the US can be traced back to the Constitution and its goal of achieving status-based equality for all American citizens. The process clearly stumbled at a number of junctures along the way but progressive and gradual changes to the social, political and legal horizons, and notably the success of the civil rights movement since the Second World War, have played a key role in challenging attitudes and discrimination in a number of social spheres. The outcome of this journey, perhaps inevitably, has been the enactment of a number of pieces of legislation designed to combat hate crime, and we shall briefly consider a selection of these here.

Modern hate crime legislation in the United States

Federal legislation

We noted above the significance of the Civil Rights Act of 1968 as something of a catalyst for modern hate crime legislation. The Act prohibits interference with federally protected rights by way of violence or threat of violence because of a person's race, colour, religion or national origin (US Department of Justice, 1999). These protected federal rights include, for example, the right to vote, to obtain government benefits, the right to public education, participation in state programs, obtaining employment, participation in jury service, interstate travel, and the right to the benefits of various types of public places and services (Levin, 2002).

Although not aimed at hate crimes *per se*, Streissguth (2003) states that this has historically been the statute under which hate crimes have been prosecuted. However, he also suggests that the high burden of proof required to secure convictions under the Act is responsible for the small number of crimes actually prosecuted (37 cases between 1991 and 2001). This, he continues, has in practice had the effect of handing responsibility for hate crime prosecutions over to local law enforcement, and has therefore played a significant role in the emergence and development of the state legislation that we shall discuss in due course.

As we have already seen, the term 'hate crime' was officially coined in 1985 by three members of the US House of Representatives sponsoring a Bill seeking a 'Hate Crime Statistics Act'. The Bill sought the annual collection and publication of hate crime data from various law enforcement and voluntary agencies across the US by the Department of Justice and was something of a response to a perceived rise in the number of offences motivated by prejudice and bigotry and subsequent lobbying by a number of civil rights groups (US Department of Justice, 1997).

The Hate Crime Statistics Act was ultimately passed by the US Congress in 1990 and the FBI Uniform Crime Reporting system was designated by the Attorney General as the official method for the collection of hate crime data. The original 1990 Act required the collection of data relating to offences motivated by race, religion, sexual orientation and ethnicity and thus represented the first official recognition of prejudice motivated offending as a specific form of offending deserving of attention in its own right. The offences covered by the original Act included homicide, non-negligent manslaughter, forcible rape, assault, intimidation, arson and destruction, damage or vandalism of property (US Department of Justice, 1997).

Jacobs and Potter (1998) state that the aims of this early legislation were fourfold. First, it was hoped that the collection of hate crime data would enable the criminal justice system as a whole to respond more efficiently and effectively to incidents of hate crime. Second, that the Act would improve the law enforcement response by increasing its sensitivity to and awareness of incidents of hate crime. Third, that the Act would raise public awareness of the hate crime 'problem', and finally, that a clear message would be sent to the American public that crimes motivated by prejudice and bigotry will not be tolerated.

Perhaps illustrative of the process of identity politics, whilst there was considerable debate about whether or not to collect data on offences motivated by homophobia, the category of sexual orientation was ultimately included in the Hate Crime Statistics Act. Significantly, however, the categories of gender and disability were not. The failure to include gender as a distinct category within the Hate Crime Statistics Act sparked much heated debate. The rationales for omitting gender centred on a number of issues. First, it was argued by opponents that statistics on rape and domestic violence were already collected by the Federal Government and therefore did not need to be included again. Second, the argument was made that in the majority of offences against women the victim was acquainted with their attacker. The reasoning here was that such offences could not be hate crimes because perpetrators predominantly targeted one woman whom they knew, and not women *per se*. In this sense then, the victim is not necessarily interchangeable as is the case for other forms of hate crime where the victim is targeted because of their membership of a particular group rather than their individual identity (Jacobs and Potter, 1998).

Jacobs and Potter also suggest that a further reason for the non-inclusion of gender in the Hate Crime Statistics Act was the fear that because of the prevalence of misogynistic violence against women in the US, the inclusion of gender as a distinct category of hate crime would cause other forms of hate crime to be eclipsed in the figures.

In response, women's advocacy groups argued strongly that many forms of crime against women do not involve acquaintances and can only be explained by the offender's irrational hatred of women (Jacobs and Potter, 1998). In such incidents the victim clearly becomes interchangeable thereby transforming an 'ordinary' crime into a hate crime. As such, following the lobbying of Congress by various advocacy groups, the Violence Against Women Act was passed in 1994 as part of the Violent Crime Control and Law Enforcement Act. Congress found that:

> Crimes motivated by the victim's gender constitute bias crimes in violation of the victim's right to be free from discrimination on the basis of gender.
>
> (Public Law 102–322: 1994, title iv)

The Act includes provisions against violent crimes committed by offenders who cross state lines to offend and those who violate a protective order. In addition, the Act allows for civil lawsuits whereby victims can claim financial reparation from their attacker (Streissguth, 2003). Jacobs and Potter argue however that the symbolic significance of the Violence Against Women Act is far greater than its practical value as its success in achieving convictions has been limited. Nevertheless, the Act saw the inclusion of gender as a specific category of hate crime for the first time.

Another crucial part of the Violent Crime Control and Law Enforcement Act 1994 saw the introduction of the Hate Crimes Sentencing Enhancement Act which allowed for increased sentences of up to 30 per cent to be passed down on offenders committing hate crimes where it can be proved that offence was motivated by the perpetrator's prejudice against the victim's race, religion, colour, national origin, ethnicity, gender, disability or sexual orientation. Note here the inclusion of disability as a distinct category of hate crime victimisation for the first time.

In response to an increasing number of hate attacks on churches and other places of worship, the Church Arson Prevention Act 1996 established the National Church Arson Task Force to oversee the investigation and prosecution of these forms of hate crimes. The Task Force brought federal agencies from the Justice and Treasury departments into partnership with state and local law enforcement and prosecutorial agencies to enhance efforts to combat attacks against religious premises, and also allowed broader federal criminal jurisdiction to aid criminal prosecutions. In addition:

> the law enhances penalties for damaging religious property or obstruct-
> ing any person's free exercise of religious freedom ... The law also pro-
> vides compensation to churches that fall prey to arsons and extends
> Federal hate crime and crime victim protections to churches attacked
> because of the ethnic or racial composition of their memberships.
>
> (US Department of Justice, 1997: 18)

In addition, the Act allows for the federal guarantee of private loans of up to $5 million for the rebuilding of damaged or destroyed religious properties. In addition, the Act also reauthorised (in effect renewed) the original Hate Crime Statistics Act of 1990 (Department of Justice, 2003).

Finally, the long mooted Matthew Shepard and James Byrd Jr Hate Crimes Prevention Act 2009, named after the victims of two of America's most infamous hate crimes, was signed into federal law by President Obama on 28 October 2009, as a part of the National Defense Authorization Act of 2010. Its purpose is to expand upon the original 1968 legislation, above, in a number of ways. First, it adds gender, sexual orientation, gender identity and disability to the list of protected characteristics. Second, the prerequisite of engaging in a federally protected activity has been removed. Third, greater powers have been given to the federal authorities to intervene in hate crime investigations not pursued at a local level. Fourth, it provides for financial aid and technical assistance for local investigations and prosecu-tions. And finally, the FBI are now also required to collate statistics on gender and gender identity motivated offences.

State legislation

Thus far we have discussed federal legislation in the US. Whilst significant because it outlaws interference with a person's right to engage in federally protected activities and upholds the federal, Constitutional and statutory civil rights of American citizens, it is quite different to state and local hate crime laws.

As Jacobs and Potter (1998: 42) explain, federal laws:

> provide federal insurance that crime will be prosecuted if state and local
> law enforcement authorities default in carrying out their responsibilities.

At the state and local level, however, the situation is far more intricate. Most states have enacted their own forms of hate crime legislation, and it is at this level that the majority of hate crimes are dealt with. The first to do so (in the modern sense) was California in 1987, which closely replicated the Civil Rights Act of 1968. Many other states have since utilised a model of hate crime legislation produced in 1981 by the Anti-Defamation League. The model (which can be retrieved from www.adl.org) was created to assist states keen to outlaw criminal acts motivated by prejudice and essentially provides a template document where state legislators can 'fill in the blanks' to suit their individual requirements about which criminal acts and which categories of prejudice are to be included.

The relative legal autonomy of each state has, however, meant that different states have adopted different forms of legislation covering different criminal acts and outlawing different prejudices at different times. Thus, what is a hate crime in one state may not be in another, and what is a protected group in one state may also not be in another. Jacobs and Potter continue by explaining that:

> There are significant differences in the ways that federal and state legislatures define hate crimes. A number of states ... treat hate crime as a low-level offence, such as intimidation or harassment. Other states have more general hate crime laws and sentence enhancements that mandate higher sentences for most or all crimes when motivated by prejudice. The statutes also differ as to which prejudices transform ordinary crime into hate crime and as to whether those prejudices must be manifest in the criminal conduct itself or can be proved by evidence concerning the defendant's beliefs, opinion and character. The diversity of hate crime laws means that we cannot assume that people are talking about the same thing when they discuss 'hate crime' or that hate crime reports and statistics from one jurisdiction can be compared with reports and statistics from other jurisdictions.
>
> (1998: 43–4)

This would suggest that in addition to the variation in legislation across the different states, the law is also in a seemingly continual state of change and revision across those states. This makes it difficult to keep up to date with current provisions in every instance and any similar attempt that I might include here will likely be out of date relatively quickly. In light of this the reader is advised to visit the website of the Anti-Defamation League who provide information on the current legal situation in each state in a simple tabular form. This can be found at www.adl.org/99hatecrime/provisions.-asp#al and outlines the statutory provisions contained within each state's hate crime legislation, which, as you will see for yourself, vary greatly across America.

England and Wales

English history has a long and close association with issues of diversity, both positive and negative, largely derived from its historically varied demographic composition. Although there is not the space here to deliver anything like a comprehensive account of all the issues that might be relevant to us, we shall simply concern ourselves with a brief overview of some key historical events that will serve as useful reference points for the more contemporary issues that we shall examine in the chapters ahead.

Ackroyd's (2000) biography of London provides a wealth of information that is pertinent for our purposes. Here he presents evidence of widespread immigration that can be found in various historical accounts that document evidence of Jews, Africans and Europeans living in London at the time the Romans established it as their principal city in AD 43, from which point the city became a centre of European trade. As this position of economic importance grew, evidence further suggests that by *c.*AD 600 native and immigrant populations were well integrated, and by *c.*AD 900 London was populated by Cymric Brythons and Belgae, Danes, Norwegians, Swedes, Franks, Jutes, Angles and Germanics, and by 1440 immigrant records show that 90 per cent of London's population was made up of people of Flemish, Danish, Dutch and German descent. The demographics of London's population were also shaped over time in particular by immigration from those fleeing religious and political persecution in Europe, and more generally by immigrants from seemingly every corner of the known world (Ackroyd, 2000). Records also show that the first black slaves arrived in London in 1555, and by the 1780s, at least 5,000 black people are estimated to have been living in London (Ackroyd, 2000).

London, and Britain more generally, therefore, has a long history of diversity shaped by immigration (be it forced or voluntary) from across the world. One distinct product of this history has been that, at least *in relative terms*, Britain has generally been regarded as a beacon for tolerance. Indeed, in considering England's historical position in this regard, Ackroyd concludes that England was *the* place that was most welcoming to exiles from around the world. Consequently, Roxburgh (2002) suggests that it is precisely this legacy of the historical acceptance and embracing of diversity relative to other European countries that has played a key role in restricting the political success of far right organisations in Britain in recent times. Despite this, however, English history is also littered with examples of long-standing prejudices towards minority groups and what we would now term 'hate crimes' resulting from those prejudices.

Ackroyd (2000) documents, for example, widespread anti-Semitism not just amongst the populace in general but also from those in power. Documentary evidence from 1189 records a number of murderous attacks on London's Jewish quarter and a pogrom from 1215 where Jews were required to wear a symbol of their race on their clothes to identify themselves as Jewish. Interestingly, Hibbert (2003) suggests that it was the men who had returned from a Crusade that were frequently the most ferocious in the massacres of Jews. Evidence can also be found of the hanging of hundreds of Jews in 1272 on suspicion of adulterating the coinage, and in 1290, at a time of economic want and widespread suspicion of illegal financial practices, an Edict of Expulsion issued by Edward I banished all Jews from England. Jews remained banned for 366 years until Oliver Cromwell permitted their readmission in 1656, although they did not finally receive full emancipation until 1858. Despite their formal readmission to the country and the immigration and integration that followed, Jews (together with the Irish and the French) remained the long-standing targets of public opprobrium (Ackroyd, 2000).

Of course, violence motivated by prejudice against Jews and Judaism is not the only form of religious persecution to be found. Indeed, much of England's history has been characterised and shaped by wider religious events. As Hibbert (2003) notes, those who had committed crimes against God and the Church had long been liable to severe punishments, but examples of religious persecution and violence (often bound up with issues of politics and treason) can be found in relation to the Crusades, the Reformation, the Inquisition, long-standing Protestant–Catholic hostility, heresy, and so on.

With regard to the issues of xenophobia, immigration and the presence of 'foreigners', many early documented expressions of prejudice echo concerns frequently expressed today, and Ackroyd (2000: 702) provides a number of interesting examples in relation to London. In 1185, for example, Richard of Devizes stated that *'I do not like that city. All sorts of men crowd there from every country under the heavens. Each brings its own vices and its own customs to the city'.* Similarly, in 1255 chronicler Matthew Paris documented concerns relating to London being 'overflowing' with immigrants.

Similarly, in 1596 Elizabeth I expressed her concerns about the number of black people living in the country, ultimately resulting in a (wholly ineffective) royal proclamation in 1601 instructing that black people should be deported from the country. In a letter to the lord mayors of England's major cities, Elizabeth wrote:

> Her Majestie understanding that there are of late divers Blackmoores brought into the Realme, of which kinde of people there are all ready here to manie, consideringe howe God hath blessed this land with great increase of people of our owne Nation as anie Countrie in the world, wherof manie for want of Service and meanes to sett them on worck fall to Idlenesse and to great extremytie; Her Majesty's pleasure therefore ys, that those kinde of people should be sent forthe of the lande.
>
> (National Archives, n.d.)

Notwithstanding the use of sixteenth-century English, one can identify the monarch's concern about seemingly stretched resources and the availability of employment for the indigenous population, similarly reflected in her proclamation of 1601 where she acknowledges the apparent concerns of her people relating to economic strain and the usurpation of 'relief':

> the Queen's majesty, tendering the good and welfare of her own natural subjects, greatly distressed in these hard times of dearth, is highly

discontented to understand the great number of Negroes and black-amoors which (as she is informed) are carried into this realm since the troubles between her highness and the King of Spain; who are fostered and powered here, to the great annoyance of her own liege people that which covet the relief which these people consume, as also for that the most of them are infidels having no understanding of Christ or his Gospel.

(National Archives, n.d.)

Elizabeth's concerns are perhaps more understandable in the context of repeated harvest failure, hunger and disease in the 1590s, and therefore arguably the need to find a scapegoat for these and wider existing social problems (National Archives, n.d.). In a broader context, though, both the history of scapegoating and the importance of (often erroneous) perception and stereotyping to the indigenous population, is highlighted by Ackroyd (2000: 707–8) who, in relation to Ashkenazi Jews arriving in London in the eighteenth century, notes that:

> they were not welcomed, principally because they were poor. It was suggested that they would 'deluge the kingdom with brokers, usurers and beggars'; once more emerges the irrational but instinctive fear of being 'swamped'. They were also accused of taking jobs from native Londoners, although, since they could not be apprenticed to Christian masters, the fear of usurping available employment was a false one. But, in London, such fears have always been widely advertised and believed; in a society where financial want and insecurity were endemic among the working population, any suggestion of unfair labouring practices could arouse great discontent.

Ackroyd also notes similar hostility to Irish immigrants, traditionally typecast as the poorest of the poor, dating back to the early seventeenth century:

> It is a question, in the modern term, of 'stereotyping' which afflicts all migrant populations. The irony, of course, is that certain groups seem unable to escape this matrix of false expectations and misperceptions ... This has always been one of the cries against the immigrants of London: that they are lazy, living off hand-outs like beggars, and thus demoralising the resident population. The assumption here must be that immigrants are a threat because they undermine the will to work, and provide examples of successful idleness; they are also receiving help or charity which, paradoxically, the native population claims by right to itself.

Identical stereotypes have of course been applied to modern day immigrants (as we shall see again in subsequent chapters) in London and indeed similar views have been found to be common elsewhere (Stonewall, 2004, see chapter five). As we shall also see in chapters five and six, the blaming of minority groups by the majority for social problems, and the perceived competition for scarce resources, is often used as an explanation for the commission of hate crimes, or more appropriately, for the creation of a climate from which hatred and bigotry can emerge. Indeed Sibbitt (1997), whose work we shall return to in future chapters, suggests that racist violence is a logical and predictable expression of prejudicial attitudes in society at large. Similarly, as we shall also see in chapter six, the perception that immigrants in particular are 'culturally polluting' white areas and threatening the future of white people and white culture is a key ideology adopted by organised hate groups, and indeed is a view held by many others outside of these groups, to justify their beliefs and actions.

Interestingly, the 2011 population census for England and Wales (Office for National Statistics, 2012) shows that, since 2001, the number of foreign-born residents in England and Wales has risen by nearly three million to 7.5 million, and that London has become the first region where white British people have become a minority. Perhaps unsurprisingly these figures have brought with them calls for immigration to be more tightly controlled, expressions of concern that the current rate of immigration is unsustainable and hinders integration, and in particular that it places unacceptable strains on resources (see, for example, Migration Watch UK, 2012). Indeed in a speech in December 2012, Labour leader David Miliband acknowledged a *profound anxiety about immigration* amongst some of the British population, noting the role of economics in the development of those anxieties, and the issues of immigration and economics have continued as topics of lively political debate into 2013. Given London's historical diversity, then, such concerns are clearly nothing new.

However, despite having a longer history of prejudice, suspicion and hate motivated violence, and despite subscribing to various anti-discrimination legislation for several decades, the focus on hate crime in England and Wales is much more recent than in the US. Indeed, the emergence of hate crime as a contemporary socio-legal issue in England and Wales is somewhat married to the more recent history of race and racism in this country.

Crimes motivated by racial prejudice in Britain have a long history, yet official recognition of the problem can be traced back to as recently as the early 1980s. Bowling and Phillips (2003) suggest that this is largely because the period from the Second World War to the late 1970s represented one of the most viciously racist periods in British history during which many British people strongly resented and resisted the immigration and integration of blacks and Asians into the country. Between 1939 and 1964 Britain's black population increased from approximately 10,000 to one million, and examples of notable events in and around that time period include the Notting Hill riots in 1958, the winning of the constituency of Smethwick in the West Midlands in the 1964 general election by a Conservative candidate using the campaign slogan *'if you want a Nigger for a neighbour, vote Labour'*, and Enoch Powell's now infamous 'Rivers of Blood' speech.

But despite the ever-increasing evidence to the contrary, the British government persistently denied the racist content of much of the existent racist violence, and attempted to downplay its impact on ethnic minority communities (Bowling and Phillips, 2003). Bowling and Phillips state that evidence of racist victimisation collected by campaigning groups in the late 1970s and early 1980s eventually led the government and the police to officially acknowledge the severity of the situation in a Home Office report published in 1981. This suggests that the 'identity politics' that Jacobs and Potter see as central to contemporary concern with hate crime also played a role in its emergence in Britain. But the problem of racism was further highlighted in the early 1980s by public disorder across the country between minority groups and their supporters and the far right and the police (Scarman, 1981; Bowling and Phillips, 2003).

In addition, the re-emergence of victimology as a significant social science in its own right, and in particular the subsequent development of victim surveys, began to reveal the extent, nature and impact of racist victimisation. Similarly, the problem of racist victimisation was further highlighted by other surveys, studies, inquiries and official reports throughout the 1980s and the 1990s. Together, these issues ensured that racism could no longer be ignored, particularly as earlier official denials of the problem were justified by an apparent lack of reliable information (Bowling and Phillips, 2003).

However, arguably the most significant single event that was ultimately to propel the problem of violent racism to the top of the political and social agenda was the murder of black teenager, Stephen Lawrence, in April 1993. At approximately 22:30 on the evening of 22 April 1993, 18-year-old Stephen and his friend, Duwayne Brooks, were subjected to an unprovoked racist attack by five white youths in Well Hall Road, Eltham, south-east London. Stephen Lawrence was stabbed twice during the attack and died shortly afterwards. The police investigation failed to bring the killers to justice (a situation that would remain until January 2012 when two men were convicted for Stephen's murder) and was later to be condemned as flawed and incompetent, and the police labelled as institutionally racist (Macpherson, 1999).

At the time, however, the Conservative government rejected a request from Stephen's parents for a public inquiry into their son's death and the failure of the police investigation. In the same year that Stephen Lawrence was murdered, the first calls for racially motivated violence to be made a specific offence were made by the Commission for Racial Equality, but these calls were also rejected by the Conservative government, as were the Commission's calls for a strengthening of existing anti-discrimination legislation. Burney and Rose (2002) suggest that political pressure for specific legislation had been growing since the 1980s. They highlight the fact that two private member's Bills, the last in 1992, had been unsuccessful and despite the

Parliamentary Home Affair Committee's endorsement of the need for specific legislation in 1994, the then Home Secretary, Michael Howard, rejected them on the grounds that such offences could be adequately dealt with by existing criminal law (a point to which I shall return in chapter nine). Despite these rejections, John Major, the then Prime Minister, strongly condemned racism in a speech to the Board of Deputies of British Jews, and tackling racist offending was also named as the top priority of the Metropolitan Police Service in London (Bowling and Phillips, 2003).

Nevertheless, Bowling and Phillips (2003) note that in reality very little practical action occurred for a number of years. However, they suggest, support for action against racism was present amongst a number of Labour backbench Members of Parliament, and with the then shadow Home Secretary, Jack Straw, who expressed hopes in the run-up to the 1997 general election that, if elected, a public inquiry into the murder of Stephen Lawrence would be possible. Following their landslide election victory, Jack Straw announced a full public inquiry into the matters arising from the murder of Stephen Lawrence to be conducted by Sir William Macpherson of Cluny.

The Stephen Lawrence Inquiry was by no means the first report to critically examine the issues of race, policing and criminal justice. However, Sir William Macpherson's report into matters arising from the death of Stephen Lawrence has been described as *'the most radical official statement on race, policing and criminal justice ever produced in this country'* (McLaughlin, 1999: 13). The Stephen Lawrence Inquiry was divided into two parts. Part one was concerned with the matters arising from the death of Stephen Lawrence and part two with the lessons to be learned for the investigation and prosecution of racially motivated crimes. The Inquiry concluded that the investigation was *'marred by a combination of professional incompetence, institutional racism and a failure of leadership by senior officers'* (Macpherson, 1999: 46.1) and made 70 recommendations, including a new Ministerial Priority for all police services *'to increase trust and confidence in policing amongst minority ethnic communities'* (1999: Rec. 1).

For those of us involved in hate crime scholarship, and those involved in criminal justice policy and practice in the UK, this was undoubtedly our watershed moment. The murder, and in particular the public inquiry (that published with damning conclusions and sweeping recommendations that went far beyond just issues of policing), with the benefit of hindsight, was *the* single most important event in bringing issues of hate crime to the fore in Britain. This was not just because of the Inquiry's focus on racism, victimisation and the responses to it, and not just because of the far-reaching implications for change that it was to have across the board (see Hall, Grieve and Savage, 2009, for a discussion of the 'legacies of Lawrence'. See also chapter ten), but also because the Lawrences' fight with 'the system' has left a legacy that has allowed other voices to be heard where they previously would not have been. Ultimately, a deep sense of injustice relating to racism, and the unwavering commitment of Doreen and Neville Lawrence in their search for truth, has opened the door for the proper and formal recognition of other forms of targeted victimisation, and given us our academic and political focus on what we now call 'hate crime'.

This shift is evident in the attention now paid by researchers, law and policymakers and practitioners alike to hate crimes motivated by prejudices other than just race, often themselves highlighted by high-profile and tragic cases. Such examples include, but are not limited to, the manslaughter of Johnny Delaney in Cheshire in 2003 and murder of Sophie Lancaster in Lancashire in 2007 (which have respectively served to bring Gypsy and Traveller and alternative lifestyle issues to the fore), the homophobic murder of Jody Dubrowski in London in 2005, and a number of murders of, and other serious offences against, people with disabilities, which are documented in the Equality and Human Rights Commission's (2011) inquiry into disability-related harassment. As Mason-Bish (2010) rightly states, the role of various campaign groups has been central to the way that policy has developed in the UK in recent years, and the victim groups included in the formal definitions discussed in the previous chapter represent those who have activists and campaigners working on their behalf, many of whom will have benefitted either directly or indirectly from the efforts of the Lawrence family (see, for example, Tyson, Giannasi and Hall, 2013, for a discussion of this issue in relation to disability hate crime).

'Hate' legislation in England and Wales

Although specific 'hate' motivated offences are a relatively recent development in law in this country, the need for protection from discrimination has been recognised for a longer period. A number of Acts and Conventions have set out various legislative provisions aimed at challenging discrimination in a number of social arenas. Some of the key pieces of legislation in this regard are Article 1 of the 1945 United Nations Charter, Article 7 of the 1948 Universal Declaration of Human Rights, Article 14 of the European Convention on Human Rights, the 1965 International Convention on the Elimination of All Forms of Racial Discrimination, the Race Relations Acts of 1965, 1968 and 1976, section 95 of the 1991 Criminal Justice Act, the 1995 Disability Discrimination Act, the 1998 Human Rights Act, the Race Relations (Amendment Act 2000) and the Equalities Act 2010 (which has subsumed the disability and race relations acts respectively).

Each of these legislative provisions extends the principle of legal equality and protection from discrimination to varying degrees in different areas of social life, although until relatively recently these have been predominantly along the lines of race (see Bowling and Phillips, 2003, for a critique). However, none of these Acts or Conventions creates a specific criminal offence of 'hate'. Indeed the term 'hate crime' does not specifically appear in any British legislation and therefore does not officially exist as a distinct category of criminal behaviour in itself. Instead, other, more recent legislation prohibits certain acts, which are already outlawed in other legislation, but allows for increased penalties to be imposed by the courts when those acts are proved to be motivated or aggravated by certain officially designated prejudices.

The key piece of legislation in this respect, as we saw in the previous chapter, is the Crime and Disorder Act 1998 (CDA), which allows for enhanced sentencing for racially and, following amendment by the Anti-terrorism, Crime and Security Act of 2001, religiously motivated assaults, criminal damage, public order offences and harassment. These criminal acts are already legislated against by the Offences Against the Person Act 1861, the Criminal Damage Act 1971, the Public Order Act 1986 and the Protection from Harassment Act 1997 respectively. However, where these existing offences can be proved to be aggravated by racial or religious hostility then the CDA allows for additional penalties to reflect the offender's prejudice towards the victim. In addition to the categories of offences outlined above, section 82 of the CDA provides a requirement for the courts to consider racist motives as aggravating factors when determining a sentence for any offence not specifically listed in the Act.

In short, the CDA effectively created nine new racially aggravated offences based upon pre-existing offences contained in other legislation. The CDA allows for sentence enhancement for offences where it can be proved that racial aggravation was present at the time of the offence, except where offences already carry a maximum life sentence. The CDA also allows for the courts (with the exception of the magistrates' courts) to increase sentences for other non-specified offences aggravated by racial hostility. Thus, some offences that would normally be summary only have become either-way offences (magistrates are able to commit racist offenders to the Crown Court for sentence), and maximum sentences have increased to the 'next level' on the sentencing tariff. The provisions for enhanced sentencing also include increased fines, community sentences and compensation (Burney and Rose, 2002), and require the courts to explicitly pronounce in open court that the offence was racially motivated.

Whilst the CDA was not the first piece of legislation to draw attention to the issue of 'hate', the provisions contained within it were in part necessary to overcome the practical difficulties associated with other legislation in this area. The promotion of racial hatred had already been outlawed by the Race Relations Acts of 1965 and 1976, and also by provisions contained within the Public Order Act 1986, and the Football (Disorder) Act 1991 and later revised by the Football (Offences and Disorder) Act in 1999.

Although there was no specific scope for sentence enhancement in any of this legislation (the courts may, however, have taken the racism into account at the sentencing stage but increased penalties were not incorporated into the wording of the law), the significance of the racist element of crime was at least recognised. Section 17 of Public Order Act 1986 in particular states that:

> A person who uses threatening, abusive or insulting words or behaviour, or displays any written material which is threatening, abusive or insulting, is guilty of an offence if (a) he intends to stir up racial hatred, or (b) having regard to all the circumstances racial hatred is likely to be stirred up thereby.

Additionally, a subsequent amendment to that Act made reference to the intentional causing of alarm, harassment or distress, which was aimed at responding to racially aggravated behaviour. However, the problems associated with this particular piece of legislation are highlighted by the fact that only 41 cases were brought for prosecution between 1990 and 1997. Iganski (1999a) asserts that this low number of prosecutions, and thus the limited effectiveness of the legislation, can be attributed first to the low incidence of offences covered by the Act, second to the limitations of the provisions of the legislation and finally (and crucially), to the ambiguous language used to define what is actually unlawful.

Of particular concern for Iganski is the use of the word 'hatred' which he explains implies a rather severe sentiment that may in reality exclude other lesser or more subtle acts, behaviours or language (written or verbal) that may nevertheless lead to criminal behaviour and may still stir up racial hatred. In essence then, prosecuting 'hatred' is difficult, but prosecuting 'hostility' as the Crime and Disorder Act does, should (in theory at least) allow for a far greater breadth of 'prejudice in action' to be taken into account. The focus on wider prejudice rather than hatred is therefore deliberate and supports the contention within other definitions that hate crime isn't predominantly about 'hate'.

More recent legislation has sought to protect groups other than those identified by race or religion, and has incorporated offences other than those specifically stated by the Crime and Disorder Act 1998. For example, section 153 of the Powers of Criminal Courts (Sentencing Act) Act 2000 requires the courts to consider racial or religious hostility as an aggravating factor when deciding on the sentence for any offence which is not specifically stated under the Crime and Disorder Act. This means that racial or religious aggravation can be taken into consideration by the court in sentencing for any offence.

Similarly, the Criminal Justice Act 2003 allows for homophobia and disability (mental and physical) bias to be taken into account as aggravating factors at sentencing, but stops short of making them specific offences in the same way that the Crime and Disorder Act does for offences relating to race and religion. Likewise, in Northern Ireland, the Criminal Justice (No. 2) Northern Ireland Order, introduced in September 2004, whilst not creating any new 'hate' offences, does allow for hostility based on religion, race, sexual orientation or disability to be taken into account on conviction when sentencing. The Criminal Justice Act 2003 does however state that it is immaterial whether or not the offender's hostility is also based, to any extent, on any other factor. The expression of prejudice, however strong or in whatever way, is the key issue.

More recently, the Racial and Religious Hatred Act 2008 amended the Public Order Act 1986 to create new offences of stirring up hatred against persons on religious grounds. This is, in part, to take into account the decisions of the courts that have variously deemed Jews and Sikhs to be racial groups and Muslims and Christians to be religious groups. The inclusion of religious hatred here, in theory at least, makes the law more inclusive, not least because it also includes atheism within its provisions. Similarly, the Criminal Justice and Immigration Act 2008 also amends the Public Order Act 1986, making it an offence to use threatening words or behaviour, or display any material which is threatening, with the intention to stir up hatred against a group of people defined by reference to their *sexual orientation*. In addition, the Legal Aid, Sentencing and Punishment of Offenders Act 2012 has amended the Criminal Justice Act 2003, and in doing so doubles the starting point for sentences for murders motivated by hate on grounds of disability or transgender to thirty years, in line with other hate motivated murders.

Finally, in December 2012 the government asked the Law Commission to consider whether the two existing groups of offences relating to hate crime (race and religion) should be extended to include disability, sexual orientation or gender identity. This involves a consideration of the Public Order Act 1986 and the Crime and Disorder Act 1998, and whether and how they should be changed to include all five characteristics. The Commission's views are due to be reported in the Spring of 2014.

Concluding comments

This chapter has considered the historical evolution of 'hate crime' as a social problem worthy of state attention, epitomised by the extent to which, gradually, legislation has been enacted to respond to it. As we have seen, the journey towards this formally recognised status in the US and in England and Wales is the product of a number of combining factors. In short, hate crime is nothing new. What is relatively new, however, is societal concern with the issue, and this chapter has suggested that there are a number of different reasons underpinning the emergence of hate crime as a contemporary social problem in need of specific attention. Whilst 'identity politics' has to a certain extent played a key role in the recognition of the plight of some minority groups, arguably best illustrated by the pivotal role played by various causes célèbres in shaping public concern and political debate in both jurisdictions, much of this formal recognition is based on very real concerns about the long-standing and disproportionate victimisation of people based upon aspects of their core identity. Of course, it is not just the US and England and Wales that have (relatively) recently begun to formally recognise hate crime. Many other countries have done likewise, and it is to this wider international picture that we now turn.

3 The international geography of hate

Barbara Perry (2001) suggests that there are few endeavours so frustrating as trying to estimate and establish the extent of hate crime. Part of the reason for this, as we saw in chapter one, is that hate crime is essentially a social construct and that the size of the problem depends almost entirely on how we define and conceptualise it (as illustrated by Jacobs and Potter's, 1998, model) which of course will vary from place to place, and from time to time. As such, the geography of *where* hate crime is occurring, and *how much* of it is occurring in any given location, presents a further interesting but complicated avenue for exploration.

Nevertheless, various attempts have been made both at domestic and international levels, by a range of bodies, to measure the extent and nature of the hate crime 'problem' in different parts of the world. One of the key sources of information of this type is published annually by the Organization for Security and Co-operation in Europe (OSCE). By using the 2011 and 2012 OSCE reports (utilising the two allows for occasional gaps in the data in one or the other to be filled thereby providing a more holistic overview) as a framework to examine the international geography of 'hate', and by drawing upon wider information derived from other relevant national and international organisations, this chapter will, as far as is possible, present an overview of the international hate crime picture.

The OSCE region

Tracing its origins to the détente phase of the early 1970s, when the Conference on Security and Co-operation in Europe (CSCE) was created to serve as a multilateral forum for dialogue and negotiation between East and West, the OSCE is the world's largest regional security organisation, with members from 57 states across Europe, Central Asia and North America (OSCE, 2012). It offers a forum for political negotiations and decision-making in the fields of early warning, conflict prevention, crisis management and post-conflict rehabilitation. The OSCE's approach to security encompasses politico-military, economic and environmental, and human aspects, and therefore addresses a wide range of security-related concerns, including arms control, confidence- and security-building measures, human rights, national minorities, democratisation, policing strategies, counter-terrorism, and economic and environmental activities. All 57 participating States share equal status, and decisions are taken by consensus on a politically, but not legally binding basis (OSCE, 2012).

Participating States of the Organization for Security and Co-operation in Europe have repeatedly condemned hate crimes and, in theory if not always in practice, pledged to take action against them. In 1990, the organisation expressed concerns about crimes based on prejudice, discrimination, hostility or hatred (OSCE, 2012), and this was reaffirmed at the Maastricht Ministerial Council Meeting of 2003 when the term 'hate crimes' appeared for the first time in an OSCE Ministerial Council decision. Today, there are a broad range of OSCE commitments dealing directly with the problem, including commitments to train police to respond to hate crimes, to review legislation, to assist efforts by civil society and to collect reliable data (OSCE, 2012). It is predominantly the latter of these commitments that we shall examine in this chapter.

Each year the OSCE publishes a report documenting hate crimes in the region. The primary objective of this report is to provide information on the prevalence of, and government responses to, hate crimes in the OSCE region, in accordance with the decisions of the OSCE Ministerial Council made in 2006, which pledged, amongst other things, to collect and make publicly available, information on hate crimes from its member States. This mandate was developed further in 2009 when member States committed to a range of undertakings, including enacting legislation to tackle hate crimes and to develop measures to encourage the reporting of hate incidents.

Despite these pledges, the OSCE (2012) are clear that there are substantial challenges to overcome in assessing the extent of hate crimes. They rightly acknowledge that such crimes are significantly under-reported by victims, and many participating States have no effective monitoring or reporting systems in place to gather relevant information, perhaps indicating the extent to which hate crime is a social and/or political priority (an issue I shall return to in chapter ten). Whilst the governments of many participating States are indeed able to provide some statistics on hate crimes, the OSCE note that these numbers almost certainly under-report their prevalence. Reports from Non-Governmental Organisations (NGOs), Intergovernmental Organisations (IGOs) and others help fill out the 'OSCE picture', but this unofficial information cannot always be verified (OSCE, 2012), and of course one must keep in mind the role of some of these groups in activities that constitute part of the process of identity politics. Thus, whilst the annual OSCE reports aim to present a comprehensive picture of the prevalence of hate crimes, it can, they suggest, be more accurately seen as a compilation of reported hate crimes, primarily from participating States, supported by data compiled from reports by NGOs, IGOs and the media, and submitted to the OSCE's Office for Democratic Institutions and Human Rights (ODIHR), collected via an online questionnaire.

Counting what, where?

The OSCE (2012: 14) recognise hate crimes thus:

> A hate crime is a criminal act committed with a bias motive. ODIHR uses this definition as the analytical filter through which the data submitted by participating States, NGOs, IGOs and others are considered and presented. Every hate crime has two elements. The first element is that an act is committed that constitutes a criminal offence under ordinary criminal law. The second element is that the offender intentionally chose a target with a protected characteristic. A protected characteristic is a characteristic shared by a group, such as 'race', language, religion, ethnicity, nationality or any other similar common factor. For example, if a person is assaulted because of his or her real or perceived ethnicity, this constitutes a hate crime.

Similarly:

> The term 'hate incident' or 'hate-motivated incident' is used to describe an incident or act committed with a bias motive that does not reach the threshold of a hate crime, either because a criminal offence was not proven or because the act may not have been a criminal offence under a particular state's legislation. Nonetheless, hate-motivated incidents may precede, accompany or provide the context for hate crimes. Since hate-motivated incidents can be precursors to more serious crimes, records of such incidents can be useful to demonstrate not only a context of harassment, but also evidence of escalating patterns of violence.
> (2012: 14)

Despite agreement on these definitions, and what ODIHR believe are gradually improving responses received from participating States, there is, they point out, still an overall paucity of clear, reliable and detailed data on the nature and scope of hate crimes in the OSCE area (OSCE, 2012).

They rightly point out that even where statistics exist, they are not always disaggregated according to bias motivation, type of crime or outcome of prosecution. In the absence of data of this type, they state, it is impossible to determine the frequency with which particular types of hate crimes occur in the OSCE region, whether hate crimes are on the rise, or which groups are most often targeted. Since different participating States keep statistics in different ways, it is also not always possible to make meaningful comparative judgements on the extent of hate crimes (OSCE, 2012).

Despite these (albeit significant) caveats, the work of the OSCE never-theless provides arguably the most comprehensive official account of hate crime occurrence around the world presently available, and as such its find-ings do indeed shed some interesting light on the 'problem' in hand.

Hate crime across the OSCE region

The most recent OSCE report at the time of writing is that published in November 2012, which provides information relating to 2011. Of the 50 states that report collecting data (Luxembourg and the FYR Macedonia do not collect data, and, somewhat curiously, Malta, Monaco and San Marino did not state whether they did or did not collect data), ODIHR had received 30 completed questionnaires, as well as general information from Bosnia and Herzegovina, Germany, Ireland, Moldova, Kazakhstan and Uzbekistan. ODIHR had also received statistics or other relevant information on inci-dents of hate crimes from government agencies in 24 participating States at the time their report was completed (OSCE, 2012).

Nevertheless, the data that was collected reveals some interesting infor-mation. Of the participating States, 35 collect information relating to victi-misation based on 'ethnicity/national origin'; 34 recognise 'religion'; 33 include 'race/colour'; 19 recognise 'sexual orientation'; 17 acknowledge 'citizenship'; 15 record 'gender'; 13 'language'; 13 'disability'; 9 'transgen-der'; and 14 record 'other', which might include, for example, 'social status' (as in Croatia), 'education' (Belgium), and 'foreigner' (Ukraine).

In terms of the crimes that can be classified as 'hate crimes', 38 states include 'homicide'; 37 'physical assault'; 34 'damage to property'; 32 'grave desecration'; 34 'vandalism'; 35 'threats/threatening behaviour'; 25 'attacks on places of worship'; and 24 'other'. With reference to the latter, countries such as Austria, the Czech Republic, Germany, Slovakia, Switzerland and the Russian Federation collect data on 'extremism' which relates to crimes committed for political or ideological purposes (OSCE, 2012). Similarly, some countries collect data on 'incitement to hatred', 'hate speech', and 'crimes of discrimination'. ODIHR note that most states use this data to formulate policy and to address domestic security issues – a critical issue to which we shall return in chapter ten.

Even from this very simple overview, it is clear that we are left with something of a 'patchwork quilt' when it comes to accounting for 'hate crimes' between different countries. This becomes even more apparent when one considers the statistics in relation to how much of what is recorded, as illustrated in the tables compiled by the OSCE (available from http://tandis. odihr.pl/hcr2011/pdf/Hate_Crime_Report_full_version.pdf, pages 23–5).

The table lists the states that comprise the OSCE region (with the excep-tion of Mongolia, who only joined in November 2012), together with a summary of the type of data collected, and the information that was submitted by each state relating to the number of hate crimes recorded by the police, the number of cases prosecuted, and the number of cases sentenced for the years 2009 to 2011. It is important of course to interpret the data with caution. A number of caveats have already been identified above relating to considerable variations between countries in relation to what is recorded, when it is recorded, how it is recorded, and so on, but the data does nevertheless serve as a useful indicator of, as the OSCE (2012: 22) put it, 'incidents acknowledged by the authorities as hate crimes or reported by victims'.

The most striking features of the statistics are, in my view, first the significant variation in the numbers of hate crimes recorded, prosecuted and sentenced between states; second, how few hate crimes are officially recorded across the region; and third, just how far the data from the United Kingdom stands out when compared to every other state (with the possible exception of Sweden who become somewhat more comparable once demographic factors are taken into account). Whilst it seems that, numerically at least, the UK is the hate crime capital of the OSCE region, one must keep in mind the definitional and conceptual issues that we discussed in chapter one when seeking to find meaning in these figures. The hate crime statistics for the UK in comparative terms is an issue I shall return to later in this chapter.

Of course, having collective figures for hate crimes tells us nothing about the nature of the victimisation that is occurring. Helpfully, however, the OSCE also break down the information into a number of categories which further aid our understanding of what is occurring in different countries. There is not the scope here to consider all of the information available, so an overview of some of the key issues will have to suffice.

Racism and xenophobia

Given the importance of race as a key motivating factor in the emergence of hate crime as a contemporary socio-legal issue (as discussed in the previous chapter), it should not be too surprising that issues of race and racism are frequently the most cited cases of hate crime in many countries. This situation was, again in theory if not always in practice, furthered by the EU Framework Decision, adopted in November 2008, on combating certain forms and expressions of racism and xenophobia by means of criminal law (European Union, 2008). As the OSCE point out, this decision seeks to ensure harmonisation across the EU of clear and comprehensive legislation on racist and xenophobic crimes, and Article 4 of the decision requires that racist and xenophobic motives for criminal acts be considered as aggravating features of crimes that courts should take account of when imposing sentences. Furthermore, as an organisation, the OSCE has long recognised the threat to international security posed by racism, xenophobia and related forms of intolerance and has, through various charters, agreements, declarations and commitments, sought to address these issues across member States (OSCE, 2012).

Once again caution needs to be exercised when interpreting the data, not least because different States have different interpretations of what constitutes 'racism' and 'xenophobia', and some disaggregate their data into more discrete categories whilst others do not. Nevertheless, from the OSCE data, some interesting 'official' patterns emerge. Belarus, Bosnia and Herzegovina, Canada, Czech Republic, Finland, France, Greece, Hungary, FYR Macedonia, Moldova, Russian Federation, Serbia, Spain, and Ukraine reported *no* data on racist and xenophobic hate crimes. At the other end of the scale, Germany recorded 2,528 xenophobic crimes and 484 racist crimes; Sweden recorded 3,936 xenophobic/racist crimes; and the UK recorded 35,875 racist offences in England, Wales and Northern Ireland. Scattered in between were Poland with 222; Ireland with 136; Austria with 57; Italy with 24; Croatia with 12; Kazakhstan with 10 (all murders); Latvia with 4; Lithuania with 5; and Belgium with 2 recorded racist hate crimes.

Even with all the caveats associated with official data collection, one is still entitled to express considerable surprise at many, if not all, of these statistics. However, because of concerns over the accuracy of official statistics, the OSCE also collect information about countries from other non-government sources. Unsurprisingly, for some (although not all) States, these alternative sources provide evidence of offences not recorded by the authorities. Again, these can vary in their interpretation of both the motive and the offence both between and within States. There is not the space here to consider all of the issues, but three examples will serve to illustrate some of the key points associated with official statistics.

The Russian Federation

No racist or xenophobic crimes were reported by the Russian Federation to ODIHR for the year 2011 (OSCE, 2012). However, a number of relevant and independent organisations report starkly different findings. For example, for the same year, the SOVA Center for Information and Analysis (2012) recorded 22 racist murders and 128 racist physical assaults. For the previous year, another Moscow-based NGO reported 3 murders and 22 physical assaults (Moscow Protestant Task Force on Racial Violence, 2011), whilst another reported 19 murders and 89 physical assaults (Moscow Bureau for Human Rights, 2010). More recently, Human Rights Watch (2012) state that whilst racist murders in Russia declined in 2011, aggressive racism and xenophobia continued to rise, as evidenced by the nationalist riots of December 2010, and that 'human rights defenders' are vulnerable to harassment and physical attack. Furthermore, in 2013 the European Commission Against Racism and Intolerance (ECRI) will publish a follow-up report to one previously published in 2006 which:

> highlighted the problem of racial discrimination in the system of residence registration leaving members of visible minorities without access

to basic rights; the escalation of racist violence, in particular perpetrated by young skinheads, and interethnic clashes; the spread of racist statements and publications, especially in the media; and the large numbers of foreign workers employed illegally and exposed to severe exploitation as well as racism and xenophobia.

(ECRI, 2012b)

Greece

Greece also recorded no racist hate crimes for 2011. In the previous year two racist attacks were reported, as was also the case in 2009. Similarly to the situation with the Russian Federation, above, a range of NGOs have reported quite different findings over these three years. For example, the United Nations High Commissioner for Refugees (UNHCR) reported *multiple instances of physical assaults on refugees* to ODIHR in 2011 (OSCE, 2011: 47) – a finding that was echoed in 2012. Another NGO, Praksis, reported 206 hate motivated incidents against refugees, asylum seekers, and undocumented migrants (OSCE, 2011). More recently, Human Rights Watch (2012: 32) have expressed their serious concern at increasing levels of xenophobic violence against migrants and asylum seekers over the past decade which, they suggest, is 'the product of the failure of successive Greek governments to adopt coherent migration policies, chronic mismanagement of the asylum system, and, most recently, the deep economic crisis and resulting austerity', whilst the European Network Against Racism (2012) has warned of increasing hostility towards homosexuals and people with disabilities. Of course Greece is not the only country to be affected by the global economic crisis, and ECRI (2012a) has warned that 'welfare cuts, diminished job opportunities and a consequent rise in intolerance towards both immigrant groups and older historical minorities are worrying trends' emerging across Europe.

The United Kingdom

Part of the rationale for changing the definition of a hate crime to one that is predominantly victim-oriented following the Stephen Lawrence Inquiry (see chapter one) was to encourage the reporting of these offences to the authorities, thereby reducing the so called 'dark figure' of unreported crime. On the face of it, in relative terms at least, the statistics from the OSCE suggest a certain degree of success in shedding some light on the 'dark figure', with 35,875 racist incidents recorded in England and Wales and Northern Ireland. Nevertheless, information from the British Crime Survey (BCS, 2012) demonstrates that despite officially recording figures far in excess of any other country in the OSCE region, the UK, or more specifically England, Wales and Northern Ireland, still only touches the tip of the iceberg in terms of the number of incidents occurring. Indeed, having combined the findings of 2009/10 and 2010/11 in order to provide more robust results, the British Crime Survey estimates that an average of 136,000 racist incidents occur annually. And as we shall see in the next chapter, this too is likely to be an underestimation of the 'true' occurrence of racist incidents.

Anti-Semitism

Similarly to racism and xenophobia, crimes motivated by anti-Semitism have long been a concern for the OSCE. Although 21 states collect specific data on anti-Semitic incidents, at the time the OSCE compiled their 2012 report, only Germany, Italy, Sweden and the UK had submitted official statistics, recording 1,239; 30; 194; and 438 respectively. Interestingly, NGO and other reports of anti-Semitic incidents were also generally very low across the OSCE region, and for the countries that did submit official data, all of these were higher in number than those submitted by the NGOs monitoring anti-Semitism in their respective state. In other words, more anti-Semitic hate crimes were recorded by the authorities than by NGOs, although anti-Semitism, it seems, remains considerably under-reported all round.

Anti-Muslim hate crimes

A somewhat more recent concern for the OSCE is the issue of anti-Muslim hate crimes, and their commitments to combating this form of crime date back to 2002 (OSCE, 2012). Conceptualising and measuring 'Islamophobia' as a form of hate crime is particularly complex (Bleich, 2011), but the 2012 OSCE report notes that 18 states currently collect specific data on this (others, such as the UK, Denmark and Liechtenstein, do not specifically disaggregate hate crimes perpetrated against religious groups), although only Switzerland and Sweden had submitted this specific data by the time the report was compiled, with 1 and 278 incidents respectively. Again, as with anti-Semitism, reports from NGOs and others were generally quite low. For example, the various NGOs in respective countries recorded 2 incidents in the US; Canada, 5; Bulgaria, approximately 23; France, 23 and Bosnia and Herzegovina, 63. Again, this may be a product of not disaggregating data beyond simply 'race' and 'religion' more generally, but it does seem that, like anti-Semitism, anti-Muslim hate crime is widely under-reported.

Religion

As noted above, some countries do not disaggregate anti-Muslim crime from the broader issue of religiously motivated hate crime, the latter of which the OSCE have concentrated on since 2004 under the heading of *Christians and members of other religions*. According to the OSCE (2012) 35 states collect data on religiously motivated hate crimes, although once again few of those had submitted data by the time the report was compiled. Sweden specifically recorded 651 anti-religious hate crimes of which 162 were anti-Christian. Germany and the United Kingdom submitted aggregated religious hate crimes, recording 319 and 1,773 respectively. Unsurprisingly perhaps, the Holy See provided information on anti-Christian incidents in 11 states, but again, reports from NGOs were predominantly restricted to examples of rather isolated incidents across the region.

Crimes against Roma and Sinti

Although the OSCE's concern with hostility and hatred towards Roma and Sinti dates back to 1990, information concerning their victimisation is rather limited. One must keep in mind that data here might not necessarily be disaggregated from the wider issue of race and ethnicity, with just 13 OSCE States specifically monitoring this issue. At the time of publication, however, only Sweden had reported any such crimes to the OSCE, with a total of 184, whilst Bulgaria, Czech Republic, Hungary and Serbia had reported information on specific cases. In keeping with the under-reporting of the problem, the OSCE note that just eight NGOs in six states reported the occurrence of any incidents.

However, a plethora of reports produced by a range of organisations in recent years paint a very different picture indeed. For example, Human Rights First (2008) variously cite widespread examples of violence, hostility, intimidation, discrimination, human rights abuses and inciteful rhetoric in countries such as Italy, Bulgaria, the Czech Republic, Greece, Romania, the Russian Federation, Serbia, Slovakia, Slovenia, Ukraine and the United Kingdom.

Indeed, in describing the Roma people, the European Court of Human Rights, in the case of *Orsus* v. *Croatia* in 2010, declared that as a result of their history the Roma have become a specific type of disadvantaged group and vulnerable minority requiring special protection. Similarly, the Council of Europe (2012a) state that:

> Some 10–12 million Roma people are estimated to live in Europe, present in each country. They are amongst the most deprived of all communities, facing daily discrimination and racial insults, living in extreme poverty and exclusion from the normal life that other people take for granted – going to school, seeing the doctor, applying for a job or having decent housing. Past efforts to help them have not brought the hoped-for results, and although laws do exist in Europe, they all too often fail to make an impact on the daily lives of Roma families.

Concerns over these, and other, issues have also been variously expressed by Human Rights Watch (HRW) who have highlighted a range of human rights issues and/or hostility affecting the Roma in, for example, Bosnia and Herzegovina, France, Italy, Serbia and Montenegro, Bulgaria, Romania, Croatia, Moldova, Norway, Hungary and the FR Yugoslavia. Closer to home, the Equalities and Human Rights Commission (2009a) have highlighted similar concerns over the inequalities experienced by Gypsy and Traveller communities in the UK (see chapter four).

Lesbian, gay, bisexual, transgender (LGBT)

As of 2012, 19 OSCE States collected data on crimes motivated by bias against lesbian, gay, bisexual or transgender (LGBT) people. Of those, nine included crimes against transgender people as a separate category, although at the time the OSCE report was compiled only four states had submitted any data. A marginally better picture can be drawn from the 2011 OSCE report, although Denmark, Finland, Germany, Latvia, Sweden and the United Kingdom were the only participating States to have provided data to ODIHR, recording 17; 128; 187; 1; 770; and 4,833 (plus 357 on the grounds of transgender bias) respectively. However, perhaps signalling the relative strength of LGBT advocacy, 32 (31 in 2012) NGOs in 28 participating States provided information on crimes against LGBT people (OSCE, 2011). Indeed, in numerous countries where no LGBT crimes were officially reported, NGOs were able to provide information relating to a range of occurrences and, in several cases, details of violent hate crimes including serious physical assaults, rape and murder (see also FRA, 2013).

Similarly, Human Rights Watch have variously documented concerns over a number of years relating to LGBT human rights abuses in numerous countries, including Uganda, Zimbabwe, Bulgaria, South Africa, Cameroon, Jamaica, Lebanon, Burundi, Russia, Hungary, Malaysia, Honduras, Philippines, Kuwait, Iran, Nigeria and Turkey to name just a few.

In attempting to shed light on the dark figure of homophobic crime in England and Wales, the Gay British Crime Survey (Stonewall, 2008) found that one in five lesbian and gay people in Britain had been a victim of one or more homophobic hate crimes or incidents in the previous three years. According to the survey these incidents ranged from regular insults on the street to serious physical and sexual assaults. Crucially, a finding that perhaps helps to explain the relatively low official statistics reported to the OSCE by the respective authorities, highlighted that three in four victims of homophobic incidents did not report them to the police.

Disability

In 2011, 13 participating States recorded data on crimes against people with disabilities. However, at the time the report was written in 2012, Germany and the United Kingdom were the only participating States that had provided data for 2011 to ODIHR, recording 18 and 1,937 respectively.

Furthermore, ODIHR received no information from NGOs relating to crimes or incidents motivated by bias against people with disabilities.

The position in the United Kingdom is particularly interesting with regard to disability hate crime. The official figures reported above represent the most ever recorded by the police. Arguably, this is a product of the increased attention that has been drawn to the issue of disability victimisation in recent years, culminating in the EHRC's inquiry published in 2011 (as noted in chapter two). However, from the research undertaken by various disability-related organisations and others, it is apparent that this remains vastly under-reported (an issue further explored in chapter four). For example, a study by Mind (2007) found that, with reference to people with mental health problems, 71 per cent of respondents had been victimised in the community at least once in the previous two years; 41 per cent were victims of ongoing bullying; 22 per cent had been physically assaulted; 27 per cent had been sexually harassed; and 34 per cent had been victims of theft. Crucially, the reporting of these incidents was low, and in a finding that perhaps helps to explain the levels of under-reporting, 64 per cent of victims reported being dissatisfied with the overall response they received from the authorities (again, an issue we will consider in chapter seven). These findings are not unique, with other studies in the field reporting similarly (see, for example, DRCCS, 2004; Mencap, 2007; Quarmby, 2008; EHRC, 2011, 2012).

The United States

Although a member of the OSCE, the US hate crime statistics were not included in the 2011 or 2012 reports and a separate consideration is therefore necessary. In the US the collection of national hate crime data has been a legal requirement under the Hate Crime Statistics Act (HCSA) since 1990. The data is collected and published annually in the Uniform Crime Report (UCR) Program by the Federal Bureau of Investigation (FBI). The FBI currently collects data from law enforcement agencies across the US on a variety of criminal offences (murder and non-negligent manslaughter, forcible rape, aggravated assault, simple assault, intimidation and robbery, burglary, larceny–theft, motor vehicle theft, arson, and destruction, damage and vandalism to property) committed against persons, property or society that are motivated in whole or in part by one of six officially designated prejudices (race, religion, disability, sexual orientation, and ethnicity gender/ gender identity).

Whilst the original intention of the HCSA was to provide an accurate picture of hate crime across America, Perry (2001) suggests that that there are numerous shortcomings associated with the data collection that ensure that the figures are far from accurate. Unsurprisingly, given our discussion in chapter one, a key limitation that Perry identifies relates to the narrow definition used by the HCSA. Only data relating to the five (the sixth, gender/

gender identity, will be included from 2013) prejudices and 11 offences are officially collected meaning that other criminal offences and non-criminal incidents are not counted, and neither are offences motivated by prejudices other than the five listed. In this sense, only certain hate crimes are counted, whilst other offences that might have a strong claim to be included are not.

In addition, Perry questions inconsistencies between the agencies reporting offences to the UCR, which is done on a *voluntary* basis. What is and what is not classified as a hate crime varies greatly across different US states and Perry suggests that this has important implications for law enforcement agencies in terms of collecting and recording relevant data for the UCR. In short, the way that hate crime is defined by different jurisdictions greatly affects what, and how much of what, is recorded in the official figures. This situation is further amplified by inconsistencies in the extent of law enforcement training and the subsequent ability of law enforcement officers to recognise offences as being hate motivated. In other words, hate motivation is subjective and open to interpretation, which in turn affects what appears in the statistics.

Furthermore, the UCR figures are also susceptible to the limitations that affect all official crime statistics. Most significant is the issue of under-reporting and the resultant 'dark figure' of hate crime. Official statistics consist predominantly of incidents reported to the authorities by the public. This of course means that incidents that occur but are not reported to the authorities are unlikely to appear in the official statistics and will therefore remain largely unknown. This is crucial because there is evidence to suggest that this 'dark figure' of unreported crime is significantly higher for hate crimes than for other types of offences for a variety of reasons that we shall explore in due course (Weiss, 1993; Perry, 2001).

Nevertheless, despite these identified shortcomings and the need to question both what is counted and how it is counted, the official figures are not without their uses. Perry suggests that the UCR represents the most comprehensive database of hate crimes in the US and is potentially useful in identifying general trends and patterns. With this in mind, let us briefly examine the latest available UCR data.

The FBI (2012) states that 1,944 law enforcement agencies reported 6,222 hate crime incidents involving 7,254 offences (under UCR counting rules an incident can involve more than one offence) in 2011. Of these incidents 46.9 per cent were motivated by racial bias, 20.8 per cent by sexual orientation bias, 19.8 per cent by religious bias, 11.6 per cent by ethnicity/national origin bias, and 0.9 per cent by mental or physical disability bias. Of the total number of offences, 63.7 per cent were crimes against the person, 36 per cent were crimes against property, and the rest were crimes against society.

In terms of those targeted, African Americans represent the largest victim group, followed by homosexual males and Jews. The statistics also show that hate crimes are predominantly offences against the person rather than offences against property, but that the majority of hate crimes are what we might term 'low-level' offences (intimidation, harassment, common assault, criminal damage and so on) as opposed to what might on the surface be deemed to be more serious crimes (murder, robbery, rape and the like). Previous UCRs have demonstrated that many of these issues have remained broadly consistent over a number of years, although the statistics for 2011 are notable because they represent a 6 per cent drop from 2010 (with the notable exception of sexual orientation and anti-Muslim hate crimes which increased slightly on the previous year) and are at their lowest recorded level since 1994.

Nevertheless, the UCR statistics represent a significant underestimation of the 'true' volume of hate crime in the US. Indeed, in responding to the publication of the above FBI figures the Anti-Defamation League (ADL) (2012b) note that at least 79 cities with populations in excess of 100,000 either did not participate in the FBI hate crime data collection programme at all or affirmatively reported that they had recorded zero hate crimes. This long-standing issue of under-reporting is also demonstrated by data collected by various victim advocacy groups across the US. For example, in their annual audit of anti-Semitic incidents, which draws upon official figures and information provided by victims, law enforcement officers and community leaders, the Anti-Defamation League (2011) counted 1,239 incidents in 2010 (compared to 887 reported to the UCR). Similarly, the Antiviolence Project, an advocacy group for the LGBT community, estimated 2,503 homophobic incidents in 2010, as opposed to the 1,277 counted by the UCR in that year.

The wider international picture

Using the OSCE as a template to discuss international issues has provided an interesting picture of the existence of hate crime in a number of countries around the world. Of course, by using this as a framework for discussion, many countries remain unaccounted for because they are either not part of the OSCE, or did not submit data in time for the most recent report. For example, one notable omission from this chapter is Australia, where statistics are hard to come by, but where racist hate crime is known to be particularly problematic (Mason, 2012). It was never my intention to try to include every country in this chapter (judging by the size of the reports produced by the international bodies such an undertaking would probably have required a text of several volumes, let alone a single chapter in a book of this size), so a brief mention of some of the 'hate-related' issues occurring elsewhere will have to suffice.

To this end, Human Rights Watch's annual World Reports provide useful information concerning a range of human rights issues around the globe. Not all of these issues fall neatly into the politically constructed hate crime categories outlined here, but they undoubtedly represent examples of discrimination, hostility and often very violent expressions of prejudice and hatred. The reports for 2012 and 2013, for example, variously document concerns relating to:

Africa – Angola (violence against immigrants); Burundi (political violence); Ivory Coast (political violence); Democratic Republic of Congo (various human rights abuses); Equatorial Guinea (repression); Eritrea (restrictions on religious freedom); Ethiopia (political repression); Kenya (LGBT, refugee rights); Malawi (various human rights abuses); Nigeria (intercommunal and political violence; sexual orientation and gender identity); Rwanda (freedom of expression); Somalia (war crimes; abuses of internationally displaced persons); South Africa (vulnerable workers; women's rights; sexual orientation and gender identity; refugee rights); South Sudan (political and intercommunal violence); Sudan (ethnic conflict and displacement); Swaziland (freedom of expression); Uganda (sexual orientation); Zimbabwe (political violence).

Americas – Argentina (women's rights); Brazil (indigenous); Colombia (indigenous; guerrilla abuses; conflict-related violence; disability); Cuba (political repression; freedom of expression); Ecuador (freedom of expression); Guatemala (gender-based violence); Haiti (gender-based violence); Honduras (transgender); Mexico (migrants; gender-based violence); Peru (disability); Venezuela (political freedom); US (see above).

Asia – Afghanistan (gender; ethnic; religious; political); Bangladesh (gender; religious; political; indigenous groups); Burma (freedom of expression; political; ethnic conflict); Cambodia (free speech; political; freedom of association; forced evictions; refugees and asylum seekers; migrant domestic workers); China (freedom of expression, association and religion; political; disability rights; migrant rights; gender; sexual orientation and gender identity); India (ethnic; gender); Indonesia (religious violence); Malaysia (freedom of expression; migrant workers; refugees; asylum seekers; sexual orientation and gender identity; religious minorities); Nepal (sexual orientation and gender identity; refugees; disability rights); North Korea (political; religious freedom; refugees and asylum seekers); Pakistan (religious persecution; gender); Papua New Guinea (gender); Philippines (gender); Singapore (freedom of speech; sexual orientation and gender identity); Sri Lanka (political; ethnic); Thailand (political violence; freedom of expression; insurgency; refugees, asylum seekers and migrant workers); Vietnam (political; freedom of religion).

Europe and Central Asia – Azerbaijan (political; freedom of religion); Belarus (political); Bosnia and Herzegovina (Roma; refugees; ethnic and religious discrimination; ethnic); Croatia (disability); the EU (various, in line with OSCE findings, above); Kazakhstan (political; freedom of religion); Kyrgyzstan (ethnic violence); Russia (neo-Nazism; racism; xenophobia); Serbia (ethnic; Roma); Tajikistan (religion; gender); Turkey (ethnic; gender); Turkmenistan (religious freedom; political); Ukraine (refugees and asylum seekers; racism; ethnic; religion; Roma); Uzbekistan (religion).

Middle East and North Africa – Algeria (religion; gender); Bahrain (political; gender; migrant workers); Egypt (political; religion; sectarianism; refugee and migrant rights; gender); Iran (political; sexual orientation; religion; ethnic; gender); Iraq (political; gender; gender-based violence; disability); Israel/Occupied Palestinian Territories (political; religion; ethnic); Kuwait (gender; sexual orientation and gender identity); Lebanon (migrants); Libya (political); Morocco (gender); Qatar (migrants); Saudi Arabia (political; gender; migrant workers; religion); Syria (political); United Arab Emirates (political; migrants; gender); Yemen (political).

Making sense of the international figures

In essence, the information within this chapter has revealed two things: first, that 'hate crime', however so defined, occurs all around the world, and second, that we really have no idea (and probably cannot ever know) in quantitative terms how much of it is actually occurring. Nevertheless, whilst the latter may be true, Perry (2001) has suggested that this is rather less important than the fact that we know that it does exist. Whilst this might be a reasonable assumption to make, the problems associated with poor data do have serious implications for areas such as policy and practice and the development of responses to hate crime (as we shall revisit in chapters seven, eight and ten).

This is reflected, for example, in a joint critique of the OSCE (2012) report by Human Rights First and the Anti-Defamation League (2012c). They conclude that whilst the annual report is an important tool in understanding the nature and frequency of hate crimes across the OSCE region, as we noted above, such reporting is seriously undermined when states either do not collect data or fail to contribute their findings to ODIHR on time. They also express their concern relating to serious discrepancies between the data submitted by governments, IGOs and NGOs, and the varying levels of adherence to commitments made to the OSCE to combat hate crimes. If, as the OSCE has identified, countries are using their data, such as it is, to construct policies and shape practice in this area, then the cause for concern should be fairly obvious.

These concerns about the vastly disparate levels of recording bring us back to the importance of viewing hate crime as a social construct. In other words, the information considered in this chapter further illustrates that hate crime is *created* and rather than being an absolute concept is, as Quinney (1970) argues in relation to crime in general, relative to different legal systems. As with other social phenomena, hate crime may be viewed as part of a complex network of events, structures and underlying processes.

As such, the ways in which definitions of crime are *constructed* (as noted in chapter one) and *applied* in a given society (as we shall see in relation to law and law enforcement in chapter seven), become crucial to our understanding of the phenomena in question. As Quinney (1970) further suggests, we cannot be certain of an objective reality beyond man's conception of it. Of course there are multiple conceptions of 'reality', together with associated meanings, and these will be constructed differently depending on the perceptions of the actors involved. In relation to hate crime these 'actors' include not only those that experience hate crime as victims, but also those that construct hate crime (or not) as an object for law and for law enforcement. One of the purposes of this chapter has been to demonstrate the role of the latter in constructing the 'reality' of hate crime.

Quinney (1970) argues that the social reality of crime is constructed by the formulation and application of criminal definitions, the development of behaviour patterns related to those criminal definitions, and the construction of criminal conceptions. Central to this theory are questions concerning who is responsible for, and has the power to, formulate and apply criminal definitions; which segments of society have the power to shape public policy; which segments of society have the power to shape the enforcement and administration of criminal law; the extent to which people engage in actions that have relative probabilities of being defined as criminal and the ways in which conceptions of crime are constructed and diffused amongst the various segments of society. The relationship between the phenomena associated with each of these issues, Quinney argues, culminate in what is regarded as the amount and character of crime in a society at any given time.

Given that the ways in which the relevant 'actors' construct their reality of hate crime are clearly crucial in determining what, and how much of what, appears in the official statistics as formally labelled 'hate crimes' around the world, Quinney's theory presents a useful framework for explaining and understanding the huge disparity in the officially recorded rates of hate crime that we see between different countries. Whilst we shall discuss the implications of these issues for law and law enforcement in chapter seven, in terms of making sense of the official statistics in this chapter, we can simply suggest the following.

In England and Wales, for example, the *higher* rate of recorded hate crime is the product of an interaction of Quinney's propositions that construct the 'reality' of hate crime in ways that predominantly serve to *inflate* the official statistics. In particular, as discussed in chapter one, the overwhelmingly victim-led and victim-oriented approach that characterises the post-Lawrence agenda concerning hate crimes largely places the power to formulate and apply criminal definitions, to shape public policy, to shape the enforcement of criminal law and to apply the label of 'crime' to the behaviour of individuals largely (either directly or indirectly) in the hands of the public rather than those of the authorities, and most notably the police, for whom the influence of discretion and occupational culture in identifying and recording hate crimes is now *relatively* reduced.

Conversely, in the US for example (and on the available evidence, many other countries as well), the significantly *lower* rate of recorded hate crime is the product of an interaction of Quinney's propositions that construct the 'reality' of hate crime in ways that predominantly serve to *deflate* the official statistics (in some cases completely). In particular, the overwhelmingly police-led and police-oriented approach that characterises the response to hate crimes places the power to formulate and apply criminal definitions, to shape public policy, to shape the enforcement of criminal law and to apply the label of 'crime' to the behaviour of individuals firmly (either directly or indirectly) in the hands of the authorities rather than those of the public.

Consequently, the vastly different ways in which the 'reality' of hate crime is constructed in different countries means that searching for objective meaning by comparing the official statistics is extremely problematic. In many respects, with regard to what is officially recorded, hate crimes are often very different things and the official rate of hate crime cannot be meaningfully compared. The social construction of reality effectively means, in this regard, that hate crime is in the eye of the beholder and therefore the official statistics cannot be taken to reflect any difference in any 'real' hate crime prevalence as it might appear to victims, police, advocacy groups or society at large. Ultimately, perceptions of what should and what ultimately does constitute 'hate crime' are shaped by a complex network of events, structures and underlying processes that vary between different societies and are frequently determined by those whose perceptions, in official terms, are deemed to matter.

Concluding comments

In this chapter we have considered, as far as is possible given the various constraints, a 'picture' of hate-related issues around the world. We have also discussed the minefield that is trying to attach useful meaning to this data. In short, perhaps the only thing that is certain is that prejudice, hostility and hate can be found wherever humans are to be found. In this chapter, though, we have dealt primarily in numbers which, as Perry (2001) points out, is fine for identifying a range of trends and patterns, but tells us little about the qualitative elements of hate crimes because the statistics simply provide us with quantitative, rather than qualitative, information. In other words, the statistics tell us that a certain number of variously defined 'events' occurred, but very little else in qualitative terms about these 'events'.

However, quantitative accounts of victimisation are increasingly being replaced in importance by qualitative and other victim-oriented research studies and surveys. In essence these are effectively 'fleshing out' the bare bones of numerical data, thereby allowing us to gain a greater insight into this form of victimisation. Whilst these studies are relatively small in number, and similarly have various methodological and practical shortcomings, they are beginning to provide valuable information. And whilst the evidence is not conclusive beyond doubt and continues to attract critics and sceptics (see chapter nine), the literature increasingly suggests that hate crime is indeed a unique form of offending that results in unique forms of victimisation. The continuance and furtherance of research in this area is crucial not just for our understanding of hate crime but also, as Iganski (2001) suggests, because understanding the harm caused by hate crime should help us to better help its victims. It is to this body of knowledge that we shall now turn.

4 Victims and victimisation

In the last chapter we attempted to establish some sort of estimate concerning the physical manifestations of prejudice occurring in different parts of the world, but primarily through official sources. As we shall see in this chapter, whilst interesting, and indeed useful in some respects (after all, one can hardly begin to develop policies in relation to hate crime if one has no idea about its existence), these sorts of 'number-crunching' exercises are limited and necessarily mask a world of qualitative information concerning the lived experience of those who find themselves on the receiving end of negative prejudice. Indeed, as we shall see in chapter five, research in relation to prejudice, stereotypes and discrimination has long been of interest to psychology, and indeed the wider social sciences, precisely because of the potential consequences that it can have for those who experience it in a negative way, both individually and collectively. As Blaine (2008: 2) suggests, then, 'if we are to fully understand the diversity of our community ... we must appreciate that it is more than statistics about ethnicity, religious preference, or cultural background'. Therefore, to understand the real nature, and in particular the qualitative impact of hate crime victimisation, we have to look to other forms of research that go beyond just counting incidents. In this chapter then, we shall consider *some* of the available information concerning the more qualitative nature of hate crime, and in particular the impact that it can have on victims.

Uncovering the 'dark figure' of hate crime

The British Crime Survey

One way to navigate around some of the limitations associated with official statistics is through the use of victimisation surveys (the importance of which we touched upon in chapter two). One relatively long-standing example that has recently begun to pay specific attention to victims' experiences of hate crime is the British Crime Survey (BCS). This is a face-to-face victimisation survey in which people resident in households in England and Wales are interviewed about their experiences of crime in the previous 12 months. As such the survey seeks to capture offences that are not reported to, or recorded by, the police, in addition to other information concerning the experience of being a victim that would not be available from official statistics alone. When combined, the BCS and police recorded crime provide a more comprehensive picture than could be obtained from just looking at one or the other in isolation. The supplementary volume to the BCS (Smith *et al.*, 2012) that specifically examines hate crime reveals some interesting information concerning its extent, nature and impact in England and Wales. As such we shall briefly consider some of the key findings.

According to the 2009/10 and 2010/11 BCS (the two were combined to provide a more detailed picture), there were around 260,000 incidents of hate crime a year, compared with around 9,561,000 incidents of crime overall in the BCS. Of the monitored strands asked about in the 2009/10 and 2010/11 BCS (race, religion, sexual orientation and disability – data on transgender hate crime was not available at the time of the research), the strand most commonly perceived as an offender's motivation for committing a crime was the offender's attitude to the victim's race (around 136,000 incidents on average a year). The equality strand least commonly perceived as an offender's motivation for committing a crime was the victim's religion, totalling 39,000 incidents. In between, sexual orientation accounted for 50,000 incidents, and disability for 65,000 incidents (it is important to note however that the total number of hate crimes is not equal to the sum of the incidents in the equality strands because victims may have stated that the crime was motivated by more than one type of bias; Smith *et al.*, 2012). Given the discussion in chapter two it is perhaps not surprising that race dominates the data here, and one should keep in mind too that it is not unusual for race and religion to overlap in terms of what is reported, in the sense that religious motivations might often be interpreted as race, and vice versa, as noted in chapter three.

The 2009/10 and 2010/11 combined BCS shows there were around 151,000 incidents of personal hate crime and 109,000 incidents of household hate crime a year, compared with around 3,700,000 incidents of personal crime and 5,861,000 incidents of household crime a year overall in the BCS. Three per cent of crime incidents overall in the BCS (4 per cent of BCS incidents of personal crime and 2 per cent of BCS incidents of household crime) were perceived to be hate crime incidents. The proportion of incidents that were perceived to be hate crime varied by crime type from 1 per cent or fewer of household theft incidents to 10 per cent of robbery incidents. The combined 2009/10 and 2010/11 BCS estimates that 0.5 per cent of adults were victims of hate crime in the 12 months prior to interview. A similar percentage were victims of personal hate crime (0.2 per cent) and household hate crime (0.2 per cent). Overall, 21.5 per cent of adults were victims of BCS crime (Smith *et al.*, 2012).

Analysis of victimisation by personal and household characteristics showed that for personal hate crime (as with BCS crime overall), the risk of being a victim varied by socio-demographic characteristics. The risk of being a victim of personal hate crime was highest among people aged 16 to 24;

people in ethnic groups other than white; those whose marital status was single; the unemployed; those with a long-standing illness or disability that limits their daily activities or those who visit nightclubs at least once a week (Smith *et al.*, 2012). The BCS data also demonstrates that there are inter-relationships between other personal characteristics. For example, the risk of being a victim of household hate crime was highest among people who lived in flats or maisonettes; those who lived in a household with a total income of less than £10,000; those who lived in a 'multicultural' area and those who lived in an 'urban' area.

In terms of repeat victimisation, the BCS showed that almost one-third of the victims of hate crime were victimised more than once, and 18 per cent were victimised three or more times. This is similar to the extent of repeat victimisation for BCS crime overall, although BCS figures have consistently shown that levels of repeat victimisation vary by offence type (Chaplin *et al.*, 2011). The data also shows that hate crime was more likely to be repeatedly experienced for household crime offences than for personal crime offences, and that this difference is larger than that found in the BCS overall (Smith *et al.*, 2012).

As part of the follow-up questions on their crime experience, victims were asked if they had an emotional reaction after the incident and, if so, how much they were affected and in what ways. Interestingly, victims of hate crime were more likely than victims of BCS crime overall to say they were emotionally affected by the incident and more likely to be 'very much' affected. Of those who said they were emotionally affected, victims of hate crimes gave the same types of emotions experienced by victims of BCS crime overall but, with the exception of annoyance, were more likely to mention each of them. In particular, 39 per cent of hate crime victims mentioned fear and 23 per cent mentioned anxiety, compared with 14 per cent and 6 per cent respectively of victims of BCS crime overall (Smith *et al.*, 2012).

In addition, the BCS asked respondents about their perceived likelihood of being a victim of crime in the next 12 months. The findings show that, overall, 3 per cent of adults thought they were 'very' or 'fairly' likely to be harassed because of their skin colour, ethnic origin or religion, and 2 per cent said they were 'very' or 'fairly' likely to be attacked for these reasons. Adults from ethnic groups other than white were more likely than white adults to say they were 'very' or 'fairly' likely to be harassed (15 per cent compared with 1 per cent of white respondents) or attacked (10 per cent compared with 1 per cent of white respondents).

The BCS also asks respondents how worried they are about being a victim of different types of crime. Overall, 5 per cent of adults were 'very' worried about being subject to a physical attack because of their skin colour, ethnic origin or religion, and, in line with the other perception questions, this was much higher among adults from black and minority ethnic backgrounds than among white adults (16 per cent and 3 per cent respectively). According to the BCS, 6 per cent of adults thought there was a 'very' or 'fairly' big problem in their area with people being attacked or harassed because of their skin colour, ethnic origin or religion. Furthermore, adults from ethnic groups other than white were three times more likely to say there was a 'very' or 'fairly' big problem in their area than white adults (Smith *et al.*, 2012).

Information was also collected on incidents that respondents perceived to be motivated by the offender's attitude towards the victim's age or gender. Although the authors warn that estimates of age motivated hate crime should be treated with caution, the BCS estimates that in total, there were approximately 143,000 incidents of age motivated hate crime a year. In addition, there were around 120,000 incidents of gender motivated hate crime a year, with women more likely than men to say they were victims.

In short, then, the BCS identifies a number of important features associated with hate crime. First, on the basis of the findings, hate crimes are far more prevalent than official statistics suggest. Second, proportionately, hate crimes are more likely to be directed against the person than non-hate crimes. Third, hate crimes are often not isolated incidents but rather are experienced repeatedly (a point to which we shall return below). Fourth, hate crime victims often expect their victimisation to continue, or are otherwise fearful of attacks in the future. Fifth, hate crimes can have a greater emotional impact on the victim than comparable non-hate crimes, and can cause increased levels of fear and anxiety.

The United States National Crime Victimization Survey

Although there are methodological differences with the BCS (for example, crime is classified as hate crime if the victim perceived that the offender was motivated by bias because the offender used hate language, left behind hate symbols or the police investigators confirmed that the incident was a hate crime), the National Crime Victimization Survey (NCVS) is the closest comparable national source of information concerning hate crime victimisation available to us.

In reviewing the data collected between 2003 and 2009, Langton and Planty (2011) provide some interesting information concerning the estimated occurrence of hate crime in the US. The successive sweeps of the NCVS revealed that in that period an annual average of 195,000 hate crime victimisations and 179,000 hate crime incidents occurred each year against persons aged 12 or older living in the US (in the NCVS, incidents are distinguished from victimisations in that one criminal incident may have *multiple* victims or victimisations). Interestingly, the 148,400 hate crimes that occurred in 2009 represented a decline from 2003 when 239,400 hate crimes were reported to the survey. During that period, the number and rate of violent hate crimes also declined from 0.8 per 1,000 persons aged 12 or older in 2003 to 0.5 per 1,000 in 2009. Nearly 90 per cent of the hate crime victimisations occurring during the seven-year period were perceived to be racially or ethnically motivated.

Langdon and Planty's analysis also illustrates that from 2003 to 2009, hate crimes accounted for less than 1 per cent of the total offences captured by the NCVS. Nevertheless, more than four in five hate crimes involved violence (approximately 23 per cent were serious violent crimes – eight hate crime homicides were committed in 2009), and in approximately 37 per cent of violent hate crimes the offender knew the victim, whereas in violent non-hate crimes, half of all victims knew the offender. A third of hate crimes occurred at or near the victim's home, whilst more than half of non-hate crimes took place there, but twice as many hate than non-hate crime victims (18 per cent vs 9 per cent) reported that their victimisation occurred at school (a point to which I shall return later in this chapter). Young people (aged 12–24) were more likely to be victims than people aged 50 or over, and males were more likely to be victims than females, as were those with an annual income of less than $25,000. Langdon and Planty also found that the majority of violent hate crimes were interracial while the majority of non-hate violent crimes were intra-racial. Fewer than one in 10 hate crime victims stated that the offender left hate symbols at the crime scene whilst nearly all hate crime victims said that the offender used hate language. Finally, the police were notified of fewer than half (45 per cent) of all hate crimes, with victims of disability hate crime the least likely to report.

In a methodological change pertinent to our next area of discussion, below, in 2010 the Bureau of Justice Statistics (BJS) changed the way in which hate crime victimisation data is collected to account for what they term 'high frequency, or series, victimisations'. These are where incidents are similar in type but occur with such frequency that a victim is unable to recall each individual event (researchers are now permitted to identify such patterns and count these up to a maximum of ten incidents, as opposed to counting them as one as was previously the case). In addition, from 2010 the BJS included crimes motivated by gender or gender–identity bias in their hate crime data.

More recent analysis of the NCVS hate crime data (Sandholtz *et al.*, 2013) has therefore provided some further interesting findings. The 'highlights' from the research demonstrate that: from 2007 to 2011, an estimated annual average of 259,700 non-fatal violent and property hate crime victimisations occurred against persons age 12 or older residing in US households; across the periods from 2003 to 2006 and 2007 to 2011, there was no change in the annual average number of total, violent, or property hate crime victimisations; the percentage of hate crimes motivated by religious bias more than doubled between 2003 to 2006 and 2007 to 2011 (from 10 per cent to 21 per cent), while the percentage motivated by racial bias dropped slightly (from 63 per cent to 54 per cent); violent hate crime accounted for a higher percentage of all non-fatal violent crime in 2007 to 2011 (4 per cent), compared to 2003–06 (3 per cent); about 92 per cent of all hate crimes collected by the NCVS between 2007 and 2011 were violent victimisations; about a third of hate crime victimisations occurred at or near the victim's home; between 2003 to 2006 and 2007 to 2011, the percentage of hate crime victimisations reported to police declined from 46 per cent to 35 per cent; in 2007–11, whites, blacks and Hispanics had similar rates of violent hate crime victimisation; when series victimisations are counted up to a maximum of 10 victimisations, the rate of violent hate crime victimisations was stable from 2008 to 2010 and declined slightly from 2010 to 2011; and, the inclusion of crimes motivated solely by gender or gender-identity bias did not significantly change the number or rate of hate crime victimisations in 2010 or 2011 (Sandholtz *et al.*, 2013: 1–2).

Hate crime as a 'process'

The findings of the BCS and the NCVS, particularly in relation to repeat victimisation and the levels of fear that hate crime victims often experience, are particularly interesting, and in some respects the lived realities of these issues actually limit the ability of victim surveys to estimate the true volume of hate crime. One of the key limitations of statistical data (be it official statistics or crime surveys) in understanding hate crimes is inherently and unavoidably related to the very nature of this type of crime. This, as Bowling (1999: 158) explains in relation to racist victimisation, is that crime in general, and hate crime in particular, should be viewed as an ongoing *process*, rather than as a series of isolated, distinct and separate incidents:

> Conceiving of violent racism (and other forms of crime) as processes implies an analysis which is dynamic; includes the social relationships between all the actors in the process; can capture the continuity between physical violence, threat and intimidation; can capture the dynamic of repeated or systematic victimization; incorporates historical context; and takes account of the social relationships which inform definitions of appropriate and inappropriate behaviour.

Put simply, crime victimisation doesn't begin and end with the commission of an offence, and this is especially true of hate crime. Hate victimisation may involve one crime or, more likely, a great many crimes to the extent that it is not always clear where one ends and the next begins. It may also involve actions that border on being criminal offences but might not be easily defined or recognised as such (hence the inclusion of *incidents* in the official definitions employed in England and Wales). As we have seen, and will see again in due course, there is evidence to suggest that these events can nevertheless have a disproportionate effect on the victim and their community, and that the fear and intimidation that results can transcend far beyond just the moment when the incident or incidents occur.

As Bowling (1999: 189) explains in his study of racist victimisation in Newham, London:

> During the year January 1987 to January 1988, fifty-three incidents targeted against seven families in two streets were recorded by the police ... The overwhelming majority of the incidents consisted of verbal abuse and harassment, egg throwing, damage to property, and

door knocking. Conceived of as individual instances of offensive or threatening behaviour, and employing any kind of hierarchy of seriousness using legal categories, many of these incidents would be regarded as minor. However, in the context of the life of any individual family and most clearly in the life of a locality the repeated incidence of harassment is bound to have a cumulative effect.

This example of course does not include those incidents that occurred but were not reported to the police, and also highlights a fundamental mismatch between the nature of many 'hate' crimes and the workings of the criminal justice system, which is a key issue to which I shall return in chapter seven. By extracting incidents from this process, Bowling suggests, as the criminal justice system, official statistics, and crime surveys attempt to do, hate crime is reduced to collection of solitary 'events' when in fact the victimisation process transcends far beyond that tightly defined time slice.

A similar conceptualisation is explained by Hollomotz (2012) in relation to violence against people with disabilities. Such violence, she suggests, should not be understood as singular acts of physical or sexual assault because these simply represent the more severe expressions of bigotry on a spectrum of routine intrusions that include social exclusion, name calling and other hurtful language, derogatory treatment and so on. Akin to Bowling, Hollomotz (2012: 54) states that:

> the notion of a continuum seeks to draw attention to the fact that boundaries between incidents of mundane intrusions, derogatory treatment and violence are blurred, which can make it difficult for an individual to distinguish that which is seen to be 'acceptable' as part of the everyday from that which is seen, even by others and the law, as an act of violence.

Thus, attempting to measure hate crime in terms of isolated incidents will present us with a figure of some sort that can be used for various counting purposes, but as hate crime is a process and not simply a collection of discrete incidents fixed in time and space, that figure is effectively useless as a measure of the *true* extent or nature of hate crime victimisation. The expression of prejudice-based hostility is therefore more than just an incident or a collection of incidents; it is an ongoing process with a disproportionate and cumulative effect. With this in mind, we shall now explore some of the research that has sought to uncover the impacts of hate crime, using the categories officially recognised in England and Wales as an initial template.

Race and ethnicity

Given the discussion in chapter two concerning the historical links between race and ethnicity and the emergence of hate crime as a contemporary socio-legal problem, it is perhaps not surprising that the literature surrounding the impact of negative racial prejudice and discrimination is vast. Indeed, as Blaine (2008) points out, the general racism research literature is too large to attempt a comprehensive survey in a single chapter. Instead, I shall concentrate on an illustrative set of examples, starting with some of the (relatively) early research specifically relating to the impact of racially and ethnically motivated hate crime.

Early studies specific to hate crime victimisation in the field of 'ethnoviolence' are typically characterised by various methodological shortcomings, inconsistent conclusions, and a resultant inability to generalise the findings (McDevitt *et al.*, 2001). Nevertheless, some of those early studies (see, for example, Barnes and Ephross, 1994; Ehrlich *et al.*, 1994) suggested that victims of ethnoviolence suffered significant impacts as a consequence of their experiences, including increased trauma and more acute negative after-effects, including post-traumatic stress, increased levels of fear and anger, lower self-esteem, nervousness, interpersonal difficulties and behavioural changes.

Although not exclusively focused on racist victimisation, one such study which sought to overcome some of the methodological shortcomings of its predecessors surveyed a sample of comparable victims of hate and non-hate motivated aggravated assaults in Boston in an attempt to establish the extent to which hate crime has a differential impact (McDevitt *et al.*, 2001). In terms of behavioural reactions the study found no significant difference between hate and non-hate victims in their post-victimisation behaviour. The majority of victims of both groups stated that they paid more attention to where they walked and that they tried to be less visible following the incident, and some stated that they had subsequently become more active in the community.

However, McDevitt *et al.* (2001) uncovered significant differences between hate and non-hate victims in terms of their psychological reactions. Overall, the study found that hate victims experienced adverse and intense psychological sequelae more often than non-hate victims, were found to have greater difficulty coping with their victimisation, and experienced problems with their recovery process because of increased fear and more frequent intrusive thoughts. In addition, the research suggests that hate crime victims experience increased fear and reduced feelings of safety than non-hate victims following an attack, largely, McDevitt *et al.* suggest, because of concern over the likelihood of future attacks often based upon the experience of repeat victimisation in the past (thereby highlighting the importance of viewing hate crime as a process). With regard to other consequences of victimisation, the research found that hate victims were more likely to lose their job, suffer health problems, experience more post-incident traumatic events and have greater difficulty in overcoming the incident.

More recent research by Craig-Henderson and Sloan (2003) argued that victims of racist hate crime experience a range of unique reactions and are different from both crime victims generally, and also victims of other forms of hate crime in at least two ways. The first is that because race hate victims are targeted specifically because of their race (or ethnicity), the characteristics of which are always visible and easily recognised, victims are unable to take comfort in the belief that the offence was simply random and could have happened to anyone. Rather, they are forced to view their experience as an attack on their identity. The researchers suggest that this differs from other victims of crime, and indeed many other victims of hate crime, because their race (or more broadly, the reason for their victimisation) cannot be hidden from the view of others and therefore the attack cannot be easily attributed to other factors.

Craig-Henderson and Sloan (2003) argue that the second factor that distinguishes race hate victims from other hate crime victims is that they are almost always members of extremely negatively stereotyped or stigmatised social groups. Furthermore, the recognition of these factors is predominantly present in the motivation of offenders and is usually pervasive and resistant to change. It could reasonably be argued, however, that all victims of hate crime are the subjects of negative stereotypes so the extent to which this is conclusively and solely attributable to race hate victims is open to debate. Nevertheless, the researchers highlight the additional issue that anti-black hate crime in particular also has the potential to invoke emotions that relate to a lengthy history of racism and discrimination, both in terms of criminal behaviour towards blacks and discrimination in other areas of their lives such as employment and housing and so on.

Whilst most of the studies referred to above are American in origin, many of the findings are supported by a British study examining the impact of racist victimisation on the lives of those that experienced it. Chahal and Julienne (2000) found that victims were significantly hindered or affected in several key areas of their lives. Most notably, problems were associated with the victim's relationship with their partner or spouse and their children, the frequency and duration of visits from friends and family members, disruption to their routine activities and their use of space (both public and private), their general health and well-being and their overall feelings of security and safety.

It is of course not just members of the black and minority ethnic community (which, I should note, along with the other categories considered in this chapter, is something of an umbrella term that rather implies that the groups thereunder are broadly homogeneous, and that victimisation will be a relatively uniform experience for all the people the term covers – a point to which I shall return in chapters nine and ten) that experience racial hostility. An under-researched aspect of hate crime that has recently started to attract deserved attention concerns the victimisation of migrants, immigrants and asylum seekers, and indeed the racism experienced particularly by white working-class communities.

As Chakraborti and Garland (2009) acknowledge, however, the issue of 'undesirable forms of whiteness' has largely gone unrecognised across the board, but in the UK is of considerable importance, particularly following press hysteria in recent years relating to the 'dangers' of allowing migrant workers from Eastern Europe into the country following the expansion of the European Union in May 2004. Chakraborti and Garland also rightly point out that the rhetoric around immigration and asylum represents something of a shift from overt racism to xenophobia, which, as Kundnani (2001) suggests, provides an alibi for racism by making the concerns often expressed (in this case about the impact of large numbers of immigrants arriving in the UK) seem 'natural' and legitimate. The issue of political rhetoric is one that I shall return to in chapter six.

Indeed, writing back in 1998, Pettigrew highlighted the plight of the 'new minorities', including 'guest workers', refugees and other immigrants, of Western Europe. His research identified four major reactions to the 'new minorities' that, he concluded, were remarkably consistent across Western Europe, namely prejudice, discrimination, political opposition and violence, which were both blatant and subtle in their execution. He also acknowledged that both direct and indirect discrimination against the 'new minorities' was pervasive and that far right, anti-immigration political parties had formed to exploit the situation. Pettigrew (1998) also noted that violence against third-world immigrants had also increased, especially in countries such as Britain and Germany where far right parties were weakest.

The situation identified by Pettigrew in many ways echoes that faced by the Roma and Sinti in Europe. Although hostility towards these groups has a long history, Mirga (2009) suggests that the situation became particularly acute following the fall of Communism and the transition towards democracy and a market economy that was accompanied by a rise in both ethnic consciousness and nationalist tendencies in a number of post-communist European states. As a consequence, Mirga suggests that the Roma and Sinti lost livelihoods and were singled out as scapegoats, often accompanied by extreme levels of violence, for the difficulties brought about by the economic transition, and that these experiences persisted as many sought to migrate west. Troublingly, Mirga suggests that the situation facing the Roma and Sinti in many parts of Europe is even worse today, where the deliberate and organised use of hate speech and incitement of violence is fuelling arson attacks on Romani houses, physical assaults, racist slurs, property destruction and police violence against these communities.

The situation highlighted by Mirga is reflected in the Human Rights First (2008) Hate Crime Survey in which is documented routine and widespread violence against the Roma in many European countries, often fuelled by political rhetoric that seeks to 'legitimise' such persecution. Referring to events in Italy in 2007 and 2008, the report (2008: 1) states that:

> the intensity of the recent anti-Roma violence in Italy should serve as a wake-up call to all of Europe. The multiple factors at work: the negative popular attitudes against Roma; the abuses that they experience at the

hands of the police; the official and unofficial discrimination in employment, housing, health care, and other aspects of public life; the violent rhetoric of exclusion and expulsion used by public officials; the failure of many states to address the challenges of the marginalisation of Roma – all combine to create a potentially explosive situation, with dire human consequences.

Indeed, the broad discrimination faced by the Roma and Sinti in many aspects of their lives appears, in a variety of ways, to reflect the experiences of Gypsy and Traveller communities in the UK. In reviewing these inequalities, Cemlyn *et al.* (2009: iii) state that:

> One core theme which arises across all topics is the pervasive and corrosive impact of experiencing racism and discrimination throughout an entire lifespan and in employment, social and public contexts. Existing evidence ... highlights high rates of anxiety, depression and at times self-destructive behaviour (for example, suicide and/or substance abuse). These are, on the face of the evidence, responses to 'cultural trauma' produced by the failings of 21st century British society and public bodies' failure to engage in an equitable manner with members of the communities. Having reviewed the strength of the evidence of the prejudice and discrimination faced by Gypsies and Travellers, the authors of the report were surprised that more members of the Gypsy and Traveller communities had not succumbed to negativity, and remained resilient in the face of what are often multiple and complex forms of exclusion.

Religion

Of course, as we have seen, one does not have to look very far into the history books to see the extent, nature and longevity of religious-based persecution. Indeed, historically many of the most violent and extreme acts of what we would now label as 'hate crimes' have been committed in the name of religion. Space does not permit a discussion of these events here, and nor does it allow for a consideration of each religious denomination, so in this section we shall confine ourselves to a brief consideration of some of the more contemporary issues in hand.

Anti-Semitism

In the UK, the conceptualisation of anti-Semitism represents a blurring of the boundaries between race and religion, where anti-Semitic crimes against *Jewish* people or communities are regarded as racist (because Jewish people are regarded as a race by legislation), and offences targeting *Judaism* that are regarded as religiously motivated. Regardless of this labelling, anti-Semitism has deep historical roots that continue to shape contemporary social and political perceptions of Jews and Judaism.

Chakraborti and Garland (2009) note that there has been a discernible rise in the number of anti-Semitic incidents within the UK, and across Europe, the US and Canada and elsewhere, in recent years, suggesting that anti-Jewish sentiment may be embedded within the cultural fabric of many societies across the world. This suggestion is perhaps reflected by the Anti-Defamation League (2012a) who have documented anti-Semitic incidents in countries including Argentina, Australia, Austria, Belgium, Chile, Canada, the Czech Republic, France, Germany, Hungary, Ireland, Morocco, New Zealand, Peru, Poland Russia, Spain, Sweden and the UK.

Interestingly however, since peaking in 2009, the Community Security Trust (2012) has recorded a decline in anti-Semitic incidents in the UK from 929 (in 2009) to 586 (in 2011). Despite this fall, the 2011 figure still represents the fourth highest figure reported to the charity since they started collecting data in 1984. In their report, the CST (2012) attribute this decline to the relative absence of 'trigger events' in 2011, such as those associated with events in the Middle East. Most of the recorded events consist of 'low-level' incidents of abusive and threatening behaviour, verbal abuse and harassment, hate literature and damage and desecration to property, although 92 incidents were recorded as violent. These findings mirror those found in research previously conducted in London by Iganski *et al.* (2005).

Anti-Muslim hate crime

As with the persecution of Jews, hostility towards Muslims also has a lengthy history spanning many centuries, but arguably it is the post-9/11 era that has really seen the emergence of 'Islamophobia' as an acute contemporary social issue. Prejudice towards Muslims is variously attributed to difficulties in assimilation into Western culture, misunderstandings of Islam, the marginalisation of Muslim communities, the focus upon negative rather than positive aspects of the faith, and, of course, the demonisation of Muslims, and those mistaken for Muslims, as (or scapegoats for) 'terrorists' and/or 'religious extremists' in the post-9/11 world (see, for example, Perry, 2003; Hunt, 2005; McGhee, 2005; Chakraborti and Garland, 2009).

Evidence to suggest the latter can be found in the significant increases in reported anti-Muslim incidents and anti-Islamic sentiment in the immediate post-9/11 period not just in the US and the UK, but also across much of Europe, Australia and elsewhere, and similarly again in the UK following the 7/7 bombings in London (Human Rights Watch, 2002; Chakraborti and Garland, 2009). More recently, the animosity that exists towards Muslims and Islam has been highlighted by the rhetoric and activities of groups such as the English Defence League and, of course, by the mass killings committed by Anders Breivik in Norway in 2011, fuelled in considerable part by his anti-Islamic sentiments. In the UK, research by Lambert and Githens-Mazer (2011) identified a range of issues affecting Muslim communities, noting too the influence of the extremist and mainstream political milieu, the perpetration of offences overwhelmingly by non-extremists, the extent of threats of violence that disproportionately impact on poor urban communities, increased levels of intimidation and violence, the potential for offences to be motivated by attitudes derived from media discourse, hate crimes against mosques, the particular targeting of Muslim women in traditional dress, a disproportionate cumulative threat of street violence, a rise in anti-Muslim demonstrations and the demonisation of Muslim leaders, all set against a backdrop of serious levels of under-reporting to the authorities resulting from fear, suspicion and alienation.

Sectarianism

The issue of sectarianism, that is, the prejudice that arises from differences between the subdivisions of a group, is a complicated issue within hate crime. We noted historical divisions between Protestants and Catholics in chapter two, and today sectarianism is most commonly associated with (but not limited to) the Troubles in Northern Ireland, where the complexity of the situation means that religious divides often blur with, for example, those of a political nature, and where hate crime can become blurred with terrorism. Although the situation in Northern Ireland has settled somewhat following the Good Friday/Belfast Agreement signed in 1998 (the name given to the agreement depends upon one's religious and political leanings, itself perhaps illustrative of the complexities of resolving such deep differences), Jarman (2005) states that sectarian hate crime remains a significant problem in Northern Ireland, but interestingly also notes an increase in racist, homophobic and disablist incidents as *overt* sectarianism, in relative terms, has started to decline. The continuation of this general trend that Jarman identifies is, however, a little less discernible from the numbers of hate incidents recorded by the Police Service of Northern Ireland where all categories of recorded hate crime, at least officially, are fewer in number than they were in 2005 (PSNI, 2012).

Of course the problem of sectarianism is not simply confined to Northern Ireland (Scotland too has a long history in this regard), and nor to just Protestant–Catholic divides. Just as prevalent are, for example, the divisions between Shia and Sunni Muslims where sectarian hostility and violence continues to occur across parts of the Middle-East, Africa and Asia. Indeed, the various reports compiled by Human Rights Watch on this, and other, forms of sectarianism highlight prejudice, hostility and violence occurring in countries such as Egypt, Iraq, Indonesia, Syria, Burma, Mali, Pakistan, Sudan, Morocco, Bahrain, Kuwait, Nigeria, Afghanistan and India, to name just a few.

Sexual orientation

One of the most comprehensive studies of hate victimisation to date is that conducted by Herek *et al.* (2002), who examined victim experiences in cases of homophobic hate crime in the US. The research built upon an earlier pilot study conducted in 1997, which found that hate crime victims experience greater long-term post-traumatic stress disorder symptoms, including higher levels of depression, anxiety and anger when compared to victims of similar non-hate motivated offences. Significantly, the 1997 research also found that some hate crime victims took up to five years to overcome the effects of the crime, compared to two years for victims of comparable non-hate offences.

The larger 2002 study supported and extended the earlier findings. Herek *et al.* (2002) found that hate crimes based on sexual orientation most frequently occurred in public locations and were perpetrated by one or more males unknown to the victim. However, the researchers point out that victimisation is not confined to these dynamics and that members of sexual minorities are effectively at risk of victimisation wherever they are identified as being gay, lesbian or bisexual. Herek, Cogan and Gillis also state that whilst hate and non-hate personal crimes did not significantly differ in their general severity, they were struck by the physical and psychological brutality of the hate crimes they encountered.

The effect of this greater brutality, they suggest, is twofold. First, victims generally suffered greater psychological distress that persisted over a longer period of time than non-hate victims. These findings are consistent with other earlier studies on hate victimisation by Ehrlich (1992) and Garofalo (1991). Second, the research also found that hate crime victimisation extends far beyond the immediate victim and has consequences for the entire gay community. Because they are motivated against an impersonal characteristic over which the victim has little or no control, Herek *et al.* argue that hate crimes act as a form of terrorism in that they send a 'message' to other members of the community who share the same traits or belong to the same social group as the victim that they are not safe either.

More recently, research by Herek (2009) has indicated that approximately 20 per cent of the US sexual minority population has experienced a crime against their person or property based on their sexual orientation since the age of 18, increasing to around 25 per cent when one includes attempted crimes. The research also suggests that harassment is considerably more widespread, with about half of sexual minority adults reporting verbal abuse at some time in their adult life as a consequence of their sexual orientation. In addition, Herek (2009) notes that the likelihood of experiencing victimisation is not uniform among sexual minorities where, for example, gay men were found to be significantly more likely than lesbians or bisexuals to experience violence and property crimes.

Furthermore, many of the findings above are echoed by those of the British Gay Crime Survey (Dick, 2008), which was briefly mentioned in chapter three, and (simply to illustrate events in another part of the world) by a study conducted in Chile, which revealed that most of the sample LGBT population reported some kind of victimisation events at some point in their lives, with ridicule being the most often reported, followed by insults or threats and physical abuse (Barrientos *et al.*, 2010).

Transgender

Although the popular term 'LGBT' often (rather unhelpfully) categorises Lesbian, Gay, Bisexual and Transgender people together, there is a small but distinct literature base emerging specifically relating to victimisation along transgender lines. Our understanding of transgender issues is however somewhat complicated by the contested nature of what itself is an umbrella term that represents anyone who 'bends' the common societal constructions of gender (Stotzer, 2009). Notwithstanding this, Stotzer (2009: 177–8), in her review of data from the US concludes that:

> Not only are transgender people suffering from physical assaults, sexual assaults, and harassment in public places by strangers, but a large portion also suffer these forms of violence in their homes from people that they know. Self-reports have offered the highest level of details about the prevalence of hate crimes, suggesting that the majority of transgender people will experience violence in their lifetimes, and that risk for violence starts at an early age.

Research examining transphobic hate crime in the European Union (Turner *et al.* 2009) has also identified issues comparable to those raised by Stotzer, above. Drawing on 2,669 survey responses, the research found that 79 per cent of respondents had experienced some form of harassment in public ranging from transphobic comments to physical or sexual abuse; that trans-people were three times more likely to experience a transphobic hate incident or hate crime than lesbians and gay men; the most common forms of harassment were (unsolicited) comments (44 per cent) and verbal abuse (27 per cent); 15 per cent of respondents had experienced threatening behaviour and 7 per cent physical abuse; that trans-women were more likely to experience harassment than trans-men; the types of harassment experienced were very similar between the different EU States; and that the vast majority of respondents from all countries were not confident that they would be treated appropriately by members of the police service as their preferred/acquired gender.

Disability

In chapter two we noted the emergence of disability hate crime as an area of contemporary concern in the UK, driven largely by a number of high-profile and tragic cases of victimisation. We have also already noted the processual nature of the victimisation of people with disabilities earlier in this chapter, and in chapter three we briefly noted some research findings concerning the extent and nature of disability hate crime. Here, then, we shall consider a little more of the available literature, but in doing so it is important to keep in mind that, like so many of the other categories adopted, 'disability' is an umbrella term that covers a multitude of different impairments, and to attempt to consider each and every one of them is far beyond the scope of a chapter (or probably even a book) of this size.

In reviewing the situation in the UK, Quarmby (2008) suggests that hate crimes against disabled people are common and widespread, and range from low-level harassment, name-calling, bullying, intimidation and vandalism to more serious crimes (often escalating in seriousness), but that they are often 'hidden' and their prevalence 'concealed'. She also argues that disablist hate crimes are different to comparable crimes motivated by other forms of pre-judice, most notably because the perpetrators of disablist hate crimes are predominantly 'friends' or carers, as opposed to strangers. She also high-lights considerable barriers in terms of accessing justice (a point to which I shall return in chapter seven), which compounds the experience of many people with disabilities.

Quarmby's findings are echoed in research from both Northern Ireland (Vincent *et al.*, 2009) and Scotland (Disability Rights Commission, 2004). The former found that people with a disability experienced a wide range of forms of hate crime, including verbal abuse, assaults and damage to property, and that such hostility occurs towards people with a wide range of forms of disability. The latter (amongst other areas of interest) considered the impact of disablist attacks, where 77 per cent of respondents stated that they were scared; 68 per cent that they were embarrassed or humiliated; 66 per cent that they were stressed; and 51 per cent reported feelings of loneliness and isolation. Other responses included anger, helplessness and self-loathing.

Selected 'others'

You will have noted through our discussions in earlier chapters that the social and political construction of hate crime in different parts of the world means that the groups that are formally recognised can vary considerably from place to place. Thus far in this chapter we have concentrated on some of the most common categories using the UK model as a framework, but of course this list is not exhaustive by any means (indeed, if you remember from chapter one, the operational definitions allow anyone to be a victim of hate crime if they perceive themselves to be so). This necessarily means that there are a number of other 'categories' that may or may not be formally recognised but who nevertheless are the victims of what we might term 'tar-geted violence'. In this section of the chapter, then, we shall briefly highlight some of the issues that 'stretch the official boundaries' of hate crime.

Gender

You may recall from the previous chapter that 15 OSCE States record hate crimes motivated by *gender*. This is an issue that has been (and indeed remains) rather contentious in many jurisdictions, and the arguments that surround the inclusion of gender as a hate crime category were neatly encapsulated by the political wrangling that took place in the US in the late 1980s and early 1990s, that we discussed in chapter two.

However, another contested aspect of gender-based hate crime concerns the issue of *rape*. In considering the inclusion of gender within US legislation, Carney (2001) noted that rape rarely resulted in hate crime charges being brought against the offender. In challenging the implication that rape is not a hate crime, Carney (2001: 319–20) argues that:

> Rape is the paradigmatic hate crime. It is a crime that violates and defiles millions of women because of their gender, and still fails to be recognized as a hate crime. Like other hate crime victims, the rape victim is selected because she possesses an immutable characteristic – her gender. Like other hate crimes, rape inflicts grave psychological consequences upon the victim and results in an increased sense of communal fear ... Rape is not an act of violence that simply happens to women – it is an act of hate that happens to women because they are women.

The debate around the conceptualisation of rape as a specific form of hate crime has been furthered in recent years as a result of concerns relating to what is termed 'corrective rape'. Particular concerns relating to the practice have largely centred on relatively recent events in South Africa where the country's Human Rights Commission (2008) has drawn attention to the apparent growing phenomenon of corrective rape in schools across the country, where the belief persists amongst young boys that lesbians can have their sexual orientation 'corrected' by being raped. Indeed, in reviewing the available evidence on the subject, Action Aid (2009) note that corrective rape is becoming the most widespread form of hate crime against black lesbian women in South Africa, with one Cape Town support group reporting 10 new cases each week. The charity's own interviews with survivors of corrective rape noted the persistent use of verbal abuse both before and during the event that centred on the perpetrator's perceptions of lesbians as 'abnormal' and having strayed from the societal boundaries prescribed for them, and we shall further examine notions of 'power' as a causal factor in the commission of hate crimes in chapter six.

Closely aligned to the issue of gender-based hate crime is a recently emerging area of interest in the field, namely that of hate crimes against *sex workers*. In a particularly interesting development in 2006, Merseyside Police in England agreed a policy stating that crimes against sex workers would be treated as hate crimes. As Campbell and Stoops (2010) suggest, this approach implicitly recognises that the high levels of violence against sex workers are shaped by discrimination and attitudes of hostility and prejudice. The inclusion of sex workers as a category of hate crime in Merseyside has also been justified through the acknowledgement that, as with other forms of hate crime, under-reporting of incidents is commonplace, and trust and confidence in the authorities to respond effectively is historically low.

Age

An interesting area of debate concerns the issue of age. Thus far the categories discussed in this chapter can be regarded as having been 'given', or at least being (for the most part) beyond the control of the individual throughout the whole of their life. I, for example, am male, white, heterosexual and able-bodied, and I have no particular control over these things. Furthermore, contrary to what my goddaughter will happily tell you, I am not old (for the record, I am 36 – not quite pensionable). But, assuming everything goes to plan, I will be old one day. After all, ageing is an inevitable and unavoidable part of living, and given the population demographics of many countries where more and more people are becoming elderly (and staying that way for a lot longer than at any other point in history), the category of 'age' in hate crime terms is of increasing note. As we get older the potential for age-related impairments inevitably increases and these, of course, can increase our vulnerability to crime and other forms of abuse.

For example, although we must remain careful about interpreting statistics, Hull (2009) states that in the US between 2003 and the end of 2006, the incidence of violent crime against individuals aged 65 and over increased by 75 per cent. Drawing parallels with the victimisation of people with disabilities (so starkly and graphically illustrated by the events at Winterbourne View care home near Bristol in 2011), Hull also suggests that this victimisation increases the risk of nursing home placement where the victim faces a significant risk of additional harm. This increase in violent victimisation against the elderly, Hull points out, is particularly disturbing given that the overall rate of violent crimes against individuals in all age groups declined over this same time period. As such, she suggests that age-related impairments render many elderly people uniquely vulnerable to victimisation, and that by omitting age from the list of recognised hate crime categories, many jurisdictions fail to recognise this vulnerability.

Findings similar to those identified by Hull (2009) were also revealed by a survey undertaken in the UK by Jenkins *et al.* (2000), which examined 1,421 calls made to the Action on Elder Abuse confidential telephone helpline over a two-year period between 1997 and 1999. The study found that two-fifths of calls reported psychological abuse, one-fifth each reported physical and financial abuse, 10 per cent of calls related to cases of neglect and 2 per cent to sexual abuse, with many calls reporting multiple types of abuse. The study also revealed that women are three times more likely to be abused than men.

Similarly, an extensive review of the available global literature in this area (Cooper *et al.* 2007) found that the range of prevalence of abuse reported by general population studies was wide (3.2–27.5 per cent), reflecting perhaps the true variation in abuse rates across cultures as well as the differences in defining and measuring abuse. Furthermore, the review found that nearly a quarter of older people dependent on carers reported significant psychological abuse, and a fifth reported neglect. Over a third of family carers reported perpetrating significant abuse, whilst one in six professional carers reported committing psychological abuse and one in ten physical abuse. In addition, over 80 per cent of care home staff claimed to have observed abuse. Collectively, then, these studies indicate that vulnerable elderly people are at a considerable risk of targeted abuse. Perhaps in recognition of this, crime against the elderly is at least symbolically linked to hate crime more generally by the CPS (2012), who now include information about crimes against older people within their annual hate crime report.

Alternative subcultures

In chapter two I referred to the murder of Sophie Lancaster in Lancashire, England in 2007 and noted the significance of this particular case to the current debate around the boundaries of hate crime in the UK, and in bringing the issue of hate crimes against 'alternative subcultures' to the fore. Although information on this type of victimisation is scarce, Garland (2010) summarises the little that does exist and in doing so identifies a number of similarities between this and other forms of hate crime, including prejudice, harassment, violence and the frequency of verbal abuse, often perpetrated by young people in groups.

In addition, Garland also refers to the information collected as part of the campaign to have alternative subcultures officially recognised as a category of hate crime victim that followed Sophie's death. The charity behind the campaign, Stamp Out Prejudice, Hatred and Intolerance Everywhere (SOPHIE), estimates, for example, that 70 per cent of the people who have contacted them have been the victim of some form of attack as a consequence of their alternative lifestyle. As a result of the work undertaken by Sophie's mother, Sylvia, and the SOPHIE charity, Greater Manchester Police in England included alternative subcultures as a formal category of hate crime in April 2013.

Homelessness

Another issue situated at the boundaries of hate crime concerns the victimisation of the homeless, who are often particularly vulnerable to crime. Although it is often difficult to decipher if an individual is targeted because of a specific hostility towards the homeless or because the nature of homelessness means that prolonged exposure to public spaces simply increases vulnerability to crime generally, the US National Coalition for the Homeless (NCH, 2012) have expressed their concern relating to attacks committed on the homeless by the housed in recent years. Whilst acknowledging the significant under-reporting of the issue, research conducted by the NCH (2012) nevertheless concluded that 1,184 reported acts of bias motivated violence were committed against homeless individuals between 1999 and 2010. Furthermore, the research suggested that 312 homeless individuals lost their lives as a result of the attacks, and that over the past twelve years there have been more than twice as many homeless hate crime homicides than all the other FBI-recognised hate crime categories combined (312 versus 111).

This issue is of course not confined to the US. In considering the available information, the Council to Homeless Persons and PILCH Homeless Persons Legal Clinic (2010) in Australia noted considerably higher rates of violent victimisation for the homeless as compared to the general population, and that this risk was further increased if the person was perceived by the perpetrator to be homeless *and* possessing another identifiable trait. For example, they found that people who were homeless and had mental health issues were three times more likely to be victimised than those without.

Furthermore, in the UK, research by Newburn and Rock (2005: 6) described victimisation levels of homeless people as 'staggering', where they are thirteen times more likely than the general public to have experienced violence, and forty-seven times more likely to be victims of theft, with almost one in ten having experienced sexual assault in the previous year. Reflecting many of the experiences of victims of 'recognised' categories of hate crime, Newburn and Rock (2005: 28) state that:

> A central theme running through this report, something at the very heart of the research findings is the fact that the homeless – in hostels and on the street – experience the world as an insecure, unpredictable and troubled place where one is obliged continually to be guarded and suspicious. This is the almost inevitable product of the fear, danger and powerlessness that is at the core of much of the experience of rough sleeping. Many of those living rough take themselves to be socially invisible. The homeless feel – or perhaps more accurately are made to feel – marginal, apart from the respectable world, and heavily stigmatised. Theirs is a world of exposure to frequent, if not continual abuse, and one in which they are denied 'respect'.

Bullying

Although bullying behaviour can occur anywhere, much of the literature has focused on that which occurs in and around schools. By reviewing some of the available literature on bullying generally, my colleague Carol Hayden and I (Hall and Hayden, 2007) sought to identify the extent to which parallels could be drawn between bullying and hate crime victimisation. We concluded that some forms of bullying could indeed be usefully conceptualised as hate crime.

A theme running throughout much of the bullying research suggests that feeling discriminated against and 'different' is a core part of being bullied. For example, research by Cawson *et al.* (2000) examined the reasons behind bullying and found that 26 per cent of respondents identified their size as the primary cause of victimisation; 21 per cent identified their social class; 19 per cent their intelligence; 10 per cent their hobbies or interests; 8 per cent their race; 3 per cent their disability; and 2 per cent their sexuality. Other reasons cited include the wearing of glasses and/or 'unfashionable' clothing. The issue of disproportionate harm that is frequently identified by the hate crime literature is also noted by Cawson *et al.* (2000: 7):

> It is noticeable that most of the issues about which respondents said they were bullied – their size, intelligence, social background and race – were fundamental aspects of their identity over which they had no control, so that bullying would represent a major psychological attack.

Moreover, our review of the literature (Hall and Hayden, 2007: 19) identified a range of other parallels between bullying and hate crime, most notably that: victimisation involves the deliberate targeting of the individual; the underlying motivation for the offence is prejudice against a particular identifiable trait or characteristic; the victim often has little or no control over the targeted characteristic; there is a power imbalance between the perpetrator and the victim; victimisation often consists of low-level incidents; victimisation is characterised by repetition; the impact of the victimisation is often disproportionate; offenders often engage in techniques of neutralisation (see chapter six); and incidents are significantly underreported to the authorities.

The link between bullying and hate crime is also a concern for the US Department of Justice's Civil Rights Division (CRD). In a blog posted on their website on 31 October 2012, the CRD stated that 'school bullies become tomorrow's hate crime defendants', although the evidence upon which they make this rather bold and generalised assertion is not particularly clear. Moreover, the need to address the issue is encapsulated within the proposed (but as yet unenacted) Student Non-Discrimination Act, which would prohibit discrimination on the basis of sexual orientation and gender identity (other categories are covered by other civil right statutes) and has the stated purpose of ensuring that elementary and secondary school students are protected from harassment, bullying, intimidation and violence (Feder, 2012).

Concluding comments

This chapter has considered a range of issues relating to hate crime victimisation. It sought to go beyond the rather superficial picture painted by statistical data by presenting a necessarily brief overview of *some* of the literature that has examined the extent, nature and, in particular, the impact that this form of crime can have upon those who experience it. In so doing we dipped into some of the available research in relation to both 'traditional' and some less 'traditional' hate crime categories. This process in itself is illustrative of some of the conceptual difficulties we considered in chapter one concerning which characteristics to include under the hate crime umbrella, and of course you could very easily point to a number that I have not included here. Two that immediately spring to mind are social class and classism, and size and sizism (I'll leave you to complete the list of omissions in your own time). Of course this is not to underplay the significance of victimisation along these lines, and much literature on these issues exists elsewhere should you wish to explore it. Their omission from this chapter does however illustrate one theoretical point about hate crime that I shall return to in chapter nine, namely that at some point you have to stop including categories in your definition of hate crime, otherwise the term will cease to have meaning and will simply become coterminous with crime in general.

Nevertheless, I suspect that having read the information within this chapter you will have started to notice some themes emerging from across the broad areas discussed, most notably in relation to the seemingly disproportional impact that hate victimisation can have both on individuals and the wider communities to which they belong. It is my intention to revisit these (and other) apparent themes in chapter nine, and whilst you might think it rather odd that I have chosen to discuss these outside of a chapter that examines victimisation, it is important to keep in mind that many of these issues remain highly contested within the field. As such, whilst we have discussed 'details' of victimisation in this chapter, the debates concerning general 'themes' in victimisation are, in my view, best left until later when we critically discuss this phenomenon that we call 'hate crime'. For now, however, we shall turn our attention to the nature of 'hate' and 'hatred', followed by a consideration of what we know about offenders and offending.

5   Prejudice and hatred

The various definitions of hate crime discussed in chapter one show that this form of offending isn't always about *hate*, but rather it is predominantly about *prejudice*, of which hate is just a small part. It follows then that if we want to understand hate crime then we must understand the nature of prejudice. Fortunately for us, as Stangor (2000) points out, there are few if any topics that have engaged the interests of social psychologists as much as those of prejudice, stereotypes and discrimination. This, he suggests, is a consequence of the immense practical importance that such studies hold for understanding the effects of these issues on both individuals and societies, particularly given the increasing diversity of the world we live in. However, Jacobs and Potter (1998) point out that whilst prejudice has long been an object for study, sociologists and psychologists have been unable to agree on a single definition for it, nor agree on where it comes from, or exactly what purpose it serves. Instead, a number of competing theories each seek to explain the phenomenon in different ways, but none of them it would seem are either definitive or conclusive. The aim of this chapter is therefore to present an overview of knowledge concerning the nature and origins of prejudice, and by doing so to highlight the inherent complexities surrounding the phenomenon, and the difficulties this presents for understanding hate crime.

Prejudice and discrimination

Before we can explore the various issues associated with hate crime offending, it is important that we understand the foundations of hatred, namely the psychological concept of prejudice, and its relationship to discriminatory behaviour. The first requirement of this chapter therefore is to provide an appropriate definition of 'prejudice' and 'discrimination', and to distinguish between the two. The terms 'prejudice' and 'discrimination' are often used interchangeably, but it is important to be clear about the difference between them. For our purposes, prejudice can be described as a type of *attitude* towards members of a social group, whilst discrimination can be described as a *behaviour* or an *action* arising from that attitude and directed towards members of a social group. In other words discrimination is essentially 'prejudice in action' (Baron and Byrne, 1994).

As a separate entity, discrimination can take many forms. Its expression may often be restrained by, for example, laws and social pressures but where such forces are absent or weak prejudicial attitudes may be expressed in overt forms. The nature of these expressions is discussed in more detail below (see Figure 5.1, p. 84) but as we saw when we discussed issues of victimisation in chapter four, even the subtlest forms of discrimination, whether direct or indirect, can have serious consequences for its victims. It can result in differential treatment or exclusion from services and provisions, and may of course extend further to include forms of aggression and violence.

The word 'prejudice' is derived from the Latin noun *praejudicium*, meaning *precedent*, and in the English language the term came to mean a premature or hasty judgement. More recently the term has also acquired its emotive sense of favourableness or unfavourableness now associated with such a judgement (Allport, 1954). According to one early definition, prejudice is: 'A pattern of hostility in interpersonal relations which is directed against an entire group, or against its individual members; it fulfils a specific irrational function for its bearer' (Ackerman and Jahoda, 1950: 4).

However, Gordon Allport, arguably the most prominent of all researchers and writers on this subject, disagreed with the assertion that prejudice always holds some form of irrational function for the bearer. Instead Allport argued that prejudice often has a *functional significance*, but nevertheless is often simply a matter of blind conformity with some prevailing common ideology (and therefore has no functional significance whatsoever for the bearer). As such he defines prejudice as:

> An antipathy based upon a faulty and inflexible generalisation. It may be felt or expressed. It may be directed toward a group as a whole, or toward an individual because he is a member of that group. The net effect of prejudice, thus defined, is to place the object of prejudice at some disadvantage not merited by his own conduct.
>
> (Allport, 1954: 9)

Under such a definition, prejudgements become prejudices only if they are not reversible when the holder is exposed to new knowledge or evidence relating to the object of his or her erroneous judgement. According to Allport a prejudice is actively resistant to all evidence that would unseat it. Therefore, the difference between ordinary prejudgements and prejudice is that one can discuss and rectify a prejudgement without emotional resistance.

However, Brown (1995) takes issue with both of the above definitions. He argues that by referring to an 'inflexible generalisation' or to an 'irrational function' these writers are making unwise suppositions. Whilst at the time their definitions may have been wholly accurate given the existing level of knowledge, Brown suggests that to think of prejudice as being impervious to change or as having no rational function for its bearer is to fail to appreciate the variety and complexity of the forms prejudice can take, and its tendency to be unstable in its nature and to change under certain circumstances. Thus, to take account of these issues, Brown (1995: 8) defines prejudice as: 'The holding of derogatory social attitudes or cognitive beliefs, the expression of negative affect, or the display of hostile or discriminatory behaviour towards members of a group on account of their membership of that group'.

Similarly, and more simply, Baron and Byrne (1994: 218) define prejudice as: 'An attitude (usually negative) toward the members of some group, based solely on their membership in that group'. Here the definition implies that a prejudiced individual evaluates members of a particular social group in a specific manner simply because they belong to that social group, and thus the individual traits or behaviours of the target hold little significance for the prejudiced person. Baron and Byrne (1994) also suggest that prejudicial attitudes often function as schemas (cognitive frameworks for organising, interpreting and recalling information). They argue that prejudiced people process information about the object of their prejudice differently from that about groups towards whom hold no prejudicial views.

As such, information consistent with their prejudices tends to receive more attention, is cognitively rehearsed and reinforced more frequently and tends to be remembered more accurately than other information. Therefore, in the absence of strong contradictory evidence, prejudice becomes a 'cognitive loop' that grows stronger and more deep-seated over time. Consequently, prejudice as an attitude can then move beyond a simple evaluation of a group to include negative feelings and emotions and stereotyping on the part of the bearer. This can in turn lead to negative actions or discriminatory behaviours directed towards the objects of the prejudice, although it is important to note that prejudicial attitudes do not always transform into discriminatory behaviour.

The origins of prejudice and discrimination

There are numerous competing perspectives that seek to identify and explain the origins of prejudice and discrimination. Arguably the most significant early contribution was that of Gordon Allport in his seminal work, *The Nature of Prejudice*. Although competing ideas have since been advocated, Brown (1995) acknowledges that Allport's work has come to be regarded as the departure point for all modern research into aspects of prejudice. Furthermore, Brown states that so significant was Allport's contribution that his theorising has provided the basis for programmes designed to improve race relations in American schools for the past 60 years or so. Allport's work is encyclopaedic in its nature but it is important to begin with a brief overview of some of his thoughts regarding the origin of prejudice before moving on to examining some more recent perspectives.

According to Allport (1954) prejudice is a normal and rational (that is to say, predictable) human behaviour by virtue of our need to organise all the cognitive data our brain receives through the formation of generalisations, concepts and categories whose content represents an oversimplification of our world and experiences therein. This process is essential to our daily living and the forming of generalisations, categories and concepts based on experience and probability helps us to guide our daily activities and to make sense of the world around us. As a result, when we categorise, we think of things in terms of groups, rather than as unique individual entities, and we assume that these categories are informative and salient.

For example, as Allport suggests, if we see heavy black clouds in the sky we may prejudge that there is a high probability based on past experience that rain will fall and we adjust our behaviour accordingly (for example, by wearing a raincoat and taking an umbrella with us), but of course not all black clouds produce rain. Similarly, for the most part, it is also easier for us to overgeneralise about a subject or issue (for example 'all students are lazy'), or to quickly make an assumption that enables us to make life easier (for example, if we see a car being driven erratically it is easier for us to prejudge that the driver is drunk than it is to actually take the trouble to find out for certain).

Allport also suggests that we form certain concepts that have not only a 'meaning', but also provide a 'feeling'. Take, for example, the concept of a 'Londoner'. The vast majority of us will know what a 'Londoner' is, but our individual concept of a 'Londoner' may stir an accompanying personal feeling that we may harbour towards 'Londoners' in general even though it is highly unlikely that we will have met every single one. In this sense our oversimplification of the world leads us to one of Allport's more significant points – that the formation of our generalisations is just as likely to lead to irrational generalisations, concepts and categories as it is to rational ones.

Similarly, Allport suggests that in order to further simplify our lives, human beings naturally homogenise, often for no other reason than convenience, which in turn creates separateness amongst groups. According to Allport, humans tend to relate to other humans with similar presuppositions for the purpose of comfort, ease and congeniality. However, it is this separateness, coupled with our need to form generalisations and categories, which lays the foundations for psychological elaboration and the development of prejudice. Allport argues that people that stay separate have fewer channels of communication, are likely to exaggerate and misunderstand the differences between groups and develop genuine and imaginary conflicts of interests. It is this, according to Allport, that contributes largely to the formation of 'in-groups' and 'out-groups' and therefore to the *potential* formation and development of in-group loyalty and out-group rejection and the subsequent *potential* expression of prejudice and discriminatory behaviour towards those out-groups. This contributes to the development and maintenance of our social identity and therefore to our feelings of well-being.

Although this is a simplified account of the foundations of prejudice as defined by Allport (readers are advised to see Allport, 1954, for a comprehensive account), it is from this basis, he argues, that people develop their prejudicial nature, both positive and negative. Allport also believed that any negative attitude tends somehow to express itself in action, although the degree of action will vary greatly based upon the individual and the strength of the prejudice. To illustrate this Allport (1954: 14) provides a five-point scale, presented in Figure 5.1, to distinguish different degrees of negative action. *Antilocution* is simply the discussion of prejudices, usually with like-minded friends. *Avoidance* represents a more intense prejudice and leads the bearer to avoid members of the disliked group, although he or she does not inflict direct harm upon them. *Discrimination* is where the prejudiced individual makes detrimental distinctions of an active sort. Under conditions of heightened emotion prejudice may lead to acts of violence or semi-violence, categorised as *Physical attack*. Finally, *Extermination* marks the ultimate degree of violent expression of prejudice. Perhaps the best example of this is the Hitlerian programme of genocide during the Second World War, although the model can just as easily be applied to other genocides. Allport is at pains to point out however that most people never go beyond antilocution, and those that do will not necessarily move progressively up the scale, but it does serve to call attention to the range of potential activities that may occur as a direct result of prejudiced attitudes and beliefs.

Whilst remaining inspirational and hugely significant, Allport's work is now clearly somewhat dated and therefore it is necessary to examine some of the issues relating to the origins and development of prejudice in light of

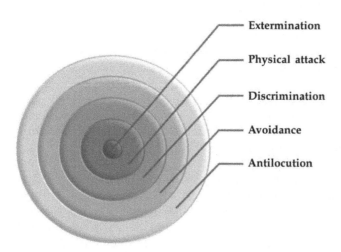

Extermination

Physical attack

Discrimination

Avoidance

Antilocution

Figure 5.1 Allport's (1954) five-point scale of prejudice.

some more recent theorising, much of which has been influenced by Allport's original ideas, particularly those concerning 'in' and 'out' groups.

Unsurprisingly a large number of competing perspectives exist, many of which are complex. What necessarily follows, therefore, is a simplified overview of some of the key theories and concepts put forward to explain the origins of prejudice. For a more comprehensive account, readers are advised to see, for example, Brown (1995), Baron and Byrne (1994) and Stangor (2000).

Stereotyping

A further important concept relating to the development and spread of prejudicial views is that of stereotyping. Brown (1995: 82) states that:

> To stereotype someone is to attribute to that person some characteristics which are seen to be shared by all or most of his or her fellow group members. A stereotype is, in other words, an inference drawn from the assignment of a person to a particular category ... [stereotypes] are embedded in the culture in which we are raised and live, and they are conveyed and reproduced in all the usual socio-cultural ways – through socialisation in the family and at school, through repeated exposure to images in books, television and newspaper.

Therefore, the fact that we tend to believe that the social categories we form are informative is a product of our capacity for stereotyping. As Stangor (2000) suggests, as we learn about groups, stereotypes become part of our memory, which are then stored and retrieved as cognitive representations that contain links between a social category and the traits that we associate with that category. These stereotypes might be cultural, in the sense that they are widely shared, or individual, in that they are somewhat limited in the numbers who share them. Similarly, he continues, our past experiences with people from social groups are remembered so that when we subsequently encounter someone from that group, our memories are triggered and our pre-existing stereotypes come into play once again. As Blaine (2008) suggests, when we know little about members of another group, we rely on personal contact with, or observations of, them to inform our beliefs about the whole group.

Furthermore, Allport (1954) and Brown (1995) both suggest an additional explanation for the origin of stereotypes, referred to as the *grain of truth* theory. Here, stereotypes derive from some aspect of social reality, regardless of how tenuous that link to reality might be (after all, if stereotypes were consistently wildly inaccurate, they would serve no useful purpose and would in all probability cease to exist). For example, if a university lecturer has a class that he or she deems to be particularly lazy, then that view may be attributed by that lecturer to his or her other classes, and perhaps indeed to the student population as a whole, which whilst true for some students can by no means be applied to all. Thus, Allport (1954: 191) defines stereo-types as:

> An exaggerated belief associated with a category. Its function is to jus-tify (rationalise) our conduct in relation to that category. The stereotype acts both as a justificatory device for categorical acceptance or rejection of a group, and as a screening or selective device to maintain simplicity in perception and in thinking.

The second half of the last sentence of Allport's definition clearly indicates that stereotypes act as schemas (cognitive frameworks) which Baron and Byrne (1994) suggest exert a strong effect on the ways in which we process social information. Essentially, they argue, stereotypes lead the bearer to pay attention to specific types of social information consistent with their pre-judice, and to actively refute information that is inconsistent with their beliefs. Thus, stereotypes lead to the biased processing and interpretation of social information that in turn leads to a situation whereby they become self-confirming and self-maintaining, and this in turn ensures continued prejudiced attitudes.

Illusory correlations

Closely related to this cognitive aspect of stereotyping is the notion of *illusory correlations* (Hamilton and Gifford, 1976), which consist of per-ceived relationships between different variables where no such relationship exists. As Risen *et al.* (2007) explain, Hamilton and Gifford argued that ste-reotypes sometimes arise not from base human motivations or intergroup conflict, but rather from the faulty workings of human memory. Their argu-ment is, in essence, that because negative behaviours are relatively numeri-cally rare, as are (by definition) members of minority groups, when the latter perform the former these behaviours become disproportionately memorable. This can lead to later impressions that minority group members are respon-sible for a disproportionate amount of these undesirable behaviours, not least because rare behaviour is more arresting than common behaviour and therefore more likely to prompt thought and elaboration and to trigger thoughts that lead to an association between a group and a particular beha-viour (Risen *et al.*, 2007). In other words, illusory correlations can occur where relatively rare events draw our attention and are remembered more readily than common events, particularly where these are negative.

As a result of illusory correlations, then, the actions of members of a minority group can have implications for the way in which the whole of that group is perceived by members of the majority. This point was poignantly illustrated by Anne Frank (1947, 1993) in her diary when she noted that 'what one Christian does is his own responsibility, what one Jew does is thrown back at all Jews' (1993: 239). As a more recent example, and perhaps illustrative of political rhetoric, if we take the former Home Secretary, Jack Straw's comments of a few years ago that *'Scousers are always up to something'* (BBC News, 1999) it is possible that an illusory correlation suggesting a strong link between people from Liverpool and criminal activity will emerge. Whilst it is undoubtedly true that a proportion of Liverpudlians are involved in crime, the illusory correlation may lead people to assume that the relationship between Liverpudlians and criminal activity is actually higher than it is. Furthermore, people may draw the conclusion that Liverpudlians commit crime simply because they are from Liverpool, and not because of other social and criminogenic factors. As Baron and Byrne (1994) suggest, individuals pay just enough attention to sources of information, be it from friends, family or the media, to form an erroneous perception of the social world.

Social identity and group dynamics

Hogg (2006) defines social identity theory as a social psychological analysis of the role of self-conception in group membership, group processes and intergroup relations. As such, he suggests, it addresses phenomena including prejudice, discrimination, ethnocentrism, stereotyping, intergroup conflict, conformity, normative behaviour, group polarisation, deviance and group cohesiveness, and, in particular since the 1990s, has become one of the discipline's most significant general theories of the relationship between self and group (Hogg, 2006).

As Ashforth and Mael (1989) point out, according to social identity theory and in keeping with Allport's hypothesis, people tend to classify themselves and others into various social categories, and this social categorisation essentially serves two functions. First, Ashforth and Mael note, it cognitively segments and orders the social environment and thus provides the individual with a systematic means of defining others, which as we have already seen above, is not necessarily an accurate and reliable undertaking. Second, this process of classification allows us to locate or define ourselves within the social environment. According to social identity theory, then, the self-concept comprises a *personal identity* encompassing idiosyncratic characteristics (for example, bodily attributes, abilities, psychological traits, interests and so on) and a *social identity* encompassing salient group classifications, and as such, social identification is the perception of being at one with, or belonging to, some human aggregate.

On this basis, Tajfel (1982) suggests that the need for individuals to enhance their self-esteem by identifying themselves with specific social groups is significant in the development of prejudice. This identification inevitably leads people to view their social group (their in-group) as somehow superior to other, competing social groups and, since all groups form and develop in the same way, prejudice can arise out of the resulting clash of social perceptions. For example, whites may see themselves as superior to blacks, men as superior to women, the able-bodied superior to people with disabilities, one nationality superior to another and so on.

More specifically, when we examine the perpetrators of hate crimes in chapter six one of the notable features of the available literature is that hate crimes are often committed by young people in groups. The impact of group dynamics is therefore significant, and Gerstenfeld (2004) notes this point. She draws attention to numerous psychological studies that have highlighted the influence of social situations on human behaviour, and in particular the importance of group conformity, to the extent that many hate crimes may not in fact be motivated solely by prejudice, but rather by pressure to follow the group.

The key processes here, she suggests, are first, *deindividuation*, whereby people feel more anonymous as part of a group and therefore take less responsibility for their actions. Second, through *identification* an individual will assume the attitudes and behaviours of a group that they find attractive or admirable and want to be a part of. Third, individuals often *internalise* the beliefs of the group that they admire and want to be a part of. Gerstenfeld suggests that the group attitudes can become a permanent and important part of the individual's belief system, and can be extremely resistant to change.

She also suggests that *internalisation* can occur because of *cognitive dissonance*. Here it is held that people actively avoid inconsistencies in their belief systems. Where inconsistencies emerge then individuals must either change their beliefs or develop new ones to avoid such inconsistencies. In other words, where beliefs are challenged by, for example, exposure to new information about the subject of those beliefs, then the prejudiced individual will likely change their ideas in a way that allows the original prejudice to remain justifiable. The existence of cognitive dissonance is reflected in research evidence that suggests that hate offenders will often denigrate or dehumanise their victim, or see them as deserving of their treatment, so as to justify their behaviour towards them (a point we shall return to in chapter six). The processes associated with social identity and group dynamics are significant in the development of prejudice and therefore, as Gerstenfeld suggests, are important for understanding why *some* people commit hate crimes.

Realistic conflict theory

Describing the central hypothesis – that real conflict of group interests causes intergroup conflict – as *deceptively simple* and *intuitively convincing*, Tajfel and Turner (1986) suggest that realistic conflict theory (Sherif and Sherif, 1953; Sherif, 1966) provides both an aetiology of intergroup hostility and a theory of competition as realistic and instrumental in character, motivated by rewards which in principle are extrinsic to the intergroup situation. As such, realistic conflict theory proposes that conflicting interests develop through competition into overt social conflict, and that these conflicts create antagonistic intergroup relations whilst simultaneously increasing identification and positive attachment to the in-group (Tajfel and Turner, 1979). Thus, prejudice can stem from a sense of relative deprivation derived from competition between social groups for valued commodities (such as, for example, jobs, land, power and so on) or opportunities (Bobo, 1983), and as the competition for these scarce economic resources intensifies members of competing social groups will come to view each other in increasingly negative terms that if permitted to foster will develop into emotion-laden prejudice (White, 1977).

Hovland and Sears (1940), for example, argued that competition for scarce resources was particularly applicable in explaining the widespread lynchings of African Americans in the south of the country during a period of particularly harsh economic conditions endured in the fifty years or so prior to their research. Similarly, the popularity of the Ku Klux Klan has historically peaked in times when white interests have come under a perceived threat from 'outsiders'. More recent research has also supported the link between economic decline and the development of prejudice, and the subsequent hostility and violence – a particularly pertinent issue given the current global financial crisis. Interestingly, however, these research studies tend to suggest that prejudice is only inevitable when group interests are threatened, and that when an individual's interests are similarly challenged the development of prejudice is far less certain. The role of economics and social strain will be examined further in the next chapter.

Integrated threat theory

Stephan and Stephan (1996) have expanded upon the principles of realistic conflict theory to propose that there are essentially four types of threats that lead to intergroup prejudice and conflict: *realistic threats, symbolic threats, intergroup anxiety* and *negative stereotypes*, which may occur collectively or individually, and whose influence on the development of prejudice will necessarily depend upon the relationship between the groups involved.

The first, *realistic threats*, as we have seen typically arise as a result of competition for scarce resources. But, as Stephan *et al.* (1998) point out, in the wider sense these threats posed by the out-group relate to the very existence of the in-group, to its political and economic power, and its physical or material wellbeing. *Symbolic threats* differ and relate to group differences in morals, values, norms, standards, beliefs and attitudes, and represent threats to the world-view of the in-group that arise as a consequence of a belief in the moral rightness of the in-group's system of values combined with perceptions that an out-group is undermining those values (Stephan *et al.*, 1998).

Prejudice can also arise from *intergroup anxiety* that can occur, Stephan *et al.* state, because of the way people feel in intergroup interactions. They suggest that people tend to be particularly anxious when the groups involved in the interaction have a history of antagonism, little prior personal contact, are ethnocentric, perceive each other as dissimilar, are ignorant of each other, or when the interaction takes place in a relatively unstructured and competitive situation where the in-group is in the minority (perhaps explaining localised anxieties concerning immigrants 'swamping' an area – see Sibbitt, 1997, below) or is of a lower status than the out-group. Finally, Stephan *et al.* suggest that *negative stereotypes* typically embody threats to the in-group because, as we have seen, they serve as a basis of expectations concerning the behaviour of members of the out-group. As we have also seen, these expectations are frequently negative and as such, the link between negative stereotyping and prejudice means that conflictual interactions are likely to be anticipated (Stephan *et al.*, 1998).

In testing the impact of these threats, Stephan *et al.* (1998) found considerable support for integrated threat theory in explaining attitudes towards immigrants where each threat (but not all four simultaneously or collectively) was a significant predictor of prejudicial attitudes, thereby highlighting the importance of *threat* as a general underlying causal factor in the development of prejudice. Whilst Stephan *et al.* concentrated on attitudes towards Moroccan immigrants to Spain and Russian and Ethiopian immigrants to Israel, similar support for elements of integrated threat theory has been identified, for example, in relation to prejudice towards Muslims in The Netherlands (Velasco González *et al.*, 2008), attitudes towards people with terminal cancer and AIDS (Berrenberg *et al.*, 2007) and Hindu–Muslim relations in India (Tausch *et al.* 2008).

Social learning and authoritarianism

Social learning theories suggest that prejudicial attitudes are learned in childhood through contact with older and influential figures who reward children (with, for example, love and praise) for adopting their views (Pettigrew, 1969). Indeed, Brown (1995) suggests that children as young as 3 years of age are aware of two of the major social categories, namely gender and ethnicity, and from that age children can readily identify with some categories rather than others, and can demonstrate clear attitudinal and behavioural preferences among these categories. Similarly, Baron and Byrne (1994) explain that children and adolescents also adopt and conform to the social norms of the group to which they belong, resulting in the development and expression of prejudicial attitudes towards others.

Allport (1954) suggested that in this regard parenting styles play an important part in the development of a child's prejudice. Allport drew particular attention to parents with authoritarian personalities, whom he argued raised their children in a strict, authoritarian and conservative way, with an emphasis on the significance of authority, power and inequality in society. These values are then reflected in the child's attitudes and behaviours towards those they perceive to be subordinate or weak. In this sense, then, hate offenders are not born, but bred, and the development of a child's prejudice is influenced by their parents, but also by other elders, and by localised social norms.

Some of the studies examining the perpetrators of hate crimes, for example, point to the influence of elder family members, friends and acquaintances on the development of negative prejudice in the young. In particular, Sibbitt's (1997) typology of racist offenders identified precisely this point. Sibbitt argues that the pensioners involved in her study of two London boroughs, having witnessed periods of significant demographic change and deteriorating social conditions, often saw ethnic minorities as 'invading' both their country and, more broadly, their lives in general and thus viewed them as scapegoats for their, and the country's, problems. Despite in many cases being friendly with black neighbours, their general negative attitudes towards ethnic minorities were found to influence the attitudes of younger members of their family.

Sibbitt also found that the attitudes of elders profoundly affected the racist tendencies of the second group in her typology, 'the people next door'. These are adults who have grown up listening to the views of their elders and in turn racialise their own problems and insecurities, for example, unemployment, housing and so on. Sibbitt suggests that such people will engage in racist behaviour where, for example, they perceive biased allocation of desired resources to minority groups, or as part of a general offending behaviour, or as retaliation for a perceived misdemeanour by a member of a minority group.

The 'problem family' represent a third category of offender. Such people, Sibbitt suggests, experience a number of problems, for example poor health and aggressive tendencies, and see themselves as persecuted and rejected by society. As such racist offending forms part of wider antisocial behaviour, particularly where community racism is already in existence.

A fourth and particularly problematic category of offender identified by Sibbitt is that of the '15–18-year-olds'. Typically, these individuals have been subject to the views of their elders, and at school will likely have associated with older youths with racist attitudes and engaged in other forms of antisocial behaviour. On leaving school, Sibbitt suggests that these individuals will have a sense of limited prospects and will often find themselves with little to occupy their time, together with a need to develop some sense of identity for themselves. They may find it easy to attach themselves to far right ideologies that provide them with both a sense of belonging and with scapegoats for their plight. These people, according to Sibbitt's research, often engage in abusive and threatening behaviour, offend as part of a group, and may be responsible for extremely violent attacks.

The '11–14-year-old' category, the fifth in Sibbitt's study, had predominantly grown up in areas where racist attitudes were common and regularly expressed. Many of these children were found to have low self-esteem and to bully other children who they perceived to be weaker than them, primarily to gain status among their peers. Some of the bullying was racist in its content, and in particular ethnic minority children were bullied in areas where wider community racism was common, often in an attempt to impress others. Again, the racist behaviour occurred in a group context.

The final category of offender that Sibbitt identifies is the '4–10-year-olds'. Again, racist language has been a part of their upbringing and is reflected in their own language. Indeed, racist views are held to be normal and may be regularly expressed by the child. Sibbitt found that 'offenders' in this category often engage in bullying which continues away from the school environment in the form of wider harassment and intimidation. Again, this type of behaviour may be related to a sense of boredom, and may also be positively reinforced by older family members.

However, Brown (1995) argues that using a child's 'passive absorption' of existing prejudices in society as an explanation of the development of prejudice is perhaps a little too simplistic. He suggests that other factors relating to a child's social and cognitive development may in fact hold the key to a more comprehensive understanding of the origins of prejudice (for an explanation of these, see Brown, 1995). Furthermore, the suggestion that hate offenders develop and learn their hatred, for example from their parents, might partially explain hate crime, but it can never fully do so given that at some point in history that hatred must have developed in the individual by some process other than simply learning it. In other words, where did the first hater in the family acquire their hatred? Other factors must, as a matter of necessity, play a part.

Social learning and stereotype formation can also occur via other avenues, most notably through the media. As Blaine (2008) points out, the influence of television is of particular interest given the amount of time many people, including children, now spend absorbing information from that source, and whose cultural education might be limited to what they see and hear on television. He suggests that whilst programmes on television have become more racially diverse in recent years, portrayals of other groups have largely failed to follow suit to the same degree, thereby potentially feeding a range of stereotypes about these groups.

Illustrating 'everyday' prejudice

Two relatively recent English studies by the advocacy group Stonewall (2003; 2004) have identified a number of factors that appear to have a bearing on the development of prejudice, and the findings of these studies illustrate a number of the theoretical points raised in this chapter.

The first study in 2003 comprised a survey of a representative sample of 1,700 adults throughout England. Of that number, 64 per cent expressed a prejudice against at least one minority group. The second study, conducted for Stonewall by Valentine and McDonald (2004) comprised a series of focus groups and single interviews with the aim of providing a deeper understanding of the factors that cause and sustain prejudice against minority groups.

The results of the research indicated five types of prejudice characterised by different levels of social acceptability and by varying forms of justification. The first category is that of *unintentional prejudice*. This form of prejudice includes attitudes or behaviours that whilst unwitting nevertheless demonstrate ignorance of diversity on the part of the holder. The second category, *cathartic prejudice*, is characterised by views that are recognised as being less positive about minority groups and socially unacceptable, but crucially that are in some way justified by the holder in order to render them acceptable.

The third category identified by the Stonewall study is that of *benevolent prejudice*. This is defined as the expression of positive views about minority groups that may in reality produce negative or discriminatory consequences. For example, some of the views expressed in the research illustrated caring stereotypes of people with disabilities, labelling them as vulnerable or helpless. Whilst such views are not intended to offend they are often negatively received. Stonewall suggest that benevolent prejudices demonstrate a lack of understanding of the reality of belonging to a minority group, and may indeed play an important role in the social exclusion of the group in question because such labels often imply incompetence and powerlessness.

The fourth category is *banal prejudice*. Stonewall suggest that this type of prejudice is evident towards all minority groups. It is defined as mundane or implicit examples of less positive attitudes that may be intentional or unintentional that nevertheless pass unnoticed. The final category is *aggressive prejudice*, which is defined as open and explicit animosity that is often backed up by the threat of violence.

The research also identified nine separate factors likely to affect the development of the prejudices described above. The first, *perceived economic injustice*, is an issue that I shall return to in greater detail in chapter six, but the Stonewall study suggested that resentment concerning the allocation of, and competition for, scarce economic resources (housing, jobs, benefits and so on) is frequently used to justify negative attitudes towards minority groups. Similarly, concerns relating to a *perceived cultural injustice* are also important in the development of prejudice. Mirroring the historical perceptions discussed in chapter two, participants in the Stonewall study spoke of being 'invaded' or 'taken over' by minority groups, and often cited differences between 'us' and 'them' in relation to religion, language, morality, values and so on. Some participants felt that white English culture was being undervalued and shown a lack of respect, whilst public resources unjustly supported minority cultures. In a somewhat contradictory fashion, many participants attempted to negate their prejudice by declaring that it is acceptable for minorities to engage in their cultural or religious practices so long as this occurs in private and not in public. Public displays of 'difference' were frequently greeted with hostility.

A further influencing factor is a *lack of personal contact*. Stonewall found that the two groups identified as the most threatening (asylum seekers and

Travellers) were the only groups that most participants had never come into contact with, suggesting perhaps the importance of ignorance in the shaping of prejudice. Conversely, disabled people were the subject of the least hostility, but were also the minority group with which the participants had had the most contact. The implication here is that contact, familiarity and knowledge of the object of one's prejudice will lead to a reduction in that prejudice. As we shall see in chapter eight, however, this is a far from certain outcome. Rather, it is the quality of the contact that is important, and *negative encounters* with members of minority groups can lead to powerful negative stereotypes across the group as a whole. Significantly, however, the Stonewall study found that positive encounters did not lead to positive stereotypes of the whole group. In such instances that particular individual member of the minority group was viewed favourably, rather than the group as a whole. In other words, it seems that negative encounters affect prejudice to a far greater extent than positive ones.

The role of the *media* was also found to be crucial in the development of prejudice amongst the participants of the Stonewall study. Whilst the interviewees denied that the media caused any of the prejudices outlined above, the researchers were able to identify a strong media influence. The results suggest that the media (particularly television and newspapers) provide much of the material that individuals use to justify their beliefs, and that these media stories are frequently held to be accurate and independent thereby corroborating the individual's view. The media were also found to encourage latent feelings, of which anger and disgust were common, and to produce a sense of powerlessness amongst the white majority group that nothing could be done about their concerns. Examples of this can be found throughout this book, and I shall specifically return to this issue in chapter eight.

Closely allied to media messages is the role of *rumour* in the development of prejudice. Stonewall's study suggested that participants lacked trust in official sources of information and gave far more credence to informal sources and gossip from friends and acquaintances. This is significant because discussing similar views with likeminded others (via the process of antilocution suggested by Allport, above) serves to justify and reinforce the prejudices in question. In other words, negative prejudice becomes justifiable because 'other people think the same way'.

Stonewall's findings relating to *intergenerational prejudice* challenge many of the social learning theories discussed above. The results suggest that contrary to previous studies, prejudice is *not* passed down through families and that intergenerational differences in views are common. The extent to which this finding is generalisable is however unclear.

The penultimate influencing factor relates to *the Church*, although little is said other than that some participants in the study identified the Church as promoting prejudiced and intolerant views. As we saw in chapter two (and will return to in the next chapter) however, religious views have been significant in the history of hate crime, and remain so in contemporary analyses of the problem.

The final factor that Stonewall identified as important is that *prejudice serves positive ends for the prejudiced person*. For example, Stonewall suggest that homophobia may reinforce an individual's view of themselves as a good Christian, or that prejudice against asylum seekers enables the individual to reinforce their sense of community belonging. In other words, prejudice serves a rational function for the holder that in turn enables the justification of that prejudice.

Themes from the prejudice literature

So far in this chapter I have presented some of the key theories of prejudice and attempted to illustrate some of the ways in which it manifests itself. Of course, this overview is necessarily limited on both counts, not least because of the sheer volume of scholarship in this particular field. However, following an extensive review of the prejudice literature, Abrams (2010) has identified a number of prominent themes that help to summarise what we know about this rather complex concept. For Abrams (2010), and reflecting many of the key messages from this chapter, the following themes are crucial to an understanding of prejudice (and therefore 'hate'):

1. Prejudice arises in an intergroup context, often as a product of conflicting goals or demands;
2. There are several powerful bases of prejudice. As such, when certain values are regarded as important, prejudices become directed towards those groups that are perceived to challenge or undermine those values. These prejudices then serve to justify discriminatory practices in pursuit of upholding the values in question;
3. Membership of a social category can generate biased perceptions and attitudes, leading to the formation of stereotypes (and the basis for accompanying emotions) and thereby creating the potential for discrimination by reinforcing differences between groups;
4. The role of *identity* is central;
5. There are multiple manifestations of prejudice, and not all prejudices are the same;
6. The size of an out-group does not necessarily dictate how threatening it is perceived to be, and nor does it determine the extent and nature of the prejudice directed towards it;
7. Prejudice can be powerfully expressed through language (as well as stereotypes, attitudes and so on);
8. People's engagement with, and experience of, prejudice takes a number of different forms;
9. Prejudice is amenable to social- and self-control, both of which can either increase or inhibit prejudice depending on issues of context;

10. Prejudice is best understood as a phenomenon involving a common set of social psychological processes, and an understanding of these is central to measuring, predicting and preventing prejudice.

Concluding comments

The chapter has presented an overview of some of the key theorising regarding the nature and origins of prejudice and discrimination. Just as there is no single definition of prejudice, so we find there is little consensus for theories that seek to explain this phenomenon. Clearly, prejudice underpins hatred as a human emotion. However, it is important to note that it is not a crime to hold prejudicial views and nor is it a crime to hate. Indeed, unless that prejudice manifests itself in some form of physical or verbal action how would we know that an individual harbours negative views towards another? Significantly, however, as noted by Allport (1954), prejudicial views will almost inevitably be expressed in word or deed at some point in time.

It is also clear that there are many kinds of prejudice that vary greatly and have different psychological dynamics underpinning them, and as we shall see, this has important implications for responding to hate crimes. Furthermore, because prejudices are independent psychological responses they can be expressed, as Allport illustrates, in a bewildering number of ways, ranging from a mild dislike or general aversion to others to extreme acts of violence. But (and this is crucial for our understanding of hate motivated offending) as Green *et al.* (2003: 27) suggest: *It might take the better part of a lifetime to read the prodigious research literature on prejudice ... yet scarcely any of this research examines directly and systematically the question of why prejudice erupts into violence.*

So, when we talk about hate in the context of hate crime, we are really referring to prejudice. But despite the wide research that has been conducted into prejudice as a psychological phenomenon, we still cannot say with any degree of certainty why it is that prejudice leads to violent behaviour. But, as Gaylin (2003) argues, to suggest that *hatred* (but not in its contemporary politically constructed sense) is normal to the human condition is too simplistic an argument to sustain. After all, he suggests, even given the opportunity and freedom to hate or express hatred without obstruction or sanction, most of us would still not choose to do so. Yet when this does occur, we do not know enough about prejudice to say how or why.

Whilst prejudice is seemingly normal and universal, hatred, it seems, is not. But in our definitions of hate crime we often fail to make a clear distinction between prejudice and hate. We label offences as 'hate' crimes, but the application of this label is determined by whether or not an offence was motivated or aggravated by *prejudice*, or wholly or partially by deliberate hostility towards a particular group. There is little talk of hate anywhere and there is a danger that by focusing on prejudice rather than on hate as an extreme and problematic element, that in fact we are targeting the wrong thing, if indeed it can be targeted at all. Whilst this is a debate that we will explore further in chapter nine, for now we need to concern ourselves with exploring explanatory frameworks that might help us to fill the gaps left by the psychological literature, and explain why it is that prejudice becomes the motivating factor for criminal behaviour.

6 Explaining hate crime

As we noted in chapter two, Bowling (1999) suggests that academic and professional interest in issues of race and racism in relation to crime (and therefore, by analogy, the emergence of 'pre-Lawrence' interest in hate crime) can be traced back to the early 1980s in the UK through two key events. The first was the urban riots of 1981, most notably in Brixton, south London, that saw the emergence of race, prejudice and discrimination as significant social issues. The second was the re-emergence of victimology in the late 1970s and early 1980s as a significant social science in its own right, and the subsequent development of social surveys that for the first time began to provide a wealth of data relating to the plight of the victim, and in particular the disproportionate victimisation of certain minority groups.

Together, these two events served to ensure that the victim was placed at the centre of the criminal justice, criminological and political focus – a situation that largely remains to date. Whilst this is of course absolutely right and the victim of any crime should be of central concern to all parties in the criminal justice system, this focus on the victim has meant that the perpetrator as an actor in the equation has hitherto been largely ignored. This is particularly true for perpetrators of hate crime and poses something of a problem for our understanding of this form of offending behaviour. The following two quotes from Ben Bowling, which as we shall see still resonate today, adequately outline the consequent challenges facing those seeking to explain hate motivated offending as a result of the predominantly victim-oriented focus. First:

> There has been almost no research on perpetrators. Whilst the most basic of descriptions have been formulated, they remain something of an effigy in the criminological literature ... The perpetrator is unknown and, consequently, the possibility for any understanding or interpretation of his or her behaviour becomes impossible.

(1999: 163)

And second:

> What is needed for the purposes of explaining [hate crime] is for
> attention to be turned away from an analysis of the characteristics of
> victims to focus on the characteristics of offenders: their relationship
> with those they victimise; the social milieux in which anger, aggression,
> hostility, and violence are fostered; and the social processes by which
> violence becomes directed against minority groups ... Criminologists
> operate with scant evidence about what is going on in the lives of these
> people. Instead, we have only a devilish effigy for symbolic sacrifice.
>
> (1999: 305)

Writing of this situation from North America, Barbara Perry (2003) has
argued similarly. In addition to the impact of the victim-oriented focus of
which Bowling speaks, Perry has suggested that theorising about
perpetrators has been scant partially because hate crime, as we have seen, is
'new' to the criminological horizon, and also because of the lack of agreement that we noted in chapter one about how exactly we should define 'hate
crime', and of course, the implications that necessarily follow for the production of reliable data upon which to base research and to construct conceptual frameworks (Perry, 2009). In addition, Perry has pointed to the fact
that historically, when criminology has taken an interest in minority groups
per se the focus has tended to be on their criminality, rather than on crimes
committed against them.

Despite Bowling and Perry's concerns being a decade or more old, it is
perhaps something of an indictment on the social sciences that Perry was
able to reiterate these sentiments as recently as 2009, lamenting that:

> It is curious that hate crime has not been an object of extensive theore-
> tical inquiry. Conceptually, it lies at the intersection of several themes
> that are currently to the fore, for example, violence, victimisation, race/
> ethnicity, gender, sexuality, and difference. In spite of the centrality of
> violence as a means of policing the relative boundaries of identity, few
> attempts have been made to understand theoretically the place of hate
> crime in the contemporary arsenal of oppression. It is not an area that
> has been seriously examined through a theoretical lens ... The goal of
> hate crime theory, then, is to conceptualise this particular form of vio-
> lence within the psychological, cultural, or political contexts that con-
> dition hostile perceptions of, and reactions to, the Other.
>
> (2009: 56)

In light of the various concerns expressed above, this chapter will present an
overview of current knowledge in relation to the perpetrators of hate crime.
We will attempt, as far as is possible given the available literature and the
space available to discuss it, to shed some light on both what is known

about the perpetrators of hate crime and what causes this type of offending, and in so doing present something (hopefully) a little more useful than the *'devilish effigy'* we have thus far largely been confined to.

Understanding 'hate crime': perspectives from the social sciences

Perhaps unsurprisingly given the often secular nature of the social sciences, explanations of hate and hate crime offending have been proffered in a rather disparate and often isolated manner, leaving us with a somewhat disjointed framework of analysis. Here, then, we shall briefly consider what some of the social sciences have to say about our area of study.

Psychology

We have already spent quite a bit of time examining psychological explanations of prejudice and hate, so I do not intend to dwell on the area for too much longer. You will have noted from our discussion of definitions of hate crime in chapter one that the words 'prejudice', 'discrimination' and 'bigotry' frequently appear, and, as Perry (2003) suggests, these concepts mark the starting point for theorising about the perpetrators of hate crime. Indeed, she notes that the literature to date has been dominated by psychological and social–psychological accounts that necessarily emphasise individual-level analyses (2009: 56). But as we saw in the previous chapter, for all our theorising about these concepts, the existing literature tells us remarkably little about how prejudice transforms into actions that would constitute hate crimes.

Stern (2005) reiterates this point. Whilst psychology informs us that most people are capable of hatred and gives us some insights into the relationship between identity and hate, its rather narrow focus on the individual as an explanation is necessarily limited and needs, if it is to provide more comprehensive answers, to be integrated into a larger framework. As we saw in the previous chapter, social psychology, which considers the individual in social situations where certain attributes may come to the fore, offers arguably greater insight into intergroup conflict and, as Stern points out, this *'treasure trove'* of research also suggests some possibilities for responding to the problem (as we shall see in chapter eight). Nevertheless, whilst psychology has some important contributions to make to our understanding of hate, as we saw in the previous chapter, these individual-level analyses do not provide the complete explanation of hate motivated offending that we might hope for.

History

In chapter two we traced the historical evolution of hate crime as a social, legal and political concern. In doing so, we charted some historical events which served our purpose of trying to explain and illustrate how it is that hate crime came to attract the attention that it now does. But history more generally also provides some useful insights into hate offending.

For example, in her examination of hate crimes in the US, Carolyn Petro-sino (1999) provides an interesting comparative analysis of past and present hate crimes and, by comparing historical events with contemporary hate crimes, she finds a number of striking similarities. To summarise, Petrosino's work illustrates a number of important themes, many of which are just as applicable to the UK as they are to the US. First, that the hate crime 'prob-lem' is not a distinctly modern phenomenon and dates back to at least the seventeenth century (and much further in the UK and elsewhere in the world). Second, that hate crime has deep historical roots. Third, that hate crime was at least as prevalent in the past as it is today. Fourth, that most hate crimes relate to racial prejudice. Fifth, that diversity is not generally well tolerated. Sixth, that offence, victim and perpetrator characteristics have remained broadly similar over the past 400 or more years. Seventh, perpe-trators are predominantly white males. Eighth, that minority groups are used as scapegoats for perceived social problems suggesting a *'culture of hate'* (see below). And finally, in something of a historical contrast, that hate crimes are characteristically less violent today than in the past. History tells us, then, that there are many distinct parallels that can be drawn between past and present-day hate crimes over a range of indicators. Petrosino's historical analysis therefore lends support to our earlier contention in chapter two, namely that hate crime is nothing new whilst society's response to it is.

Moreover, as Stern (2005: 5) rightly points out:

> History is the study of the past and, as such, provides a framework for understanding hatred and how it has manifested itself at different times and places. It focuses our attention on the societal origins of intergroup hate, on the rise and lifespan of various ideologies and theologies, on the role of dehumanization, on how institutions are used, and how old battles are recycled symbolically to energize new ones. It also helps us understand the "triggers," the events that combine the ingredients of hate into a combustible brew.

He also makes the important point that, in addition to recognising historical triggers (for example, events in the Middle East – *note the links to the find-ings of the CST report discussed in chapter four* – the collapse of the Soviet Union – *again note the links here to the plight of the Roma and Sinti also discussed in that chapter* – and 9/11 – *similarly discussed in relation to the demonisation of Muslims*), history is also a discipline often abused to pro-mote hatred. In particular Stern (2005) points to the issue of Holocaust denial, which is no longer just the preserve of neo-Nazis, and to the content of white supremacist, Afrocentric, and fundamentalist Islamist teachings, which respectively subvert the meaning and interpretation of historical events for nefarious purposes.

Similarly, for example, Frost (2008), argues that the hostility towards, and demonisation of, Islam today is part of a longer legacy of anti-Muslim sentiment that stretches back to Renaissance Europe during the Middle Ages. This historical legacy, she suggests, has been contemporarily shaped by a host of 'trigger' events (and the manner of the reporting of these) including the Salman Rushdie/*Satanic Verses* affair in 1988, the invasion and occupation of Iraq, the situation in the Middle East and the use of suicide bombers, 9/11 and the stereotyping of 'Islam' and 'terrorism', the Danish anti-Muslim cartoons where the responses of radical Islamists dominated the media and were held to be 'representative' of the response of all Muslims and so on.

Cultural studies

Closely aligned to the role of history in understanding hate crimes are issues relating to culture. The limitations of individual-level analyses of hate as a motivation for criminal behaviour, coupled with the 'normality' of prejudice that we have already discussed in the previous chapter, means that, as Levin and Rabrenovic (2009: 42) put it, hate hardly depends for its existence on individual pathology or abnormal psychology. This latter point is neatly illustrated by one of the most widely cited studies of hate offenders conducted by McDevitt *et al.* (2002 – variously referred to throughout this chapter and again in chapter eight) who concluded that the rarest type of hate offender (less than 1 per cent of their sample) was that which they labelled as 'mission'. Here the offender is totally committed to his or her hate and bigotry, and views the objects of their hate as an evil that must be removed from the world. These offenders are those that would fit into cell one of Jacobs and Potter's (1998) model that we discussed in chapter one.

So, for Levin and Rabrenovic, and in line with McDevitt *et al.*'s findings, hate is rarely about abnormal or 'extreme' psychology, and neither is it necessarily a form of deviance from the point of view of mainstream society. Rather, hate is, they suggest, a part of the culture of the society in which it exists and when conceived as such, it is part of the totality of an individual's learned and accumulated experiences, including beliefs, values, attitudes, roles and material possessions, which intensifies as it incorporates widely shared myths and stereotypes. Indeed research by Chandler and Tsai (2001) suggests that public views of immigration, for example, are shaped more by perceived cultural threats than by economic concerns, political ideologies or fear of crime (cited by Stacey *et al.*, 2011) – a finding that supports those identified by Stonewall that we discussed in the previous chapter.

Levin and Rabrenovic (2009) argue that cultural hate has, and does, play an important role in justifying hate crimes against those who differ from the offender in socially significant ways. This cultural element of hate, they argue, can be identified in a number of different ways, including the ability of a hatred towards a certain group to be broadly shared across a range of other groups, the spanning of hatred across generations and the acquisition of common culturally based hatreds from an early age. Indeed, as we saw in the previous chapter, Sibbitt's (1997) research examining racist offending in London suggested that the perpetrators of racist offences spanned all age ranges, from young children to old-age pensioners, and involved both sexes who often acted in groups. Sibbitt suggests that the experiences of older people are therefore crucial in providing a framework that shapes the hate-based attitudes and behaviours of others within a family or a community, and that the attitudes of younger offenders are often derived from those of their elders (although at this point we should remember the limitations of social learning theory also considered in the previous chapter).

For Levin and Rabrenovic (2009), then, cultural hate identifies appropriate targets, increases the impact of victimisation, and, crucially, maintains intergroup conflict in the face of efforts to reduce the incidence of hate crime. The study of culture and its component parts therefore seems to have much to offer in aiding our understanding of hate and hate offending.

Geography

In chapter three we discussed the international geography of hate crime. That is to say, I used the term as a collective to provide a 'rough guide' as to what is happening and where throughout a number of different countries in the world. But beyond looking at what is occurring across international borders, geography as a discipline has much to contribute to our understanding of hate crime.

As Stacey *et al.* (2011) point out, over the past decade or so hate crime research has focused increasingly on the social and ecological context in which hate crime occurs, often focusing on issues of demographic change within and between geographical locations to explain variations in rates of offending and victimisation from place to place (see for example, Green *et al.*, 1998; Grattet's 2009 research on 'defended neighbourhoods'; and Chakraborti and Garland's 2004 work on rural racism).

The influence of 'territory' in the commission of hate crimes has also been illustrated by McDevitt *et al.* (2002). In 25 per cent of the cases analysed, they categorised the motivation as being 'defensive' in its nature. In these cases, the offender committed hate offences against what he or she perceived to be outsiders or intruders in an attempt to defend or protect his or her 'territory'. Echoing the view discussed in chapter four that hate crimes are 'message crimes', the researchers found that many 'defensive' offenders believed that minority groups had undeservedly moved into their neighbourhood and that their hate crimes served to send a message to the victim and other members of the victim's group that they are unwelcome and should relocate. McDevitt *et al.* suggest that defensive attacks are often associated with demographic shifts at a local level, particularly where neighbourhoods or communities begin to experience a transition from being dominated by one ethnic group towards a more diverse population. This mirrors the findings of Sibbitt (1997) who highlighted rapid demographic changes in the UK in the 1960s as a key factor in the development of community prejudice and resentment towards ethnic minority groups – a factor held by Sibbitt to underpin racist offences against these groups.

More recently, Poirier (2010: 1) has further highlighted the depth of the importance of geography to understanding hate:

> A key concept is that bias crimes have ubiety – that is, that they occur in specific physical places. Moreover, they are legible – that is, they express (or are understood to express) facts about the safety and security in particular places of people and things (buildings, graves, ritual objects, etc.) that are identified with specific social categories. In contrast to hate speech, which is solely discursive, bias crimes engage both physical place and discursive space. In so doing they constitute a claim to territory.

In addition to pointing out the need for a physical location for hate crimes to occur (which one might suggest seems rather obvious), Poirier (2010: 2) also makes reference to an issue that is of increasing importance in the digital age:

> In contrast to physical place, discursive space can be considered nullibietous – that is, having no physical dimension ... In an age of media scrutiny, the dialogues that bias crimes engender can occur any-where. They are potentially worldwide. But they are often at the same time local. Much depends on what various media notice.

Although he acknowledges that in reality there is always a physical substrate to discourse and communication, Poirier's interpretation of geography serves to emphasise that the 'geography of hate crimes' in the twenty-first century includes both public and private spaces, but also other 'spaces' that go beyond traditional interpretations of 'geographical location', but which can have implications for a variety of ideological, political and economic per-spectives, each of which we shall touch upon in due course.

Economics

In chapter three we noted the apparent increase in hate crimes and other targeted violence in some countries where the impact of the current world financial crisis has hit particularly hard and, below, we shall discuss the importance of political rhetoric in shaping hate motivated behaviour when we briefly consider what political science has to offer as a discipline. Inex-tricably linked to both these concerns, it seems, is the issue of *economics*. This is hardly surprising given the importance attached by criminologists to the strength of a given economy as a predictor of crime levels generally.

Whilst we shall consider the theoretical issues of economic and social strain below when we discuss the contribution of sociology to our understanding of hate motivated offending, for now an illustrative example that links the past to the contemporary will serve to demonstrate the potential significance of economics to the problem of hate crime. In the previous chapter we noted an historical link between economic hardship and membership of far right groups, in that particular case the Ku Klux Klan in the US in the early part of the twentieth century. Similarly, the rise of the Nazis in Germany in the 1930s was fuelled in large part by high rates of unemployment and the resulting feelings of relative deprivation and loss of status amongst swathes of the German population (Falk and Zweimuller, 2005) that helped to make the political rhetoric of the Nazis attractive and palatable.

In this country, Sibbitt (1997), as we have seen, has presented historical evidence to suggest that in particular, the rapid demographic changes in the UK during the 1960s, coupled with the inability of some communities to cope with this change has played a part in the development of community prejudice. The situation is somewhat amplified, Sibbitt suggests, by factors such as unemployment, economic hardship and/or deprivation, competition for scarce resources (for example, housing), and a lack of community facilities (particularly in relation to youth and leisure facilities). Thus, economic strain, although not always the sole cause of hate crime, may instead provide a platform from which it can emerge. In this sense people will require a scapegoat upon which to blame the situation in which they find themselves. Here the problems experienced by certain communities are inevitably perceived as being not of their own making or a product of circumstance, but as the fault of certain groups who are seen as responsible for causing or intensifying these social problems.

In short, then, there is a prominent hypothesis that links economic hardship, often in the shape of unemployment, to far right extremism and associated offending behaviour, and to hate crime more generally. In empirically testing this hypothesis using data from Germany, Falk and Zweimuller (2005) concluded that there is indeed a significant positive relationship between unemployment and right-wing criminal activities. They also found that unemployment was closely related to both violent and non-violent crimes, although the association with non-violent crimes was much stronger. In this sense, then, unemployment, or the fear of unemployment, helps to explain negative attitudes towards foreigners who are perceived to take jobs from the majority population and who therefore fulfil the need for a scapegoat. As we saw in chapter two, this is a position that 'foreigners' have long occupied.

Notwithstanding the findings provided by Falk and Zweimuller, as a *holistic* account of hate crime occurrence, the value of economics as an explanatory framework remains a little hazy. For example, in their analysis of the impact of immigration on anti-Hispanic hate crime in the US, Stacey *et al.* (2011) note that research on the relationship between economic conditions and racially motivated hate crime has provided mixed results. In justifying this, Stacey *et al* present findings from research by Lyons (2007), which found that racially motivated hate crime was more prevalent in the more affluent neighbourhoods in Chicago, and conversely from Green *et al.* (1998), who found that changes in economic conditions in New York, specifically the unemployment rate, were not significantly related to monthly counts of hate crime incidents in the city. In their own research, Stacey *et al.* found little evidence to suggest that anti-Hispanic hate crimes were triggered by economic threat. Rather, their results appear to align more closely with the views of Levin and Rabrenovic (2009), above, by implying that the primary threat posed by immigration may be *cultural* rather than economic.

Theology and religious studies

Given the position and influence of religion in both historical and contemporary hate crime issues, the field of religious studies is of considerable importance in terms of both understanding and responding to the problem. Stern (2005) argues that religion encompasses the best and the worst of human interaction with hatred. On the one hand, he suggests, religion has set the norms for universal human dignity, whilst on the other it has served as a justification for some of the most barbaric carnage in human history, becoming most dangerous when theology and ideology are combined. Indeed, as we have seen, one doesn't have to look very far into the history books to find examples of the kind of events to which Stern alludes, but these concerns are not simply confined to those history books. They are of course reflected in contemporary anxieties over extremism, fundamentalism, radicalisation, and 'radical Muslim clerics' and other so-called 'preachers of hate'.

For Stern, though, the issue of religion goes beyond just theology and belief to include the role of religious institutions and the impact they can have on individuals, groups, their politics and so on, as we shall see below. This is particularly important in terms of understanding not just how religion is used to promote hatred, but also how it can be empowered to help combat it, which Stern acknowledges involves institutional concerns as well as theological ones. Similarly, he highlights the role of government in relation to religion, noting that the way in which governments understand and deal with religious issues will be of increasing importance, particularly in Europe, where concerns over government responses to these challenges persist.

Two contemporary examples will suffice in illustrating such concerns. The first is the post-9/11 counterterrorism strategy in the UK, which McGhee (2010) suggests has developed in the main at the expense of an appreciation of the wider contexts of radicalisation and extremism, and has arguably had the unintended consequence of further tingeing the general public's view of Muslim communities with fear and suspicion. The second is the French government's decision to outlaw the public wearing of Muslim headscarves and veils with the aim of achieving secularism – a move that seems to me to be likely to risk precisely the opposite effect to the one intended by further alienating Muslim communities.

Appleby (2012) has similar concerns both about the role of the media and a relative lack of sophistication in policy circles in conflating religion with fundamentalism, and fundamentalism with terrorism. In particular he expresses his concern at the lazy commonplace pairing of the words 'religious' and 'violence', which he argues gives the unfortunate impression of a natural connection between the two. In reviewing the extensive available literature on 'religion' and 'violence', Appleby (2012: 2–3) suggests that there are *three* lines of analysis that help us to understand when it is that religion becomes the motivation for violence, which he terms *strong religion, weak religion* and *pathological religion*:

> the term Strong Religion [is used to] cluster works that see religion itself as the source of, or justification for, deadly violence, or that emphasize distinctive religious practices, beliefs, and ideologies as the decisive ingredients in violent movements that may also draw on nationalist, ethnic, or other motivations ... Weak Religion, refers to works that present religion as a dependent variable in deadly violence, the primary source of which is secular in origin (e.g., enacted by the state or by nationalist or ethnic extremists). Finally, a network of scholars explores what might be termed Pathological Religion, namely, religious actors whose embrace of fundamentalist or extremist religious modes of behavior reflect symptoms of psycho-social deviance.

But despite this impressive attempt to simplify and categorise what Appleby refers to as an 'incoherent avalanche' of publications in this field, a general comprehensive theory of religious violence remains elusive.

Politics and political science

Of course, the two examples of government responses to religion, above, also bring us inside the discipline of *politics* and *political science*, which itself may contain all sorts of insights into the causes of hate crime. We have already considered in previous chapters the role of politics, and in particular identity politics, in bringing hate crime to the fore as a specific area of concern. Here of course the goal of making hate a political issue was so that something might be done to challenge it and, ultimately, to 'make things better'. But what about where the opposite occurs? Once again history is littered with examples where hate, and hateful rhetoric and discourse, has been used for nefarious political purposes. The various genocides that have taken place around the world offer some prime examples, but more recently (and perhaps a little more subtly) so do the issues raised in chapters three and four in relation to the political stances taken in some European countries in relation to the Roma and Sinti, and 'new migrant' communities respectively.

Another contemporary example might include Iran's anti-Israeli foreign policy (although there is some debate about whether or not Iran's former President

Ahmadinejad has explicitly called for 'Israel to be wiped off the map' – see Hasan, 2012, for an interesting discussion of the political discourse in this regard). Nevertheless, Stern (2005) states that of all the anti-Semitic discourses, political anti-Zionism (the belief that Jews do not have the right to self-determination in a land of their own) is the least understood and the most resurgent in recent years. Stern is also critical of, for example, Israel's support for Hamas from the late 1970s to counter the Palestine Liberation Organization (PLO), and the US government's support for Islamist groups in Afghanistan to fight the old Soviet Union towards the end of the Cold War – moves that may have served short-term political goals, but have had less than desirable longer-term implications.

Closer to home, and linked to domestic rather than international politics, apparent recent increases in the occurrence of disability hate crime are, in part, being attributed to what is perceived to be irresponsible political rhetoric from the British government in relation to statements concerning the numbers of people claiming incapacity benefit who are 'faking' disabilities (Riley-Smith, 2012). Research by ComRes (2012) on behalf of the disability charity Scope, for example, found that disabled people identified the small number of people falsely claiming disability benefits *and* the way the actions of this minority of claimants are reported as primary causes of public hostility. Scope concluded that it was impossible to ignore that the results came at the same time as the government continued to focus the welfare debate on a few benefit 'scroungers' as part of efforts to make the case for more radical reform to the welfare system.

Similarly, a poll on behalf of the Trades Union Congress in the UK in 2013 suggested that 'prejudice and ignorance' was being fuelled by 'myths' spread by politicians in relation to the welfare system. The poll of 1,800 people found that four out of ten people believed that the benefits system is too generous whilst three in five believed that the system has created a culture of dependency. The poll also found that those who knew *least* about the realities of the system were the *most* hostile towards benefits claimants, with more than half of such respondents declaring it too generous. Conversely, only one in three of those 'in possession of the facts' thought similarly (Grice, 2013). In other words, it seems that in this instance people's perceptions of the welfare system, and levels of hostility towards those that claim benefits, differ markedly depending upon whether they are in possession of none, some or all of the facts. Clearly, then, the disciplines of politics and political science have a contribution to make to our understanding of hate crime, both on the international and the domestic stage.

Ideology

Many of the disparate issues discussed above are often brought together in the form of ideological beliefs that are then used as justifications for hate and hate offending, most notably by what we might call 'hate groups'.

As such, it is worth briefly drawing together a number of the points considered so far in this chapter to illustrate the significance of ideology to our field of study.

In considering contemporary hate groups in the US, Barbara Perry (2001), Phyllis Gerstenfeld (2004) and others have identified a number of common core ideological claims to superiority that are used by hate groups to 'justify' their beliefs and actions. In many cases these are just as applicable to hate groups here in the UK and elsewhere in the world. Whilst a detailed examination of these is beyond the scope of this book (readers are advised to see Perry, 2001; Gerstenfeld, 2004) it is nevertheless important to briefly consider these ideologies because they allow us to gain an insight into the motivations and belief systems that serve to justify and legitimise the behaviour and actions of the members of such groups.

Gerstenfeld suggests that arguably the most important of these ideologies relates to *power*. Historically, as we saw in chapters two and five, hate groups have tended to form and grow in popularity at times where the dominant group feel somehow threatened. Indeed the history of the Ku Klux Klan is characterised by such peaks and troughs in popularity when faced with perceived threats to white dominance.

The notion of power is particularly central to white supremacist discourse and the belief that power is rightfully theirs is based largely on the misguided premise that the white race is biologically superior to all other races. Specifically, Gerstenfeld suggests that such groups believe that the power of the white race is being stolen, for example, by blacks through their criminal behaviour; by mass immigration and the taking of jobs and the 'swamping' of the white population; by a Jewish conspiracy to control government and the media; and by non-whites race-mixing and thereby 'polluting' and 'weakening' the 'pure' Aryan gene pool.

The second ideology that Gerstenfeld outlines is *racial separatism*. She suggests that most hate groups advocate either complete or at least partial racial separatism, with many members believing that their perceived superiority gives them the right to define what constitutes a natural citizen of their country and that entry into that country can only happen on their terms. Indeed, this focus on racial separatism is not restricted to white supremacists, as non-white organisations are known to advocate similarly.

The third ideology relates to *religion*. Gerstenfeld suggests that whilst not all hate groups have a religious basis, for many it is the key to their belief system. For white supremacists the most important (but not always exclusive) religious sect is that of *Christian Identity*. Gerstenfeld points out that the teachings of Christian Identity are attractive to white supremacists because they provide these groups with a 'theological seal of approval'. The sect teaches that Aryans are God's chosen people and that non-whites are subhuman, and that white people are descendents of Adam, whilst Jews are descendents of Satan. These 'facts' provide a rationale for racist views, particularly given that Christian Identity teaches that Adam's descendents are engaged in an apocalyptic struggle against the descendents of Satan. Gerstenfeld suggests that in this sense white supremacists believe that they are literally doing 'God's work'.

Two other key ideologies that Gerstenfeld and others have identified first concern a common antipathy for certain groups, particularly Jews who are frequently perceived to be descendants of the devil and who are also involved in a conspiracy to take over the world, and non-whites who are perceived to be a wholly inferior race, and second, a common antipathy for certain beliefs and actions, in particular abortion, communism, feminism and political liberalism (Gerstenfeld, 2004).

Sociology and criminology

At the start of this chapter we noted Barbara Perry's concern about the extent of theorising in relation to hate offenders – a statement that reiterated her similar concerns in 2003 that sociology, and in particular criminology, had yet to come to terms with 'hate crime'. In the remainder of this chapter, then, we shall consider, albeit briefly, some of the sociological and criminological contributions to our knowledge about hate offending.

Anomie

Many sociological accounts of hate crime have their roots in anomie, and more specifically, strain theory. Hopkins-Burke and Pollock (2004), for example, suggest that hate crime should be considered a normal, rational and fully understandable activity within our society and, as a result, sociologically informed criminological theory, in particular that founded on the European and US anomie traditions, can be adapted to explain and understand the existence and persistence of hate motivation at all levels of the social world.

In particular, they, suggest, insights can be derived from the early work of Durkheim (1933) in relation to social solidarity and the nature of social change, which they suggest, helps us to make sense of the notion that hate crime motivation has its foundations in the origins and later development of societal structure. More recent, mid-twentieth century US anomie theorising, such as that concerning adaptations (Merton, 1938 – see below), differential association (Sutherland, 1939, 1947), deviant subcultures (Cohen, 1955), and delinquency, drift and techniques of neutralisation (Matza, 1964 – see also below), they further suggest, demonstrate how hate crime motivation has not just strongly founded macro-societal origins, but can occur as the outcome of rationally developed strategies developed, or encountered, by socio-economically disaffected people, with disparate commitment levels, at a local or micro-societal level (Hopkins-Burke and Pollock, 2004: 7). Finally, they argue, more recent radical European traditions with nonetheless firm identifiable foundations in both earlier anomie traditions help to explain the

complexities and variations of hate crime motivation in contemporary frag-
mented communities. Here they point in particular to the radical, neo-
Marxist subcultural theories of the Birmingham Centre for Contemporary
Cultural Studies formulated in the 1970s. There is not the space here to
adequately consider all of these issues (but see Hopkins-Burke and Pollock,
2004, for an in-depth and interesting consideration of each of these aspects),
so we shall satisfy ourselves with an overview of some of the more commonly
utilised sociological and criminological theories in this field.

Strain

Accounts of Mertonian strain theory are widely available, so we will satisfy
ourselves with a simple overview here. Merton (1949) believed that crime
was a product of the mismatch between the goals by which western society
judges 'success' (wealth and material possessions) and the means available to
individuals to achieve those goals. Whilst society by its very nature pressures
everyone to achieve those valued goals, not everyone has the opportunity or
ability to do so legitimately (for example through hard work, education and
so on). Those who are unlikely to legitimately achieve the goals valued by
society, Merton argued, would be placed under a 'strain' to achieve them
through alternative means. In other words, it is achieving the goals that is
important, and not necessarily how you achieve them.

Given these pressures, Merton argued that people would adapt to their
situation in different ways. Some would *conform* and 'play by the rules', and
others would deviate from those rules. Of the four categories of deviants
(ritualists, retreatists, rebels and innovators) we shall concern ourselves with
innovators and *rebels* (although it should be noted that Hopkins-Burke and
Pollock, 2004, suggest that latent hate may often be present but not actua-
lised in the other categories too). Innovators, according to Merton, accept
society's goals but reject the legitimate means of achieving them. Instead,
because they are unable to legitimately achieve 'success' (for example,
because of unemployment, poor education, poor skills and so on), these
people will innovate and use illegitimate means that may prove more efficient for them to achieve the very same goals. In essence, then, the frustration, or strain, caused by the desire for 'success' and the inability to achieve
it legitimately gives rise to criminal behaviour. Moreover, Agnew (1992)
suggests that this strain often gives rise to negative emotions including dis-
appointment, depression, fear and, crucially, anger because of the situation
they find themselves in.

If we relate this theory to hate crime then it is tempting to conclude that
such offences are committed by people in response to a perceived instability
(or strain) in their lives, for example through increased competition for jobs
and other scarce resources caused by 'foreigners', exploitation and marginalisation, and people's economic security being threatened by 'outsiders'
(Perry, 2001). According to strain theory, then, hate crime is a way of

responding to *threats* to the legitimate means of achieving society's pro-scribed goals. Minority groups therefore serve to increase the perception of strain that the majority population feel, and hate crime is a product of, and a response to, that strain.

This is illustrated, for example, in a small sample of studies cited by Sibbitt (1997). In outlining the role of social factors in shaping racist attitudes, the Association of London Authorities (1993) identified the key issues as unemployment, competition for housing, a lack of facilities for young people and the need for people to find scapegoats to blame for their situation and therefore for the *strain* in their lives. In addition, Sibbitt also draws upon a study conducted in Germany by Heitmeyer in 1993 that claimed hostility towards foreigners to be a product of social and political disintegration, the search for identity, experiences of powerlessness and isolation, and anxiety relating to social conditions, most notably in relation to jobs and housing. Likewise the results of a Scandinavian study conducted by Bjorgo (1993). Such arguments are also frequently presented and fuelled by, for example, the British tabloid press in their recent coverage of immigration and asylum in this country.

With regard to *rebellion*, which Merton labelled as those people who both reject society's systems and goals *and* seek to change them, some useful theoretical insights into more extreme and contemporary aspects of hate might be derived. Hopkins-Burke and Pollock (2004) suggest, for example, that Merton's concept of anomic rebellion is particularly useful in explaining the growth of Islamic fundamentalism against the dominant capitalist world order and its culture.

However, whilst strain theory may be suitable for explaining some hate crimes, or perhaps more suitably as a part-explanation, as a comprehensive theory Mertonian strain (as a specific part of the broader anomic tradition to which Hopkins-Burke and Pollock refer) falls down at a number of critical points. Perry (2001: 37) argues that:

> there is no doubt that hate crime occurring in the historical (recession) and sociogeographical (inner city) context of economic instability may be in part a response to perceived strain. Those facing downward mobility may indeed lash out against scapegoats whom they hold to be responsible for their displacement ... However, not least of the inconsistencies here is that if strain accounted for hate crimes, then those most prevalent among the victims would instead be the perpetrators! Who is more disadvantaged – economically, socially and politically – than women and racial minorities? Yet these groups are much more likely to be victims than offenders.

In other words, if those experiencing the greatest strain should be those most likely to commit hate crimes, then minority groups should logically also be the largest perpetrator groups, but in reality this is not the case. Whilst the intention of hate crime policy is sometimes subverted and minorities may in some instances be disproportionately represented on the official statistics as perpetrators, it is minority groups who are predominantly the victims of hate crime. Perry also points to the fact that hate crime is not just committed at times when strain and cultural tension may be present, and nor is it always committed by those who are powerless in society and who are therefore most likely to perceive strain.

Indeed, Perry highlights the fact that hate crime crosses all class boundaries. She argues that the perpetrators of hate crime regularly include those who hold positions of relative power within society and not just those who are alienated or deprived. Indeed, those in the highest positions of power have perpetrated some of the worst examples of hate crimes throughout history. Perry also highlights the professional backgrounds of the leaders of certain organised hate groups and, perhaps closer to home, the historical evidence relating to the secondary victimisation of minority groups by the criminal justice system, most notably by the police who hold a clear position of power within society. Furthermore, even where offenders are relatively powerless, through hate crime they are in fact exercising a degree of power over what they perceive to be 'subordinate' groups and in doing so are maintaining their 'rightful' place in a perceived hierarchy of power within society.

Differential association, subcultures and drift

Despite Perry's criticisms of strain as an explanation of hate crime, Hopkins-Burke and Pollock (2004) imply that a more holistic take on the anomic tradition provides stronger theoretical foundations upon which to build our understanding. For example, by adding Sutherland's *'differential association'* (which holds that a person is more likely to offend via a process of social learning if they have associations with individuals engaging in similar activities) into the mix, then the link between social structural conditions and individual behaviours might be better explained, as might the transmission of 'hate' from one individual to another.

Similarly, they suggest, *subcultural theories*, rooted in Cohen's (1955) work on delinquent youths, help to further illustrate how individuals come together as groups with shared views and cultural values. Whilst Cohen and others concentrated their theorising on the subcultural responses emerging from the disjoint between disadvantaged youths and mainstream middle-class society, Hopkins-Burke and Pollock (2004) suggest that, coupled with differential association, this can usefully be adapted to explain group 'hate' (and not just that found in disadvantaged communities) by providing insights into the ways in which people become socialised into a particular world-view. This of course has links to our discussion earlier in relation to the importance of aspects of social identity and culture in shaping prejudice,

and has implications for our understanding of the far right and other organised hate groups.

One of the criticisms of subcultural theories, however, relates to their
seemingly overly deterministic nature. Matza (1964) was acutely aware of
these theoretical vulnerabilities, observing as he did the tendency of *most*
young offenders to *drift* in and out of delinquency, to find excuses for their
criminal behaviour and ultimately, to 'grow out of' crime. This theoretical
take on offending is perhaps best illustrated by research from McDevitt
et al. (2002), Sibbitt (1997) and from Byers *et al.* (1999).

For example, of the 169 cases they analysed, McDevitt *et al.* concluded
that 66 per cent (or 111 of the total) of the offences, mostly committed by
youths, were motivated by the *thrill* or for the excitement of the act. This
finding supports Sibbitt's (1997) contention that many younger racist offenders commit offences out of a sense of boredom and a need for excitement
in their lives. The former report that in 91 per cent of these 'thrill' cases the
perpetrators left their neighbourhood to search for a victim, and deliberately
selected their target because they were 'different' to themselves, and the
attacks were underpinned by an immature desire to display power and to
enhance the offender's own feeling of self-importance at the expense of
others.

Similarly, the perspectives of anomie presented here also support Sibbitt's
broader view that it is the interplay of contextual factors and the psychology
of certain individuals that produces perpetrators. Offenders, she suggests, are
likely to be involved in other forms of criminal or antisocial behaviour, of
which hate offending is a part, and will operate with the passive support (or
at least without the condemnation) of some sections of the wider community
who share similar views but who are not necessarily inclined towards criminal behaviour themselves.

Furthermore, research conducted in the US by Byers *et al.* (1999) has also
revealed some interesting insights into hate crime offending by drawing on
Sykes and Matza's (1957) techniques of neutralisation, which sought to
identify how perpetrators of crime justify their offending behaviour. Sykes
and Matza found that offenders in general often attempted to justify their
actions in a number of ways that mitigated their involvement, and that these
justification techniques provided useful information about the motivation of
criminals.

In their study of hate crimes committed against the Amish, Byers *et al.*
found that whilst some offenders showed little or no remorse for their
actions, others attempted to justify or rationalise their behaviour by using a
number of 'neutralisation techniques'. The first technique described by Byers
et al. is that of *denial of injury*. Here offenders attempted to neutralise their
behaviour by suggesting that no real harm was done to the victim, that the
offence was in effect 'harmless fun', and that the victim should in any case
be used to being subject to certain forms of abuse, all of which combined to
make the offender's behaviour somehow acceptable.

The second identified technique was that of the *denial of the victim*. According to Byers *et al.*, this makes the assumption that the victim either deserved what they got, or that the victim is effectively worthless and offences against them are inconsequential either socially or legally. Essentially, then, victims are somewhat dehumanised and seen as deserving of their victimisation.

The third identified technique is the *appeal to higher loyalties*. Here, offences may be committed through allegiance to a group. Offenders therefore may see their behaviour, and subsequently not revealing that behaviour or the behaviour of their peers, as a form of group bonding and security within their 'in-group'.

Fourth, Byers *et al.* suggest that some offenders will engage *condemnation of the condemners*. Here offenders attempt to neutralise their behaviour by questioning the right of their condemners to sit in judgement of them. This may be done by suggesting that those that condemn them are in reality no better, share similar views to the offender, and given the chance in similar circumstances would act, or may have previously acted, in a similar way to the perpetrator.

The final technique relates to a *denial of responsibility*. Here, Byers *et al.* explain, offenders attempt to neutralise their responsibility for their actions by claiming other factors to be the cause of their behaviour, such as, the researchers suggest, the offender's socialisation and the way they were brought up. In other words, the blame for their behaviour lies somewhere other than with them.

Furthermore, Byers *et al.* found that many offenders broadly fitted the 'thrill' category described by McDevitt *et al.*, above, and also pointed to the importance of peer support, which has links to Sibbitt's work on the 'perpetrator community' by highlighting the significance of shared views, and the reinforcement of those views. Offenders' attempts at justifying their actions also lend support to the view that victims are frequently dehumanised by their attackers, are subordinate to the offender and are somehow deserving of their victimisation. This in turn reflects Perry's notion of power, the expression of power, and the use of hate crime as a method for maintaining perceived social hierarchies and for 'punishing' those who attempt to disturb the social order, to which we shall now turn our attention.

Structural accounts

Barbara Perry (2001: 46) argues that the US (and therefore by analogy the UK):

> is a nation grounded in deeply embedded notions of difference that have been used to justify and construct intersecting hierarchies along lines of sexuality, race, gender, and class, to name but a few. In other words, difference has been socially constructed, but in ever-changing ways

across time and space. Nonetheless, these constructions have reinforced similarly changing practices of exclusion and marginalisation.

In other words, there is essentially a form of classification in society with different categories of 'belonging'. For example, as Perry explains, one is either male or female, black or white or Asian, Christian, Jew or Muslim and so on. Here, the boundaries are held to be fixed and impermeable, and membership, as we noted in chapter four, is usually given and not chosen. With these divisions, according to Perry, come assumptions about the members of each of the other categories. In creating an identity for itself, a group necessarily creates its antithesis. Again, similarly to Allport's (1954) findings, whilst one group perceives itself as dominant and privileged, so it also sees other groups as subordinate, disadvantaged and 'different'. Significantly, Perry (2001: 47) states that:

> difference has been constructed in negative relational terms. A dominant norm ... has been established, against which all others are (unfavourably) judged. This is the case whether we speak in terms of race, class, gender, sexuality, beauty, or any other element of identity. So it is those who are not white or male or Christian or moneyed who are marked or stigmatised as different.

So those who do not fit the 'mythical norm' of dominance and power in western society (that is, those who are not white, male, young, able-bodied, financially secure, heterosexual, Christian, physically attractive and so on) are categorised as 'different'. With the notion of 'difference', Perry argues, comes the assumption of inferiority and the assignment of a subordinate place in society. Thus we are left with a hierarchical structure of power in society based upon notions of 'difference', with the 'mythical norm' at the top and those who are 'different' assigned subordinate positions. According to Perry, these hierarchies are reinforced through labour and employment, politics, sexuality and culture, the facets of which serve to continually construct, reinforce and maintain the dominant order.

Therefore, according to Perry (2001: 55):

> when we do difference, when we engage in the process of identity formation, we do so within the confines of structural and institutional norms. In so doing – to the extent that we conform to normative conceptions of identity – we reinforce the structural order. However, not everyone always performs 'appropriately'. Frequently, we construct our gender or race or sexuality in ways that in fact challenge or threaten sociocultural arrangements. We step out of line, cross sacred boundaries, or forget our 'place'. It is in such a context that hate crime often emerges as a means of responding to the threats. The tensions between hegemonic and counterhegemonic actors may culminate in violent

efforts to reassert the dominance of the former and realign the position of the latter.

As such, through Perry's theory hate crime can be viewed as a 'tool' by which perpetrators attempt to reaffirm their perceived dominance when 'subordinate' groups attempt, for example, to 'better their lot' and threaten the 'natural' relations of superiority and inferiority within society. Such theorising, Perry contends, allows hate crime to be placed within the wider context of oppression that is found in a complex structure of power relations firmly and historically grounded in various notions of 'difference':

> In other words, hate motivated violence is used to sustain the privilege of the dominant group, and to police the boundaries between groups by reminding the Other of his/her 'place'. Perpetrators thus re-create their own masculinity, or whiteness, for example, while punishing the victims for their deviant identity performance.
>
> (Perry, 2001: 55)

However, whilst Perry's work represents a (or, arguably *the*) significant contribution to theorising hate crime, critical, structural theories such as Perry's are not without their critics. The suggestion that hate crimes are expressions of power aimed at reaffirming the offender's perceived hierarchy of appropriate social positions, some argue, masks a number of complexities associated with individual offences and offenders and indeed victims. There are effectively two problems. First, if hate crime is indeed used to sustain the privilege of the dominant group, then the implication appears to be that members of a dominant group can only ever be offenders, and conversely that members of minority groups can only ever be victims. Yet, victims of hate crimes are often members of the dominant social group, and members of minority groups are often the perpetrators of hate crime. Such a reality clearly does not sit easily with structural theories.

Second, to suggest that every hate crime is always about maintaining power is arguably a little too simplistic. This notion of power can be expressed in a variety of ways, and to differing degrees to the extent that no two motivations for hate offences can ever be said to be truly identical. Andrew Sullivan (1999) suggests that structural accounts are far better at alleging structures of power than at delineating the workings and complexities of the individual heart and mind. Structural theories necessarily tell us very little about how the victims or the offenders feel, nor indeed who the offenders might be. Power may be the underpinning factor in many cases, but as we saw in the previous chapter, prejudice and hate are expressed in many different ways, and no two 'hates' are ever qualitatively the same. The varieties of human emotion and human behaviour encapsulated by the word 'hate' are too varied to be defined or explained as straightforwardly as they are in structural accounts.

Merging theories

In considering theories of causation in relation to hate crime, Walters (2011: 314) neatly summarises many of the issues to emerge from the content of this chapter:

> while the extant literature on causation is of great epistemological value, several shortcomings can be identified. Firstly, there has been little which attempts to examine the intersections between the various theories espoused within criminology and other disciplines. The tendency to focus on disparate disciplinary analyses of hate crime has meant that the aetiology of 'hate' and more specifically hate motivated behaviour has been shaped within this or that field of study. Even within individual fields of study, researchers have failed to get to grips with linking macro level theory to individual agency. For example, within the criminological body neither strain theory nor 'doing difference' have been used to adequately explain why only some individuals commit hate crimes while others, equally affected by socio-economic strains and social constructions of 'difference', do not.

To close this theoretical gap, at least partially, Walters suggests that theories of strain and theories of structure are better understood when they are synthesised through the interconnecting emotion of *fear*. He proposes that it is the fear that Others will encroach upon dominant group identity *and* socio-economic security that fuels the climate of prejudice against them, and as this fear spreads throughout a community it can affect everyone, regardless of their socio-economic status (thereby arguably bypassing some of the shortcomings of both sets of theories). That said, however, Walters also acknowledges that even with fear as the interconnecting element, neither theory explains why only certain individuals commit hate crimes while others, equally open to the same strains and hegemonic constructions of identity, choose not to. Indeed, he notes that there is little within the hate crime literature that addresses this.

In seeking to undertake this task, Walters taps into a hitherto unused source of criminological theory, namely Gottfredson and Hirschi's (1990) theory of self-control, in which they argue that it is a lack of self-control on the part of individuals that causes them to succumb to criminal opportunity (or, conversely, the presence of self-control on the part of most that stops them succumbing to such opportunities). In so doing, Walters (2011: 328) attempts to fill the gap between macro-level causational mechanisms and micro-level offending patterns, concluding that:

> an individual's propensity to commit hate crime may ultimately turn on his or her levels of self-control. By viewing hate offending in terms of self-control we begin to understand why many disgruntled racists or homophobes remain simply that and why others' prejudiced sentiments

trigger a criminal response. Indeed, the current research body on hate perpetrator typology provides a persuasive account of offending suggesting that most perpetrators will display one or more of the following characteristics: thrill seeking, a tendency towards taking physical risks, defensive of territory, low tolerance levels of difference, a disposition towards violence and other anti-social behaviours, a lack of academic qualifications and/or low-skilled employment. The profile of hate offenders therefore creates a picture of offending which fits into almost all aspects of Gottfredson and Hirschi's theory of self control.

Although he accepts that this approach does not explain all forms of hate crime, Walters' contribution to the theoretical literature does begin to move us towards a more holistic approach to explaining hate crime and, given the rather disparate nature of the accounts offered by the different disciplines highlighted in this chapter, represents a move towards a more sophisticated way of analysing the problem of hate motivated offending.

The 'normality' of hate offending

Iganski (2008) also notes the shortcomings of abstract and deterministic theorising, and has attempted to illuminate the connections between background structures of bigotry and the foreground of offenders' actions by combining theory with empirical fieldwork. By drawing upon what Garland (2001) has labelled *'the new criminologies of everyday life'*, which encompasses criminological perspectives including *routine activities theory* (see, for example, Felson, 2002), *rational choice theory* and *situational crime prevention*, Iganski's own research makes for some uncomfortable reading.

Iganski concludes, as we have already noted elsewhere, that hate crimes are predominantly 'low-level' offences, but are overwhelmingly committed by 'ordinary' people rather than by 'extremists', as media headlines might suggest. Thus, there is a 'normality' to everyday hate crime that, for Iganski, carries with it the rather uncomfortable reality that the majority of hate offenders are not hate-fuelled bigots who actively seek out their victims in a calculated and premeditated manner, but rather are 'people like us' (2008: 42) who offend in the context of their everyday lives. The value here lies in Iganski's focus on, and discussion of, the situational dynamics and social circumstances of hate crime offending that is derived from empirical evidence drawn from the lived experience of victims, resulting in the conclusion that hate crimes predominantly result from *'the normal frictions of day-to-day life'*. Whilst this focus on lived experience predominantly relates to victims of racist and religiously motivated offences, Iganski also usefully explores the experiences of victims of disability and homophobic hate crimes and in so doing begins to fill something of a void in the existing literature. His analysis of the data therefore reveals a myriad of distinctive features of city life that provide potential opportunities for 'everyday' hate victimisation.

Linking the 'ordinary' to the 'extraordinary'

Iganski's (2008) work provides an interesting insight into the everyday nature of hate offending and reiterates some of the issues raised in the previous chapter about the universal and inevitable nature of prejudice. But it is not just the 'everyday' hate offences committed by 'ordinary' people that are relevant here. Similarly uncomfortable reading can also be found in explanations of genocide and mass killing, which represent the 'extraordinary' end of the spectrum of hate offending.

Whilst we may be tempted to draw a distinction between 'ordinary' and 'extraordinary' offenders when we think of genocide, the distinction is perhaps more appropriate for the *crimes* than for the *criminals*. Killing on a genocidal scale is clearly extraordinary, but Waller (2002) suggests that in order to understand 'extraordinary evil' we in fact have to understand its 'ordinariness'. In other words, the perpetrators of mass killing and genocide are extraordinary because of what they do, not who they are. According to Waller, to consider the perpetrators of mass killing and genocide simply as psychopaths or monsters (that is, by employing individual-level analyses) is not sufficient to account for all the examples throughout human history. For example, Waller points out that up to 500,000 people took part in the Holocaust, and that up to 150,000 Hutus took part in the killing of at least 800,000 Tutsis in Rwanda in 1994. Not all of these perpetrators can be psychotic, or sadistic, or have some other extreme psychological label attributed to them. Rather, Waller contends, it is more fruitful to holistically understand the ways in which *ordinary* people come to commit *extraordinary* acts.

To this end, Waller suggests a synthesis of a number of factors that he combines to produce a unified theory of offender behaviour, and one that makes for similarly uncomfortable reading. The first prong of Waller's model focuses on three tendencies of human behaviour that we also examined in the previous chapter; *ethnocentrism* (the belief that one's in-group is superior to other groups), *xenophobia* (the fear of outsiders and members of 'out-groups') and the desire for *social dominance*. As we saw, these factors are universal and, given the nature of prejudice, both normal and unavoidable. However, whilst these form the foundations of hatred, we have already noted that this is not enough, and that not everyone expresses these natural tendencies in a violent way.

The second part of Waller's theory therefore focuses on the factors that shape the identities of the individual perpetrators. Here, three factors are held to be particularly significant; *cultural belief systems* (external, controlling influences; authority orientation; ideological commitment), *moral disengagement* of the perpetrator from the victim (facilitated by moral justification, euphemistic labelling of evil actions and exonerating comparisons) and *rational self-interest* (professional and personal).

The third strand of Waller's theory considers the role of the social context in influencing individuals. Of particular significance is the role of *professional socialisation* (built on escalating commitments, ritual conduct and the repression of conscience), the *binding factors of the group* (including diffusion of responsibility, deindividuation and conformity to peer pressure) and the *merger of role and person* (the significance of an organisation in changing a person within it). The final strand of the theory relates to the victims, or more accurately, how the victims are perceived. In this regard three further factors are significant; *us–them thinking, dehumanisation of the victim* and *blaming of the victims*, each of which have been considered in other chapters in this book.

Waller points out that his theoretical model is not an invocation of a single psychological state or event. Rather, it represents an analysis of the process through which perpetrators are changed from an ordinary person to an individual for whom committing extraordinarily evil acts becomes a part of their new self. The model, he suggests, specifically explicates the forces that shape human responses to authority by looking at who the perpetrators are, the situational framework they are in, and how they see 'outsiders'. By considering those factors that make humans the same (the nature of prejudice), those factors that make humans different (thoughts, feelings and behaviours), contextualising these within cultural and situational influences and by considering the psychological processes by which victims are excluded, Waller provides a framework which facilitates the commission of extraordinary evil by ordinary people. In other words, under Waller's model, the nature of prejudice leaves all humans capable of extreme hatred and extraordinary evil when activated by appropriate cues contained within the identities of the perpetrators, the social context and the perception of victims.

Rather than provide a definitive and conclusive account of why people commit acts of mass killing and genocide, Waller's model instead presents an account of the conditions under which such acts can take place. It is a complex interplay of a number of factors, and as such is similar to accounts of 'ordinary' hate crime. Simply, there is no single factor that causes people to commit crimes against 'outsiders', regardless of the scale of those crimes. What is certain, however, is that prejudice plays a central role as the underlying facilitator that is triggered by other factors.

In this sense we might reasonably return to Sibbitt's (1997) contention that 'hate' is a logical and predictable expression of underlying prejudice in society at large. In the context of genocide, it is clear that the support, or at least the indifference, of many people is often required for such acts to occur. The negative prejudices and violent actions of a minority alone are insufficient for genocide to take place.

Concluding comments

This chapter has sought to shed some light on the factors that may lead to, and cause, hate motivated offending, and has noted the contribution to this body of knowledge from a range of disciplines. What is clear is that this remains a complex issue to comprehensively (or indeed adequately) explain. It seems, then, that the views expressed by Kellina Craig more than a decade ago still ring true today. In her review of the socio-psychological literature, Craig (2002: 120) identified specific areas that relate to the characteristics of hate crime perpetrators, and in doing so noted the difficulties and limitations of theorising hate crime:

> Although several explanations may be applicable to hate crime occurrence, no existing one can fully account for all types of hate crime. This is because the factors that contribute to hate crime (i.e. perpetrators' motives, victims' characteristics, and cultural ideologies about a victim's social groups) differ markedly for each incident ... Thus, in order to explain hate crimes, a consideration of all potentially relevant explanations is necessary.

Simply then, hate crime perpetrators can effectively be motivated by one or more of a wide range of social, psychological, political, cultural and other factors. On the basis of Craig's statement, the search for a single, universal causal factor for hate crime is likely to be fruitless. Rather, it is the interplay of a number of different factors that produces perpetrators. As such, the investigation and analysis of hate motivated offending, and the search for causal explanations, within discrete disciplines has clearly yielded many avenues for us to explore. Indeed, the social sciences have much to offer, but despite this, explanatory frameworks remain rather disparate and, consequently, we cannot say with any certainty why it is hate crime occurs. Nevertheless, the conceptualisation of hate crime as a socio-legal problem in many countries around the world means that it still needs to be responded to, and it is to these issues that we now turn.

7 Law and law enforcement

As we have seen, over the past thirty or so years the enactment of hate crime legislation in the US has represented one of the most lively and significant trends in criminal law-making at both the federal and state level (Levin, 2002; Streissguth, 2003; Hall, 2005). England and Wales has followed suit with various legislative provisions against crimes motivated or aggravated by racial or religious prejudice, sexual orientation and disablism, and the incitement of racial and religious hatred. More recently, other countries (albeit with seemingly varying levels of commitment) have implemented, or are in the process of implementing, various forms of hate crime legislation. The development of legal responses to the hate and discrimination 'problem' is evident from the records of the Office for Democratic Institutions and Human Rights (ODIHR), a part of the Organization for Security and Co-operation in Europe (OSCE), who, as we saw in chapter three, collate data on the existence and development of anti-discrimination and hate crime laws in member States (see www.legislationline.org for the latest legislative developments). At the time of writing, ODIHR's records show the existence or development (albeit in different ways and to greatly varying extents) of 'hate crime' laws in over 50 different countries. Jacobs and Potter (1998) suggest, however, that hate crime laws vary but generally fall into one or more of four categories. First, there are those that enhance sentences for hate motivated offences; second, those that redefine existing criminal behaviours as a 'new' crime or as an aggravated form of an existing crime; third, those that relate specifically to civil rights issues and finally, those that concern themselves solely with matters of reporting and data collection. One or more of these categories are generally reflected in legislative provisions adopted by countries enacting 'hate crime' laws.

The rise of hate crime as a contemporary social issue has been driven by a number of different factors, as we noted in chapter two. In many countries, particularly Western democracies, a combination of the extent and nature of hate crimes, their seemingly increasing upward trend, coupled with increased public tolerance of issues of diversity and sensitivity to prejudice, and the influence of identity politics (the political processes by which certain groups might come to be recognised as disadvantaged), has forced 'hate' crimes onto the statute books. As Boeckmann and Turpin-Petrosino (2002: 207) explain:

> The juxtaposition of broad societal agreement on the values of equality and tolerance and the presence of intergroup tensions arising from long-standing differences in society as well as increasing ethnic and social diversity have created a new category of criminalised behaviour: hate crime. Hate crime laws represent official recognition of the harm of intergroup aggression and the importance of applying sanctions against it.

Although their creation has been, and remains, a contentious issue (see chapter nine), in essence the rationale behind hate crime laws is fairly commonsensical. Proponents argue that specific legislation represents an official recognition of an apparent emerging and increasing threat to society, and signifies the importance attached by government (at least in theory) to combating this threat. Where provisions exist, the potential for the increased punishment of the offender signifies an appreciation of the apparent disproportionate harm that hate crime can have on the victim and wider communities and provides a deterrent to potential offenders by clearly stating that hate crimes will not be tolerated and that firm action will be taken against those that perpetrate them. Hate crime laws also promote social cohesion by officially declaring that the victimisation of 'different' groups is not acceptable, and the very existence of law arguably provides a symbolic message designed to force social change in relation to prejudiced attitudes and behaviours.

Given the expansion of legislative provisions in many countries designed to combat the apparent growing problem of hate crime, this chapter considers theoretical and practical issues relating to the law and law enforcement in relation to hate crimes. By drawing predominantly on the UK and the US experience, it is argued that because hate crimes are complex events, they pose significant challenges to law-makers, the police and prosecutors. The chapter suggests that there are many issues both internal and external to those individuals and agencies responsible for law enforcement, and over which they have varying degrees of control, that inevitably impact upon their ability to enforce the law and to respond effectively and to provide a service appropriate to the needs of victims and wider communities.

The limits of effective legal action

Before examining the enforcement of law in this area, it is necessary to consider, albeit briefly, some of the sociological issues concerning the purpose of law and, in particular, its relationship to social change. Grossman and Grossman (1971) suggest that social change can be viewed in three stages. First, social change may be *incremental*, in which patterns of individual behaviour may be altered. Second, it may be *comprehensive*, in which group norms or patterns of relations between groups may be altered. Third, social change may be *revolutionary*, in which society's values may be altered. As such, much social research on law has largely concentrated on two related issues: the ability of law to influence social change and, conversely, the ability of social change to influence law. Within this literature there has been a particular emphasis on the former, with the latter often viewed (erroneously) as 'too obvious to require discussion' (Cotterrell, 1992: 49). The powerful effect of social change on shaping hate crime legislation is evident from the influence of identity politics (see Jacobs and Potter, 1998), and other historical events that we considered in chapter two.

Opinion within the literature concerning the ability of law to influence social change is however divided. Some argue that law serves important educative and symbolic functions (Lester and Bindman, 1972) that promote social integration and unity (Arnold, 1935) and can influence people's beliefs as well as their behaviours (Berger, 1952). Conversely, others suggest that the ability of the law in this regard is grossly exaggerated (Erlich, 1936; Kahn-Freund, 1969) and that the direct use of law in promoting social change is problematic. Others have argued, however, that law may indirectly influence social change by shaping social institutions (including the institutional framework and policy priorities and the legal duties of such institutions) that have a direct influence on the rate and character of social change (Dror, 1959). In sum, Cotterrell (1992: 61) suggests that it is best to view legal strategies 'as part of a long-term process of negotiation of attitudes and perceptions of interests in which political and legal action constitute only one element in a complex network of influences on social change'.

It is also important for the context of this chapter to consider some issues relating to the wider limitations of legal effectiveness. Cotterrell (1992) suggests that modern studies of the limits of effective legal action can be traced to the work of Roscoe Pound (1917) who laid down a number of principles that, despite being the best part of a century old, remain pertinent to a consideration of hate crime legislation and its effective enforcement. First, Pound (1917) suggested that law can only deal with the outside and not the inside of people. In other words, for a host of reasons including problems relating to proof, Pound argues that law cannot attempt to control attitudes or beliefs, only observable behaviour. As will become evident in this chapter and again in chapter nine, this point has served as the crux of the debate concerning the legitimacy and efficacy of hate crime laws.

A second relevant point relates to the fact that law necessarily requires an external agency (usually, but not exclusively, the police) to put its machinery in motion that itself (in most cases) requires invocation from the public. In other words, in this context, hate crime laws do not enforce themselves. Rather they are enforced by the police who in turn frequently require the input of the public (often as victims or witnesses) to start and pursue the process. This, in turn, raises some important prerequisites for the effectiveness of law, most notably that it must be, and be seen to be, in the interests of those upon whom the law depends for either its invocation or enforcement to set the process in motion (Cotterrell, 1992). For hate crime laws to be effective, victims must have enough confidence in the law (and its enforcement agencies) to achieve the ends for which it is intended to make it worthwhile reporting crimes committed against them. In addition, law enforcement agencies, and the individuals working within, must have both the *ability* and the *desire* to enforce the law.

Another important point raised by Pound (1917) is the notion that whilst there are interests and demands that it might be desirable for the law to recognise, the reality of such demands means that by their very nature they cannot be safeguarded by law. In this regard, Pound refers specifically to issues of clarity concerning legal precepts and the limitations of law, which arise from the difficulty of ascertaining the facts on which law is to operate. In other words, to be effectively enforced by state officials working in state agencies, law requires a high degree of clarity, particularly concerning issues of proof (Cotterrell, 1992). As will become clear in due course, clarity of proof in hate crime cases where evidence is frequently problematic is another issue of concern.

Finally, Pound (1917) also notes that in some areas of social life the sanctions of state law appear useless and can disrupt rather than repair social relations. More recent writers in this field have drawn on this point by suggesting that the law may simply serve to bureaucratise social and moral relations and in so doing create uncertainty, hostility and distrust (Cotterrell, 1992), a point to which we shall return in chapter nine. Such issues are particularly acute if the purpose of law is held to be the creation of social change, but arguably less so if the opposite is true. Either way, each of Pound's points hold particular relevance for effectively legislating against hate crimes. Furthermore, as Pound (1917) suggested, law does not enforce itself and therefore the points he makes extend to law enforcement agencies. Such concern necessarily brings us to the role of the police upon which, as the gatekeepers of the criminal justice system, so much subsequently depends.

The problem of motive

As we have seen, the vast majority of hate motivated incidents are breaches of existing criminal law. In this sense, hate crimes are in essence like any other crime. However, to accept such a view is to be ignorant of the (arguably) distinct nature of hate crime (see Perry, 2001; Hall, 2005; also chapters four and nine), and of the potentially devastating impact these crimes can have on the victim and the wider community. As Holdaway (1996: 45) states:

> the question of how far a [hate] motive changes the nature of an assault or act of criminal damage brings to the fore wider issues about the

social context within which people from minority ... groups live and the appropriate response of legislators and policy.

As noted in the introduction to this chapter, the response of law-makers in many countries (most notably in England and Wales and the US, but also elsewhere) to growing concerns about hate crime has been to introduce new hate-based offences to the statute books. Consequently, the expression of hate motivation by an offender when committing existing offences attracts stiffer sentences from the courts and in doing so places hate crimes in a unique position in terms of the law.

Prior to such legislation the determination of criminal liability for all offences had essentially concentrated upon an act and upon whether the defendant intentionally, recklessly or knowingly committed it. At this point it is important to be aware of the difference between motive and intent. Whilst the motive gives rise to the intent, it was the latter and not the former that made an act criminal. Thus, suspects were only convicted for intentionally committing an act and *not* for having a motive. In the past, therefore, the law has punished acts and not motivations, and as such the issue of motive has been entirely distinct from *intent* or *purpose*.

However, the inclusion of specific hate offences in criminal law changes this situation. Not only are new crimes created, but the most significant aspect of these offences is the motivation behind their commission. Notwithstanding issues concerning the parameters of legislation determined by case law (see Streissguth, 2003; Hall, 2005), the criminalisation of hate motivation argu-ably represents a shift in the focus of the criminal law from *deed* to *thought*. As a result, the courts are now required to establish the offender's motives and therefore 'what is really being punished is a criminal's thoughts, however objectionable they may be. The actions – incitement, vandalism, assault, murder – are already against the law' (Haberman, 1999: 2).

This significant change represents, at least in principle, the importance attached by policymakers to tackling hate crime. This is important because, as Holdaway suggests, 'both victims and offenders learn from the messages contained in the attack and from the nature and quality of legal and policy responses by institutions' (1996: 47). The impact that this has on policing is crucial because in order for legal and policy responses to achieve their aims, the police are required to provide evidence of both motive *and* intent. Without proof of motive (be it prejudice, bias, hostility or hatred), a hate crime is simply an ordinary crime. This necessarily raises serious questions concerning the ability of the police to accurately identify and subsequently provide evidence of the motivation behind an offence – a task that they are not required to do for any other crime (Bell, 2002).

Although some cases are clear-cut, the successful prosecution of most hate crimes is difficult because of the need to prove beyond reasonable doubt that the offender was motivated by prejudice, and also because of the diffi-culty in proving that prejudice was a causal factor in the commission of the offence. These two issues, Jacobs and Potter (1998) suggest, often make hate crime cases more difficult to prosecute than crimes committed without the hate element. In England and Wales the Crown Prosecution Service (CPS, 2003) also recognise the inherent difficulty in proving bias motivation (see also Burney and Rose, 2002).

For the police, the issue of accurately identifying motive is problematic. As we saw in the previous chapter, existing literature on perpetrators demonstrates that a whole host of motivations might be present in the commission of a hate offence. The literature, as we have seen, further suggests that no two hate crimes are ever the same in terms of the precise motivation behind them (Craig, 2002). This raises an interesting question – if decades of research into prejudice and hate has failed to conclusively identify the motivations behind these crimes, can we reasonably expect a police officer to do so to the extent that motivation is proved beyond reasonable doubt? Assisting officers in making these decisions is therefore crucial. However, neither the law in the US nor in England and Wales, or to my knowledge anywhere else, provides any guidance concerning what hate motivation might look like in practice; officers simply have to work it out for themselves, albeit often with assistance from prosecutorial bodies.

The police as decision-makers

As the 'gatekeepers' of the criminal justice system, the decisions made by police officers, and in particular those of the lower ranks, are crucial in determining what, and how much of what, ultimately comes to the attention of the rest of the justice system. Given the amount of discretion inevitably afforded to officers of lower ranks, their decisions concerning both *whether* and *how* to enforce the law in individual cases (decisions that for the most part remain unchecked by others in the justice system) become crucial (Lipsky, 1980; Bell, 2002).

Whilst the decision-making of officers is relevant to all types of incident in terms of determining how much further official attention that incident receives, it is acutely important in hate crime cases. This is because, as noted above, officers not only have to make decisions concerning the crime, but decisions also have to be made concerning the motive behind the crime. It is the decisions made concerning the latter that ultimately determine whether a crime becomes a hate crime. In short, a crime is not officially a hate crime until the police decide that it is. This is certainly the case in the US, and the statistics presented in chapter three suggest similarly for many other countries. It also remains the case in England and Wales despite definitional changes that allow anyone to apply the hate label for reporting and recording purposes. Ultimately, at some point a police officer has to make decisions concerning motivation (is this a crime or a hate crime?) and then decide whether to *charge* a suspect with an ordinary offence or a hate motivated or aggravated offence. In so doing, it is the police that officially apply the hate label, albeit in most cases in England and Wales this now occurs further down the policing process than was the case prior to the post-Lawrence definitional changes, and with guidance from the CPS. The nature and workings of police discretion and police decision-making are therefore crucial to the success of legal and policy responses to hate crime.

In relation to hate crimes, Cronin *et al.* (2007) suggest that the decision-making of patrol officers, whose decisions concerning potential motivations for an offence to a large extent determine whether a hate crime is ever officially recognised as such, is affected by issues of *ambiguity* (where multiple motivations might be evident), *uncertainty* (where only limited information about an incident might be available) and *infrequency* (where hate crimes are so infrequent that officers may never gain experience in responding to them). Any of these issues, they argue, can affect the accuracy of hate crime classifications made by the police, as of course can the attitudes, beliefs and practices of individual investigating officers (Franklin, 2002).

In terms of shaping police decision-making, Grimshaw and Jefferson (1987) have highlighted the existence of a *'hierarchy of police relevance'* that officers use, often subconsciously, which determines their response to any given incident. At the top of the hierarchy are what Bowling (1999) terms *'good crimes'*. These are clear criminal offences with innocent, reliable and credible victims, perpetrators who are 'real' criminals, and that offer a clear opportunity of detection and arrest and a good result in terms of securing a conviction. Further down the hierarchy are *'rubbish crimes'*, in which the 'quality' of the victim and perpetrator may be poor, where there is a much reduced chance of detection and arrest, or where there is an increased likelihood that the victim will withdraw the allegation at a later date. At the bottom end of the hierarchy are what Bowling terms *'disputes'* or *'disturbances'*, which are frequently perceived to be legally ambiguous and of limited police relevance.

In his interviews with police officers Bowling (1999) found that with the exception of certain crimes (such as robbery, assault and theft) where the legal relevance to the police is clear, racist offences tended to be viewed as being at the lower end of the hierarchy of police relevance. Bowling found that the perpetrators of racist hate crimes were largely perceived by the police as being 'yobs' or 'hooligans', and that racist incidents were regarded as acts of 'yobbishness' (a perception largely supported by McDevitt *et al.*'s 2002 offender typology – see chapters six and eight). In this sense, both the offence and the offender often fall into the category of 'rubbish', and receive less attention from the police than 'real' crimes. Similarly, Bowling's research highlighted the extent to which, from a police perspective, racist incidents routinely fall short of the criteria required to classify them as 'good crimes' and are regarded as 'disputes' or 'disturbances' (although the extent to which this remains the case in post-Lawrence policing in England and Wales is the subject of some debate – see Crane and Hall, 2009 and Hall *et al.*, 2009, for a consideration of this issue).

In other words, in all but the most serious crimes, racist incidents tend to appear at the lower end of the hierarchy of police relevance, and as such receive less police attention than crimes where the legal duty to respond is unambiguous. Crucially, Bowling's research illustrated that this placing of racist incidents on the hierarchy, most notably by rank and file officers, remained consistent despite changes in force policy and force prioritisation of racist offences. In assuming that the majority of hate offences are simply minor incidents, the disproportionate impact that these can have on victims is often not appreciated and is overlooked by the police. The result of this clash of perceptions is that victims may feel that their victimisation is not taken seriously by the police.

The extent of police discretion and the rudimentary decision-making process, predominantly by rank and file officers, of course has important implications for the number of hate crimes that are ultimately recorded and investigated. The hierarchy of relevance indicates a historical propensity for racist incidents not to be recorded, or treated appropriately, except where the offences are particularly serious. In turn this helped to create a lack of trust in the police amongst minority groups that subsequently led to a dis-inclination to report offences committed against them (Macpherson, 1999). This of course is crucial because if hate crimes are not reported to the police, then for the most part they cannot be responded to by them.

Other influences on police decision-making in this area relate to the nature of both individuals and organisations. There is a plethora of historical evidence to suggest that the police in both England and Wales and the US have, and indeed still do, exercised their discretion disproportionately and unfavourably with regard to minority groups. Traditional explanations for this discrimination include the individual (Scarman, 1981) and institutional (Macpherson, 1999) prejudice of police officers and police organisations, and the occupational culture of the police, research into which has consistently highlighted issues of police prejudice particularly along race, gender and sexuality lines (Skolnick, 1966; Reiner, 1992; Chan, 1997; Waddington, 1999). The importance of these biases is noted by Lipsky (1980: 85) who suggests that:

> Routines and simplifications are subject to workers' occupational and personal biases, including the prejudices that blatantly and subtly permeate the society. These biases expressed in street-level work may be expected to be manifested in proportion to the freedom workers have in defining their work life and the slack in effective controls to suppress those biases. Since street-level bureaucrats have wide discretion about clients, are usually free from direct observation by supervisors or the general public, and are not much affected by client preferences, their routines and simplifications deserve considerable scrutiny.

With regard to the police, almost without exception, police services in England and Wales and the US have been, and indeed largely remain, white, male-dominated organisations with attitudes that largely reflect those held by mainstream society; after all, historically police officers have been, and still are, predominantly drawn from the majority population. Given the historical and contemporary societal prejudice held by the mainstream towards minority groups (Allport, 1954; Sibbitt, 1997; Hall, 2009; see also chapters two and five) it should therefore not be too surprising that minority groups' experience of, and trust in, policing is qualitatively different to that experienced by the majority group, and this is reflected in the views historically articulated by minority groups (Bradley, 1998; Macpherson, 1999).

Furthermore, there is evidence from both England and Wales and the US that police officers are often reluctant to enforce hate crime legislation (Bell, 2002; John, 2003; Hall, 2005, 2009, 2012; AVP, 2007). Whilst this might be a product of individual, institutional or cultural discrimination, there are a number of other important issues that are specific to hate crime. First, it is important to remember that the enforcement of hate crime laws effectively reverses long-documented stereotypical police perceptions about minority groups, and in particular, minority ethnic groups. Research has highlighted the historically grounded stereotype held by British police officers that black males are disproportionately involved in crime as perpetrators (Gordon, 1983), and American studies of racial profiling and excessive use of police force suggest similarly (Bell, 2002; Johnson, 2003). Indeed, the origins of some American police departments have been traced to a goal of controlling the 'problematic' black population both during slavery and after emancipation (Bolton and Feagin, 2004). In theory at least, however, the concept of hate crime necessarily reverses this stereotype in the sense that minorities are more likely to be victims than perpetrators, a situation that does not sit comfortably with the findings from studies of police occupational culture. Given the extent of discretion afforded to police officers, this has potentially significant implications for both the amount and quality of service afforded to hate crime victims by the police.

Second, police officers may be reluctant to make decisions about hate motivation because, in effect, they may feel that they simply don't have to, or that their job would be easier if the crime didn't have the hate label applied to it. Hate crimes are already criminal offences, and without the hate element are of course categories of offences that officers are more used to dealing with. The decision not to label a crime as a hate crime may therefore enable officers to bypass many of the aforementioned problems associated with identifying motivation, whilst still being able to get a 'result' for the underlying offence. Furthermore, officers may decide against applying the hate label simply because they may fail to understand or recognise the qualitative differences between a crime and a hate crime in terms of the potential impact on victims (Hall, 2009).

A third issue that may affect police decision-making relates to the politicisation of hate crime. In the current climate both in England and Wales and the US in particular, hate crimes are potentially subject to disproportionate and/or excessive public scrutiny. For example, a hate-motivated assault is likely to generate greater public and/or media interest than a comparable regular assault. Even where incidents of hate crime do not attract attention in this way, given the impact that they can have on the wider community, the police may still find themselves under added pressure from that community, or from advocacy groups, to label a crime as hate-motivated and to act accordingly. Conversely, there may also be conflicting pressures not to label too many incidents as motivated by hate for fear of portraying an image of intolerance and disharmony in their jurisdiction, or because of a general lack of political will to respond (a justification that may indeed help to explain some of the international statistics presented in chapter three, where we discussed the potential for the politically driven *deflation* of official figures). As Bell (2002: 4) points out with regard to the policing of hate crime in the US:

> The 'politics of hate' influences nearly every stage of the process, including what gets reported, the help the [police] receive to investigate incidents, whether witnesses come forward, whether the community and City Hall pressure the [police] to investigate or not to investigate, and finally, the action the district attorney will take on a case. If an incident makes it through the investigation process without being dropped or classified as unfounded, it must then make it over a different set of hurdles when prosecutors and the courts come into play.

The police as policymakers

The ability of police officers to make key decisions concerning individual cases means that not only are they decision-makers, but they are also in effect policymakers as well. Lipsky (1980) states that the policymaking roles of *'street-level bureaucrats'* such as the police are built upon two interrelated facets of their positions, namely relatively high degrees of discretion coupled with relative autonomy from organisational authority. He argues that 'although they are normally regarded as low-level employees, the actions of most public service workers actually constitute the services "delivered" by government. Moreover, when taken together the individual decisions of these workers become, or add up to, agency policy' (1980: 3). He further suggests that 'unlike lower-level workers in most organisations, street-level bureaucrats have considerable discretion in determining the nature, amount, and quality of benefits and sanctions provided by their agencies' (1980: 13).

Of course the issues described above are not the only factors that influence police decision-making. As Bell (2002) suggests, any police investigation is a complicated process in which officers use the law, official policies and procedures, prior training, routines and practices to shape their decisions and to establish 'fact' in a given case. Lipsky (1980) acknowledges the importance of policies, rules and regulations in restraining, at least to some degree, the discretion of street-level bureaucrats, but points to what he sees as the impossibility of severely reducing or removing discretion from this type of work. This is because, he argues, the work of street-level bureaucrats involves complex tasks for which the elaboration of rules, guidelines or instructions cannot circumscribe the alternatives. The situations in which street-level bureaucrats work are too complicated to be reduced to programmatic formats, and these situations often require responses to the human dimensions of situations that are responsive to the unique circumstances of individual clients. The need to be compassionate and flexible on the one hand, yet at the same time to be impartial and rigidly apply the rules on the other represents, for Lipsky, a dialectic of public service reform.

As a consequence of the issues discussed here, it is widely accepted that there will be slippage between orders and the carrying out of orders, either as result of poor communication, inadequate resourcing, inadequate sanctions for non-compliance, or workers' disagreement with organisational goals and objectives and their consequent withholding of cooperation in the exercise of their duties (Lipsky, 1980). The issue of slippage between policy and practice is of particular interest.

The reality is, then, that changes to prescriptive policy are not a guarantee that success will be achieved 'in the real world'. Indeed there is substantial historical evidence that suggests that the transformation of police policy into effective practice is a complex and vulnerable process, particularly in the field of police–community relations. For example, in their study of beat policing, Grimshaw and Jefferson (1987: 199) examined the transformation of police policy into police practice and noted that:

> policies involving operational and related tasks will be characterised by the values of operational common sense, and those involving administrative tasks will be characterised by rational scientific management values ... the 'success' of policy in influencing practice will be task related. Thus, the impact of those policies bearing on operational and related tasks where occupational common sense is to the fore will be less decisively calculable and more unpredictable in effect than those policies bearing on administrative tasks.

In other words, gaps between what is supposed to happen (policy) and what actually happens (practice) when responding to an incident are likely to appear where the actions of the police in any given situation are guided by operational common sense afforded to them through the opportunity to use their own discretion, rather than being strictly guided by the requirements of law or management directives which restrict their discretion. This is significant because, as Bowling (1999) has argued, the discretion afforded to police officers when responding to racist incidents has historically been problematic, and has contributed to the failure of police policy to improve operational performance. As such, he argues that despite force prioritisation of racist incidents throughout the 1980s and 1990s in England and Wales, for deep-rooted legal, organisational, structural and cultural reasons, operational practice remained largely unchanged throughout.

There is therefore a long held belief amongst minority groups based on experience that the police are either unable or unwilling to effectively investigate crimes against them, and that their cases are not taken seriously (Macpherson, 1999; Victim Support, 2006). This situation is compounded by research evidence that historically points to widespread and discriminatory 'over-policing' (Hunte, 1966; Landau, 1981; Willis, 1983). The extent to which such ineffective policing is the result of individual or institutional prejudice and discrimination, inadequate resources, occupational culture, poor policing at lower levels or bad management at upper levels, or a product of the nature of hate crime itself is difficult to determine and has been the subject of much debate (Human Rights Watch, 1997; Reiner, 1997).

A further factor that influences both decisions and the exercise of discretion is the issue of resourcing. As Lipsky (1980) suggests, there are several ways in which street-level bureaucracies such as the police characteristically provide fewer resources than necessary for workers to do their jobs adequately, with the most important being first the ratio of workers to clients, and second, time to deal adequately with each client in what are characteristically large caseloads.

Part of the problem of caseload size is a product of increased demand for services over time. In policing terms, hate crime has emerged (in some countries at least) as a relatively recent social problem, effectively meaning that there is political and public pressure for the police to respond that previously would not have existed. The most obvious example relates to the huge increase in recorded racist hate crimes (in effect, increased demand for police services) in England and Wales as a result of the post-Lawrence definitional change (Hall, 2005). In response to this, following the Lawrence Inquiry, police forces, and in particular London's Metropolitan Police Service, increased resourcing to help meet Macpherson's recommendations and to help challenge the problems the police faced at that time. At face value it would seem logical to expect that increases in funding and resources in this area should result in improvements in police performance. It is, however, a feature of public services that this is not likely to be the case, certainly in the long term. As Lipsky (1980: 33) explains:

> A distinct characteristic of the work setting of street-level bureaucrats is that the demand for services tends to increase to meet the supply. If additional services are made available, demand will increase to consume them. If more resources are made available, pressures for additional services utilising those resources will be forthcoming.

In other words, in public services such as the police, there will always be more people who need the services on offer than the police can provide services for. Unless it can somehow be controlled, demand will always outstrip supply, and perceived availability of a service will fuel demand for that service. The situation becomes particularly acute when the increases in resourcing are relatively moderate in quantity and relatively short in duration, as is often the case when different issues compete for political and police priority. On the other hand however, if demand for services can be controlled, for example through the exercise of discretion in decision-making, then the pressures of inadequate resourcing may be eased.

In addition to a lack of organisational resources, Lipsky also suggests that street-level bureaucrats also experience deficiencies in personal resources, in terms of inexperience, lack of training (a point not lost on the OSCE given their role in trying to improve police training across the region), and so on. Lipsky points out that part of this inadequacy is attributable to the nature of the job in the sense that some jobs simply cannot be done properly regardless of personal or organisational resources. This point may have particular relevance to the policing of hate crime because there are some important issues that exist in this area over which the individual and the organisation have less potential for control.

For example, it has been suggested, as we saw in chapter four, that hate crime is best viewed as an ongoing process. Viewing hate crime in this way can help to further explain the negative views of the police that many members of minority groups hold. The underlying rationale is that there is a fundamental mismatch between the nature of hate crime and the requirements of the criminal justice system. With reference to racist victimisation, Bowling (1999) argues that the problem is that whilst hate crime is best viewed as an ongoing *process*, the police and wider criminal justice system necessarily respond to *incidents*. Bowling suggests that racist victimisation does not occur in a moment, but rather it is ongoing, dynamic and is embedded in time, space and place, and must always be kept in context if it is to be understood and responded to effectively. However, Bowling explains that as the 'incident' is transformed from the world of the victim's experience into an object for policing it is placed in the context of the police organisational and cultural milieu, an environment that is usually antithetical to that of the victim. The net result of the process/incident contradiction, according to Bowling, is that whilst the police may feel that they have responded appropriately and effectively, the victims are frequently left with feelings of dissatisfaction, fear and a perception of being under-protected.

The social context of law and law enforcement

It should be clear, then, that law and law enforcement in relation to hate crime are subject to a number of complex variables. In seeking to make sense of these complexities, and in line with the theoretical issues discussed in this chapter, I have argued previously (Hall, 2009, 2012a) that, broadly, the factors impacting upon the policing of hate crime (and therefore impacting upon service provision to victims) can be categorised into four distinct but interrelated areas. These are identified as *law* (including operational interpretations of law in the form of policy), *law enforcement* (in the form of agencies and the officials that work therein, and including the provision of the range of available state services beyond simply enforcing the law), *the public* (including individuals, communities and representative advocacy groups) and the *context* (social, political and historical) in which the policing of hate crime takes place.

In short, in a democracy the relationship between these four factors is broadly as follows:

1. The law requires enforcement *and* enforcement agencies require the law (at least to some degree) to guide their activities;
2. Enforcement agencies (in this case the police) for the most part require the public to invoke and pursue the enforcement process (which in this case includes other services relating to the policing of hate crime) *and* the public require confidence in enforcement agencies to provide the protection promised by law and the services offered by law enforcement agencies;
3. The public require the law to provide the impetus to invoke the enforcement process *and* the law requires the broad agreement of the public for its creation, longevity and legitimacy;
4. Context (social, political and historical) influences and shapes the creation of law, the mood of the public and law enforcement responses to the social problem in question *and* the creation of law, the mood of the public, and law enforcement responses to the social problem in question influence and shape context (social, political and historical).

If we begin with the issue of *context*, a useful starting point for illustrating these complexities is to ask the question '*what is the context that gives rise to the legal recognition of a perceived social problem?*'. As we saw in chapter two, in the US and in England and Wales the legal recognition of hate crime was predominantly achieved through the process of identity politics in which perceptions of, and concerns about, an increase in the extent and nature of the problem were brought to the political fore.

The construction of law in order to respond to such concerns reflects this process, particularly in England and Wales where only racially (and latterly religiously) motivated offences are specifically legislated against, reflecting the context of the debate concerning racist violence following the murder of Stephen Lawrence in 1993 (see chapter two). The context that gives rise to legal recognition then necessarily passes the problem into the rather mechanistic world of law-making where lived reality is transformed into a form suitable for the statute books. Here answers to questions concerning what groups will be protected, what behaviours will be outlawed, what the punishment will be, and what is required from law enforcement agencies in order to meet the requirements for conviction must be constructed. As we have seen from our discussion in chapter one, the way in which hate crime is officially defined and conceptualised, often influenced by identity politics, can significantly determine both the volume and nature of recorded incidents (clearly illustrated in chapter three), which in turn has very serious implications for law enforcement in terms of workload, resourcing, investigative practices, occupational health and, of course, the amount and quality of service provision to victims.

Once the problem has been legally constructed it necessarily requires enforcement, in this case by the police. Legal requirements are then transformed into organisational policy for practical purposes, which represents the organisation's instructions to its employees for dealing with a given problem. Here the issues for consideration are widened because law enforcement is usually only one activity undertaken by the police in hate crime cases. Dependence on an organisation that is necessarily influenced by individual and occupational perceptions and beliefs, finite resources, competing priorities and so on, to enforce the law and provide other related services in response to a given problem raises a host of issues, but which can ultimately be reduced to two key points: do the police have the *ability* to respond effectively to hate crimes and do the police have the *desire* to respond effectively to hate crimes? The answers to these two questions determine the extent to which legal and organisational goals in terms of responding to the problem, which itself is determined by the context that gave rise to its construction, are met.

My own research in this area (Hall, 2009) suggests that whilst there is inevitably considerable overlap between those factors that impact upon the *ability* of the police to respond to hate crimes and those that impact upon the *desire* of the police to respond to hate crimes, the key factors impacting upon the *ability* of the police to respond are broadly as follows (see Hall, 2009 for a full discussion):

1. The operational definition and conceptualisation of hate crime
2. The volume of hate crime
3. The nature of hate crime
4. Resource availability
5. The exercise of discretion
6. The content and propriety of policy instruction
7. The investigative process and case construction
8. Quality of training
9. Internal and external pressures
10. Organisational goals and visions of 'success'

In addition, the key factors impacting upon the desire of the police to respond to hate crimes are as follows:

1. Organisational culture
2. State of staff morale

3. Levels of officer confidence in dealing with hate crime incidents
4. Extent of understanding and appreciation of the issues relating to hate crime
5. Calibre of leadership
6. Nature of formal rules and sanctions

The ability and desire of the police to respond adequately to any problem is crucial because, as Cotterrell (1992) suggests, to continue to function effectively the police must protect the social and political bases of their authority, and to do this they must demonstrate an adequate degree of success in the tasks allotted to or assumed by them. In terms of hate crime this situation is particularly acute given the social, historical and political context in which the contemporary policing of hate crime takes place. In policing terms, arguably the most important aspect of that context is the depth of trust and confidence that the public have in policing and the police. The police are largely dependent upon the public to invoke the services on offer, which in turn is dependent upon both the *ability* and the *desire* of the public to do so. Furthermore, these two caveats are themselves dependent on the public first having a degree of *knowledge* about hate crime and the services available to respond to it.

The ability and desire of the police to respond to hate crimes are therefore crucial in influencing the *ability* and *desire* of the public to engage with the police, and the relationship is reciprocal. It is this relationship that is central to 'success', however so defined, in the policing of hate crime. As both Pound (1917) and Cotterrell (1992) have stated, citizens' willingness to invoke law is therefore essential for effective enforcement by state agencies and, in my view, three interrelated areas – *knowledge, ability* and *desire* – are of central importance.

The first issue concerns the extent of public *knowledge* concerning the services available to them. In his discussion of the factors inhibiting the effective voicing of grievances, Cotterrell (1992) suggests that the poor and inarticulate in particular lack knowledge and opportunity to complain against abuses. With reference to hate crime, knowledge might well be inhibited by the issues Cotterrell identifies, but also more specifically by factors such as language and understanding of a foreign (both literally and metaphorically) criminal justice system, or perhaps by certain issues relating to a person's disability, where barriers to accessing justice can be particularly problematic.

Having knowledge of available services is one thing, but being able to invoke them is often quite another. A lack of knowledge is clearly a barrier in terms of the ability of the public to report offences against them but, inevitably, the significant under-reporting of hate crimes, starkly illustrated by victim surveys in this field (see chapters three and four), suggests problems beyond knowledge to include the *ability* and *desire* of the public to invoke the enforcement process. The issue of ability was raised by the

Stephen Lawrence Inquiry. Part of the underlying rationale for the change in definition in England and Wales was to encourage reporting of racist incidents to the police by making it easier for the public to do so. Macpherson (1999) highlighted the importance of third-party reporting, identifying the need for people to be able to report at locations other than police stations, and the ability to report 24 hours a day. In principle (if not always in practice), this opened up an avenue for victims of all hate crimes to report incidents without having to have direct contact with the police, and many third-party reporting mechanisms are in place today for this very purpose.

The *ability* of the public to invoke law enforcement services is closely related to the *desire* of the public to invoke services, which itself is largely determined by issues of experience, perception, and the extent of trust and confidence in policing. Undoubtedly a lack of trust and confidence in the police inhibits some victims' desire to invoke law enforcement services. This lack of trust and confidence is nothing new and victims of hate crime are often reluctant to report their victimisation to the police for a host of reasons, and these are well documented in the literature on both sides of the Atlantic (see for example Reiner, 1992; Human Rights Watch, 1997; Bradley, 1998; Bowling, 1999; Hall, 2005; Victim Support, 2006; AVP, 2007; Crane and Hall, 2009; Hall *et al.* 2009), where areas of dissatisfaction have included perceptions that the police do not provide enough support, their response is inadequate or ineffective, they do not keep victims informed of case progress, they are insensitive and indifferent, are verbally and/or physically abusive, they do not treat cases seriously and they are not culturally aligned to victims. In short, the interrelated issues of victims' knowledge of, and ability and desire to, invoke law enforcement play a key role in shaping both the experiences and practicalities of policing hate crimes.

Finally, the extent of trust and confidence of the public in state agencies to effectively respond to hate crimes feeds into the issue of context. For example, if public concern about a problem that is perceived to be inadequately responded to gives rise to a collective context that exerts political pressure to force or strengthen that response, then the process discussed here starts to unfold. Conversely, if state responses can consistently demonstrate an adequate degree of success by having both the ability and desire to respond appropriately, then it follows that trust and confidence in those agencies will increase, as will the ability and desire of the public to invoke state services, which in turn will serve to alleviate some of the problems associated with context.

Of course, the issues discussed in this section do not provide a panacea to the problems associated with the policing of hate crime. Too many variables are present to suggest a 'solution' to such problems. Rather, the discussion identifies a range of areas *where* problems might occur, demonstrates *how* and *why* these problems might occur, how they might manifest themselves and highlights the impact of these issues on related variables, not least victims and wider communities. It is also clear that the myriad of issues impacting upon the policing of hate crime (including the amount and quality of service provision to victims), regardless of jurisdiction, cannot and should not be viewed in isolation of each other.

Concluding comments

This chapter has considered a number of theoretical and practical issues relating to the law and law enforcement in relation to hate crimes. It has been argued that because hate crimes are complex events, they pose significant challenges to law-makers, the police and prosecutors. The chapter has suggested that there are many issues both internal and external to those individuals and agencies responsible for law enforcement, and over which they have varying degrees of control, that inevitably impact upon their ability to enforce the law, to respond effectively and to provide a service appropriate to the needs of victims and wider communities.

The theoretical perspectives discussed in this chapter highlight the potential for practical difficulties in law enforcement in hate crime cases, and it would seem, are reflected in the practical problems experienced in the prosecution of such cases, as illustrated by the relatively low rates of conviction for these offences in most countries where such laws exist. At one level, the potential for difficulty arises because, arguably, the law in this field reflects a number of the elements that Pound (1917) argued would limit legal effectiveness, not least because of the problems associated with proving the motivation behind an offence, or that the offence was aggravated by some prejudice-based hostility.

In addition, Pound (1917) rightly notes the importance of the role of law enforcement agencies, most notably the police, in the process of law enforcement. The role of the police is crucial, as noted by Cotterrell (1992: 56):

> How the law is put into effect is clearly as important as its content. The nature of the enforcement agencies used, the degree of commitment of enforcement agents to implementation of the law, their morale and – a closely related factor – the amount of resources available to ensure compliance, are all shown to be extremely significant factors. In addition, the particular strategy of coercion or persuasion employed in regulation is clearly of great importance.

The theoretical perspectives relating to the police discussed in this chapter serve to illustrate the importance of how the law is put into effect. The theoretical issues concerning 'street-level bureaucrats' demonstrate the powerful position held by those often in lower ranks of law enforcement agencies, and the potential for these employees to determine the outcomes of both law and organisational policy through their use of discretion.

With these issues in mind, it is important to note that in some countries, notably in England and Wales, law enforcement is only one aspect of the policing response to hate crimes. This is important given that the literature discussed in this chapter implies that the nature and characteristics of hate crime effectively mean that the clear-up rate is a relatively meaningless measure of police performance. It is therefore important to consider measuring 'success' in other ways – an issue of potential consternation in England and Wales given the government's sole target for the police – to reduce crime – juxtaposed with what is a clear need to encourage victims to report more hate crime, which, if achieved, would have precisely the opposite effect by inflating rather than deflating the official statistics. Rather, the 'success' of policing in relation to hate crimes might be better measured against the numbers of hate crimes reported by victims, where depending on the circumstances an increase may signify an increase in trust and confidence in the police, or by victim satisfaction with the police response, as indicated by qualitative and quantitative surveys. The latter is of significant importance in assessing the 'success' of the police and is of far greater informational value than clear-up rates.

It may also be possible to further measure 'success' against the educative role achieved by policing activities in the community, or the strength of the message conveyed to the public that hate crimes will not be tolerated and the suffering of victims will be treated seriously. One might also consider the ability of the police to respond proactively to a perceived threat or tension in a community; or the collecting and dissemination of hate-related intelligence; the training of other police officers to respond appropriately to hate crimes; or the ability of the police to liaise with advocacy groups and 'build bridges' between minority communities and the police. All of these represent significant functions undertaken by some police services which are not measurable simply by considering clear-up rates, or whether numerically hate crime goes up or down, yet the importance of which should not be underestimated, particularly given the difficulties in law enforcement in this field. In other words, enacting and attempting to enforce hate crime legislation is not a panacea to the problem of hate crime. Rather, it is one part of a much bigger picture, and it is to that bigger picture that we now turn.

8   Challenging hate and hate crime

In chapter six we considered a range of explanatory frameworks from across the social sciences that each offered useful, but rather disparate, insights into the possible causes of hate offending. Together with the psychological literature that we explored in chapter five, this collectively provides us with a wealth of information upon which to ponder, and you may well have in your mind a leaning towards a particular explanatory framework that you consider to hold the best hope of finding answers to the problem (assuming, of course, that you believe that a problem indeed exists, but we'll come back to that particular debate in chapter nine). The issue, though, as we have alluded to elsewhere, is that it is precisely this disparate nature of our existing knowledge that causes us difficulties when we come to formulate practical responses to hate and hate crime.

As Stern (2005) points out, our responses to hate and hate crime have thus far been undertaken across a number of disparate planes simultaneously. To paraphrase his illustration of our use of the various frameworks, our responses are influenced thus; if we think of hate as a mental disorder, then analysis and treatment is considered the cure; if it is economics, then economic recovery is the answer; if political events are the cause, then we need to effect social change; if it is a criminal matter, then we need criminology and an effective criminal justice system; if a lack of education is the underpinning factor, then we should educate; if hate is a product of the individual or the individual in a group context, then we need psychology or social psychology; if it is a product of the social world, the answer is in sociology; if it is caused by culture, then anthropology may come to our rescue; if politics is a causal factor, then let's turn to political science, and so on.

But, as we have already seen, none of these provide comprehensive explanations by themselves. As a consequence, we have a range of formal responses to hate crime that have different theoretical perspectives underpinning them. The purpose of this chapter, therefore, is to explore some of these responses from around the world, and to see what is being done to combat both 'hate' and 'hate crime'.

International and domestic legislative and policy responses

In chapter three we considered the findings of the OSCE's (2012) hate crime report, and, in particular, attempts to establish some sort of estimate of the extent and nature of hate crime in participating States. As a further part of their annual 'stock-take', the OSCE also provide information concerning international and domestic activity in relation to developments in efforts to challenge hate and hate crime. Moreover, in assisting states to meet their various obligations and commitments, ODIHR and the OSCE (2012) have undertaken a number of programmes and activities across member States addressing issues such as collecting and disseminating information, developing practical materials and handbooks, working with international organisations and OSCE field operations, supporting and training law enforcement agencies, and supporting and training civil society.

The OSCE also identified a number of what they term 'institutional developments' (these are responses outside of legislative change, such as law enforcement and prosecutor training, policy instruction, government action plans, victim support initiatives, data publication, cooperative protocols, working groups and so on) in Bulgaria, Croatia, Cyprus, the Czech Republic, Finland, Hungary, Liechtenstein, Lithuania, Poland, Spain and Sweden. Despite these developments, however, across its annual reporting cycle the European Commission Against Racism and Intolerance (ECRI) made various specific recommendations for improving responses to hate crime in Azerbaijan, Cyprus, Iceland, Italy, Latvia, Lithuania, Luxembourg, Montenegro, Serbia and Ukraine (OSCE, 2012), suggesting that much remains to be done in many countries around the world.

We also briefly touched upon the 2008 EU Framework Decision in chapter three, which seeks to ensure the harmonisation of 'hate' legislation across the European Union. In 2011 the EU Fundamental Rights Agency (FRA) reported that 23 member States had notified the Commission about implementing the necessary measures (compliance with which is to be reviewed by the EU by November 2013), and the OSCE (2012) recorded that Bulgaria, Croatia, Cyprus, Finland and Georgia had all enacted and/or amended various pieces of legislation in accordance with the Framework Decision in 2011/12. In addition, in May 2011 the European Commission issued a proposal for a directive of the European Parliament and the European Council seeking to establish minimum standards on the rights, support and protection of victims of crime generally, but within those proposals reference is made to the specific needs of hate crime victims based upon the distinct nature of hate crime (EC, 2011; OSCE, 2012). In this sense then, recent international policy and legislative responses have included provisions for victims as well as offenders.

Beyond these political commitments to the OSCE, and others relating to the Council of Europe and the European Union, as Human Rights First (2010) rightly point out, following the adoption of the Universal Declaration of Human Rights in 1948, governments also have a number of obligations to a range of international treaties and other bodies. In particular, these include the International Covenant on Civil and Political Rights (1966), the International Convention on the Elimination of All Forms of Racial Discrimination (1965), and the European Convention on Human Rights (1953).

Of course, despite these and other developments, it is perhaps the recorded figures that speak loudest, and the information considered in chapter three clearly illustrates that for all the legislative and policy developments, responses to hate crime in many countries remain woefully inadequate in practice (indeed, to this end the OSCE, 2012, make a raft of recommendations in areas relating to data collection, legislation, the activities of criminal justice agencies, cooperation with civil society and other programmatic activities). The possible exception here, at least in *comparative* terms, is the UK, where legislative and policy responses have been to the fore in recent times. We have already discussed legislation at some length in this book, so instead I shall briefly consider some of the policy issues to have recently emerged in the UK.

The UK government response to hate crime

In March 2012, the UK government published its action plan to tackle hate crime. Notwithstanding the content, this was *symbolically* important. If you recall from chapter two, the Conservative government (in power until 1997) showed little interest in furthering the race–hate agenda as a political and legislative concern, meaning that nearly all of the progress made in this regard has happened under a New Labour administration. Perhaps unsurprisingly, the removal of New Labour from office in the 2010 general election, replaced by a coalition government with a Conservative Prime Minister, caused considerable concern in some quarters that hate crime might start to disappear from the political agenda (this is an issue to which I shall return in chapter ten). The publication of the action plan at least suggests that, in theory at least, this is not the case.

There isn't the space here for a full consideration of the content of the action plan, but nevertheless some overarching aspects are useful for our purposes in this chapter. The government's approach to crime in general is based upon a withdrawal from top-down micro-management towards more locally administered responses that should reflect the needs of local areas and communities. As such, the government sees its role as setting strategic direction, making information available, sharing good practice and, where necessary, passing legislation (HM Government, 2012).

In the context of hate crime, the action plan (HM Government, 2012) is underpinned by three core principles, the ongoing responsibility for which is shared across government departments and the agencies of the criminal justice system: *preventing hate crime* (by challenging attitudes and early intervention); *increasing reporting and access to support* (through increased victim confidence and supporting local partnerships) and *improving operational responses* (through better identification and management of cases and dealing effectively with offenders).

Under the theme of *preventing hate crime*, the government has identified 23 action points including, for example, the need to develop and improve the evidence base upon which interventions are based, reducing negative media stereotypes of different groups, supporting educational and anti-bullying initiatives, supporting the work of charities and others (including sports organisations) involved in challenging hateful discourse, working with relevant others to address hate on the Internet, developing resources for use by local partnerships, and supporting the work of the anti-Semitism and anti-Muslim cross-government working groups.

With regard to *increasing reporting* and *access to support*, 16 points for action are identified. These are broadly based on the need for the improved collection and dissemination of data and the identification of statistical gaps, the need to engage with 'at risk' communities, working with the voluntary sector to establish and share 'good practice' in reporting and preventing hate crimes, supporting the work of True Vision (see www.report-it.org.uk) and providing funding for selected organisations and projects in the field.

Finally, with the goal of *improving operational responses*, 14 action points are highlighted, including the publishing of a hate crime manual to guide police organisations, the updating of training for all police roles, the development of various tools to assist professionals dealing with hate crimes, the amendment of legislation as necessary, the development of a hate crime framework covering prisons and the probation service to assist with the management of offenders, and to assess the scope for alternative disposals, including restorative justice (to which I shall return shortly).

Of course, the action plan is rather sketchy on specific detail and many of the undertakings within are ongoing at least until the next general election in May 2015, but the first two core principles do at least recognise and acknowledge the need for a holistic approach to the problem, rather than simply relying on a retributive response through law and the criminal justice system. We have already discussed some of the problems associated with the latter in terms of law and law enforcement, so for now we shall turn our attention to what might be done with those offenders who are successfully caught and convicted, before examining other options for 'challenging hate' that might constitute part of a more holistic approach.

Prison

As you may well have gathered by this point in this book, the policy response to hate crime in England and Wales has hitherto been largely dominated by law, policing and the judicial process, which is perhaps unsurprising given the historical evolution of the subject that we discussed in chapter two. The information already discussed in this chapter, and in chapter three, suggests that this is a trend that is being followed, in theory at least, by other countries across the world (certainly in Europe if the EU Framework Decision is to be met). We have already examined some of the difficulties associated with some key aspects of the criminal justice response in the previous chapter, but there remains a further associated issue that we have yet to consider. This punitive approach to dealing with hate crimes and hate offenders through the imposition of enhanced sanctions for those convicted of specific hate motivated offences also makes it increasingly likely that the prison system will become involved with hate offenders. It is therefore important to consider the role of the prison service in responding to hate offenders, and its role in preventing future offending.

Imprisonment of hate offenders raises a difficult dilemma. On the one hand there is the need to protect the public from dangerous offenders, but on the other there is the need to effectively address the underlying causes of the hate crime (that is, the offender's prejudice) in order to prevent future offending. Prison may achieve the former (at least for the duration of the offender's incapacitation), but it tends to fall short on the latter.

The problems associated with imprisonment as a response to hate offenders are threefold. First, because the chances of being caught, convicted and ultimately sent to prison are remote for most hate offenders the deterrent value of prison is weak at best. Second, prisons are often divided along racial, ethnic and religious lines, and are therefore 'hotbeds' for prejudice, intolerance and hate group activity and recruitment (Gerstenfeld, 2004; Blazak, 2009). Third, simply punishing offenders is not enough. If future offending is to be prevented, then some form of rehabilitation that addresses the offender's prejudicial attitudes that caused the offence to occur in the first place is crucial. In an overcrowded prison system, and in times of considerable austerity around the world, where both effective rehabilitative programmes and the opportunities to implement them are relatively rare, it is unlikely prison will offer any effective solution beyond simply removing them from society for a period of time. Indeed, Levin and McDevitt (2002) argue that imprisonment may in fact be counterproductive because hate-based views may be hardened whilst in prison thereby increasing the likelihood that they will be physically expressed following release.

In a US context, these issues are starkly illustrated by Blazak (2009). Drawing on the available statistics, Blazak calculates that of the 2.2 million people in US prisons, 95 per cent will at some point be released (estimates suggest around 650,000 people per year). Approximately 10 per cent of the prison population are involved in racist white prison gangs, meaning that (given the rate at which inmates are released back into the community) approximately 65,000 members of such gangs are released every year. Yet, he suggests, little is known about the sociology of racist prison gangs, and such prisoners are overwhelmingly released without any established strategy to respond to their increasing presence in the outside world.

Prison, therefore, does not seem to offer much by way of an effective response in itself, and certainly not in the long term following release. The best hope, it would seem, lies in a dual approach whereby offenders are rightly punished for their crime, but also in which their underlying prejudices are challenged and addressed. Rehabilitating offenders, as well as punishing them, would appear to hold the key to preventing future offending. Perhaps, then, identifying strategies for reducing prejudice and using these to inform rehabilitative efforts offer better prospects for responding to hate and hate crime.

Rehabilitation of offenders

Given both the complexity and uncertainty that is clearly involved in understanding and explaining hate offending, it will likely come as no surprise to you that formally addressing it is similarly complex and uncertain. As Craig (2002) has explained, hate crime represents a unique form of aggression and has both symbolic and instrumental functions for the perpetrator, who can be motivated by one or more of a wide range of social, psychological, political, cultural and other factors. That said, however, McDevitt *et al.*'s (2002) offender typology that we noted in chapter six also contains some clues about the likelihood of influencing, deterring and perhaps even preventing future offending. The tabulated characteristics of the four identified offender types reveal some interesting information across a range of different variables (see Table 8.1).

For our purposes here, the offender's commitment to their hatred is a significant factor, particularly in relation to whether or not they can be deterred from their actions. Thrill offenders are not particularly committed

Table 8.1 Characteristics of hate crimes by offender motivation (McDevitt *et al.* 2002: 311).

Attack characteristics	Thrill	Defensive	Retaliatory	Mission
Number of offenders	Group	Group	Single offender	Group
Age of offender(s)	Teens–young adults	Teens–young adults	Teens–young adults	Young adults–adults
Location	Victim's turf	Offender's turf	Victim's turf	Victim's or offender's turf
Weapon	Hands, feet, rocks	Hands, feet, rocks	Hands, feet, rocks, sticks, guns	Bats, guns
Victim offender history	None	Previous acts of intimidation	Often no history	None
Commitment to bias	Little	Moderate	Moderate	Full
Deterrence	Likely	Unlikely	Unlikely	Most unlikely

to their prejudice, whereas in contrast mission offenders are fully committed to their erroneous beliefs. Defensive and retaliatory offenders, it would seem, fall somewhere in between the two ends of this spectrum. These latter findings serve to highlight the complexity of prejudice as a psychological phenomenon, and reinforces the view expressed in chapter five that hate is felt and expressed in different ways by different people to different degrees. It further illustrates the point that when we talk about 'hate' as a motivation for criminal behaviour, we cannot always be referring to the same thing in every case. The hate of the mission offender, for example, is considerably different in its nature to the hate of the thrill offender (yet the term 'hate' that we apply to both sets of offenders and their offences does not discriminate between, or indeed acknowledge such differences).

Just as there are different degrees of hate, so there are different degrees of culpability. The finding that hate crimes are often committed by offenders operating in groups rather than alone has also led McDevitt *et al.* (2002) to advance a 'continuum of culpability' to assist criminal justice decision makers in determining the role of group members in the commission of an offence, and to develop sentencing options based upon that degree of culpability. Identifying differing degrees of involvement in an attack, and thereby different degrees of culpability for those operating in groups, not only serves to potentially aid prosecution decisions but also furthers our understanding of offender behaviour.

With these findings in mind, some degree of success, particularly for first-time offenders, has been achieved in the US through probation and community service sentences. Levin and McDevitt refer in particular to sentences consisting of probation including some form of community service to a local minority group or minority group organisation. Based largely on contact theory (Allport, 1954), the intention here is that the offender will learn about the community they have targeted through contact with its members whilst at the same time returning something positive to that community by repairing some of the damage and harm caused. Such an approach, however, is not always straightforward. As Levin and McDevitt (2002: 201) suggest:

> A major limitation of the community service sentencing approach is its lack of formal treatment programmes. Having a location for the assignment of offenders is one thing; putting together an effective programme to reduce hatred is quite another. Having an offender paint the exterior of a synagogue that he has defaced might return something to the community he has harmed, but it is questionable that this activity alone would teach the offender why what he did was wrong. To do that, he would need a programme that effectively addressed his misconceptions.

Similarly, writing of probation practice with regard to racially motivated offenders in the UK, Dixon and Court (2003) have acknowledged the various limitations. Given the unique nature of hate offending, they suggest that generalist offender programmes are relatively ineffective because they fail to adequately address the dynamic risk factors that are, as we have seen, inherently associated with hate as a motivation for crime. Similarly, Dixon and Court suggest that general cognitive behavioural programmes for hate offenders are ineffective because they fail to impact upon the emotional aspects of this type of criminal behaviour. Echoing Levin and McDevitt, Dixon and Court (2003: 150) argue that the complex psychological processes and the wide range of risk factors that underpin hate offending can only be effectively dealt with by developing interventions specifically tailored to hate offenders.

But what elements might such interventions contain? In light of the problems associated with the prison system and community sentences that fail to effectively tackle the offender's underlying prejudice, Levin and McDevitt (2002: 203) make a number of suggestions for the content of such offender programmes, stating that 'a model hate crime offender treatment or rehabilitation program must include the following elements: assessment, discussion of impact on victims, cultural awareness, restitution/community service, delineation of legal consequences, participation in a major cultural event, and aftercare'.

For Levin and McDevitt each stage represents an important step in the rehabilitation of hate offenders. Based upon their offender typology, the assessment allows trained professionals to understand the type of offender they are dealing with, and the strength of their prejudicial attitudes. Such understanding will serve to guide the programme in the most suitable direction. Following the assessment, Levin and McDevitt point to the importance of explaining to the offender the harm they have caused to their victim. Many hate offenders see their victims as 'different', 'inferior' or 'inhuman' and reversing this dehumanisation process is an important aim. Furthermore, Levin and McDevitt suggest that many hate offenders readily accept false and negative stereotypes of their victim's group. Thus, it is important to identify and challenge these misconceptions whilst simultaneously promoting the benefits and values of diversity within the community. Attempting to deconstruct stereotypes and misconceptions about a group is a crucial element of increasing an offender's cultural awareness and understanding.

In addition, the sentence should contain a genuine reparative and restitutive element. It should be related to the community harmed, yet tailored to avoid resentment on the part of the perpetrator. In this sense then, involving the offender in a major cultural event within the victim's community can help the offender to see the victim as a human being thereby serving both as a reparative purpose to the victim and their community and an educative experience for the offender. In addition, the legal consequences of pursuing hate motivated behaviour should be explained, particularly as many young hate offenders may be of the opinion that they can still 'get away with it', even if they are caught again.

A further suggested component of a rehabilitative programme involves 'aftercare' for the offender so that they can return to the programme to resolve any remaining issues if they feel they need to. Finally, Levin and McDevitt suggest, such offender programmes should be continuously evaluated and monitored, and amended as new and improved information about prejudice and hatred comes to light.

Such rehabilitative programmes may sound ambitious, possibly overly optimistic, and there is little doubt that adopting such an approach for hardened hate offenders may be highly unsuitable. Nevertheless, for young, first-time or thrill offenders, a carefully designed and implemented programme containing these elements may prove to be of value. Therefore, whilst acknowledging that for hardened hate offenders the only realistic option may be incarceration, Levin and McDevitt (2002: 207) optimistically suggest that for other offenders:

> Intermediate sentences – less than prison but more than probation – are necessary for assuring that hate crimes are treated more seriously than ordinary offences. However, many hatemongers can be rehabilitated – if they are fortunate enough to benefit from a serious but humane and imaginative approach to criminality.

Questions remain, however, as to what form this 'humane and imaginative' approach should take in reality, and how realistic a proposition it really is. Whatever approach is taken, Sibbitt (1997) argues that when dealing with racist offenders (and therefore by analogy, hate offenders) agencies need to look beyond the offender and recognise both the relationship between the individual and the wider 'perpetrator community' from which he or she is drawn, and the function that the hatred serves for the individual offender. Attempts to combat hatred need to extend beyond the individual offender and also consider the social situation in which the hatred was fostered and shaped, and the purpose it serves.

Once the importance of these two factors is recognised, Sibbitt argues, it will become easier to engage the offender in a constructive manner. She describes four responses that professionals might adopt in dealing with an offender's expressions of hatred. First, the professional may not respond at all, in which case the problem remains unchallenged. Second, the professional may respond with 'moral opprobrium', where the inappropriateness of the offender's views are explained and further sanctions threatened. Third, the professional may attempt to deconstruct and challenge the logic of the offender's arguments by pointing out the irrationality of their thinking, although Sibbitt cautions against making the offender feel intellectually inferior and appearing insensitive to what may be genuine underlying concerns on the offender's part. Finally, Sibbitt advocates the challenging of hatred in the context of a holistic approach in which individual perpetrators, potential perpetrators and the perpetrator community should be targeted.

With regard to individual perpetrators, Sibbitt suggests that the most appropriate intervention for the perpetrator will be dependent upon a number of issues including their criminal history both specifically in racist activity and antisocial behaviour more generally, the wishes of the victim, the risk posed to the public, the effectiveness or otherwise of previous attempts at intervention, and the perpetrator's personal circumstances. To this end, Sibbitt highlights the importance of multi-agency information sharing so that a comprehensive account of relevant information and related issues is kept and can be used to determine which agency is best suited to working with the offender, be it the police, the probation service, housing officers or youth, community or social workers.

In working with potential perpetrators, which Sibbitt defines as those who have not yet offended but who are at risk of doing so, the role of local community diversionary projects and schemes is advocated, particularly aimed at (disillusioned and often bored) youths. Agencies such as the police and probation service may play a part here by helping to identify where such schemes would be most beneficial and who might be best placed to run them. Sibbitt points to the apparent success of an established youth project in London that engaged youths on a housing estate and challenged their specific prejudices and general attitudes to criminality in a variety of ways using a variety of methods (for a detailed account, see Sibbitt, 1997).

Finally, in respect of 'perpetrator communities', professionals may play a part by challenging inappropriate language or behaviour whenever it occurs in the course of their work by, for example, using one of the four strategies suggested for individual offenders, described above. Furthermore, Sibbitt outlines the positive benefits of community projects where members of a community are required to work together to achieve a goal that is of mutual concern so that it becomes necessary to view each other in terms wider than just 'race' or 'religion' or 'sexuality' in order to achieve that common goal, such as, for example, a youth club, the acquisition of leisure facilities or through the formation of tenant associations on estates.

Theory into practice?

Many of the theoretical principles outlined above are present in the various rehabilitative programmes in place for hate offenders in different parts of the world. In a useful piece of research, Iganski and Smith (2011) published a report on behalf of the Equalities and Human Rights Commission Scotland in which they examined the existence and content of rehabilitative programmes for hate offenders in a number of different countries. Their findings make for interesting, if a little depressing, reading. Iganski and Smith identified the existence of specific programmes in Germany, Scotland, Northern Ireland, England, Sweden and the US, although by the time they published their report, most of those identified in the US had ceased to exist, primarily due to funding issues. None were identified in Australia, New Zealand or Canada.

Whilst you may express a degree of surprise that so few countries have rehabilitative programmes for hate offenders, the lessons from chapter three should temper that surprise. After all, the official statistics for the vast majority of countries around the globe hardly scream out the need for costly interventions where for the most part few, if any, hate offenders pass through the criminal justice system. Given the numbers presented in chapter three, then, it will probably not come as a surprise that Iganski and Smith identified programmes in the countries that they did. There is not the space here to discuss each of the initiatives identified (see Iganski and Smith, 2011, for a detailed account), but some interesting general themes did emerge across most (although not all) of the programmes.

The first significant theme identified by Iganski and Smith related to the importance of accepting and understanding hate offenders, rather than rejecting and condemning them and/or making moral judgements about their behaviour. Prejudice usually serves some sort of function for the holder and therefore there are inevitably reasons for its existence. As such, condemnation of an individual's prejudices without understanding what purpose they serve for the holder is likely to be counterproductive in any attempts to address them. As Trotter (2006) has suggested, approaches which blame, punish and judge rather than seek to address the individual's problems or reinforce positives, are doomed to failure, instead creating further alienation of the offender.

Group work and the utilisation of group dynamics, involving reflecting on attitudes and behaviours and relationships between group members, were also identified by Iganski and Smith as serving a useful purpose in the identified interventions. Similarly, the establishment of trust between all the parties involved was significant in the effective running of such programmes. The importance of this latter point has also been highlighted in research by Lindsay and Danner (2008), who note that positive change in this regard can only be achieved in the context of a constructive relationship between the worker and the client.

Also central to many of the programmes identified were components to address issues relating to anger management, where anger and frustration were often directed towards individuals and/or institutions who fulfilled the role of scapegoat for the offender. In addition, educational components designed to increase offenders' awareness of, and sensitivity to, bias and to promote cultural awareness were common in many of the initiatives. In a similar vein, a number of the programmes included elements of *carefully managed* community service where offenders are required to spend time working to support an organisation representing the group of the victim harmed. Such an approach is designed to address the offender's dehumanising and stereotyping of the victim by allowing them to 'get to know' members of the other group. Other educational components involve discussions of legal issues, which are held to be important because many offenders it seems do not believe their actions to be illegal. On this point we might reasonably relate back to the offenders' use of *techniques of neutralisation* that we considered in chapter six. Finally, Iganski and Smith note the importance within some interventions of the use of apology and acts of redemption, where offenders might be required to write a letter of apology or to engage in some form of mediation or restorative justice – an issue to which I shall shortly return.

The construction of an effective intervention programme for hate offenders is, then, a necessarily complicated undertaking, and the general inherent complexities involved are reflected in the recommendations for the UK that Iganski and Smith (2011) propose. The need for a national policy, an increased evidence base upon which to inform interventions, the widening of a focus beyond that of just race, commitments to funding, the sharing of conceptually sound evidence-based practice, the need for systematic evaluation of existing programmes, post-intervention follow-ups, and appropriately tailored programmes that meet a variety of relevant needs, are all crucial considerations.

To this list of difficulties we might also add problems associated with the attrition rate within a criminal justice system (which determines how many offenders are ultimately processed by the system and receive formal sanction for their offence, the complexities of which we considered in chapter seven), and those associated with offenders who are formally charged with an offence but where the 'hate' element is dropped as a result of plea bargaining (a process that should not come as too much of a surprise given the evidential issues that we also discussed in chapter seven). Put simply, the high rate of attrition coupled with plea bargaining has the potential to ensure that most hate offenders are never identified and officially labelled as such. This is particularly problematic if those running the intervention are dependent upon the courts to formally identify hate as a motivation before the programme can begin. In such instances, if the hate element remains unidentified, then it is quite irrelevant how good any interventions might be.

Mediation and restorative justice

Gerstenfeld (2004) suggests that potential success in rehabilitating hate offenders might be found in restorative justice through victim–offender mediation. This approach, which has grown in popularity in recent times, seeks to actively involve the offender, the victim and the wider community in the justice process by bringing the victim and the offender together with the aim of achieving reparation and reconciliation. Under mediated and controlled circumstances the victim has the opportunity to explain to the offender the impact that the offence had on them, and to discuss related issues and to ask questions of the offender. In response, the offender has the opportunity to explain their actions and to apologise for what they have done.

According to Shenk (2001) victim–offender mediation is ideal for responding to hate crimes for three reasons. First, because hate offenders often 'dehumanise' the objects of their stereotypes, coming face to face with their victim allows the offender to understand the harm they have caused and to view their target as an individual; as a human as opposed to a 'faceless' representative of a hated group. Such an experience can play an important role in deconstructing an offender's stereotypes. Second, both parties are afforded the opportunity for emotional release, an important factor in overcoming the effects of crime; and third, the experience may serve to encourage reporting of hate crimes by victims and curtail future offending by the perpetrator. We might also reasonably add two more benefits to this list. First, such an approach places the victim at the centre of the delivery of justice and signifies empowerment of the victim; and second, that the use of victim–offender mediation does not necessarily mean that other more punitive approaches cannot be used as well (Gerstenfeld, 2004).

More recently, Walters and Hoyle (2012) have illustrated the importance of mediated approaches in overcoming the problems associated with traditional and rather simplistic stereotypical assumptions that generally hold that the difference between the offender and victim is clear cut and unproblematic. They rightly point out that this perception of the offender as a 'stranger' necessarily excludes the 'messy' and intractable disputes between people who know each other, such as neighbours, colleagues and acquaintances that may be only partly motivated by prejudice and where distinguishing between the perpetrator and the victim may be extremely difficult. In such complex scenarios, Walters and Hoyle conclude, traditional law enforcement approaches are unlikely to provide a resolution. Rather, they found that referring such cases for community mediation, where the respective parties work through their disputes through facilitated dialogue, resulted in positive emotional benefits including reductions in anger, anxiety and fear, and crucially helped to prevent further incidents from either occurring or escalating.

However, despite its apparent benefits, we should not assume that the restorative justice/mediation approach will prove to be some kind of panacea for hate offending. There is an ongoing scholarly debate surrounding the practical efficacy of victim–offender mediation with its true value uncertain, particularly for hate offences where its success remains generally unproven, despite an increasing literature that cautiously suggests its potential benefits if administered appropriately (Gerstenfeld, 2004; Walters and Hoyle, 2010). Furthermore, this approach is often dependent on the offender being caught and convicted, the victim wishing to meet them and cooperation being established between the two parties. There may also be the possibility that the offender's hatred of the victim's group may be so strong as to render the process useless. As such, to the extent that it can be done at all, the cases suitable for mediation need to be chosen carefully.

Preventing 'hate'?

Thus far in this chapter we have considered responses to and interventions with individuals who have already developed and expressed negative prejudice. But if we accept the assumption that when we are born we are free from prejudice, it naturally follows that we must somehow learn or acquire our beliefs as we grow up. Is it perhaps reasonable to assume then that if we can learn or acquire negative prejudices, then we might also learn to be tolerant, given the right circumstances? With this in mind, preventing the development of negative prejudice rather than responding to it once it manifests itself and becomes physically expressed might hold more hope for success in addressing hate crimes. For this reason, educating and schooling individuals in a manner that will promote the value of diversity and reduce negative prejudice has become an important issue for consideration, particularly in the case of children before their prejudices fully develop.

The significance of educative approaches has long been recognised. Allport, writing back in 1954, stated that there were too many educational programmes (for both adults and children) for him to report in one volume, but broadly categorised them under six headings (*informational, vicarious, community study-action, exhibits, festivals and pageants, small-group process* and *individual conference*; see Allport for a full examination of these categories). At the time, Allport was only able to speculate on the effectiveness of these approaches, stating that 'desirable effects' were achieved in approximately two-thirds of the programmes, particularly in relation to those that adopted indirect approaches that focused not on *knowledge of* but on *acquaintance with* the subject in question.

More recently, Bigler (1999: 689) has highlighted the 'broad array of specific strategies for integrating multiracial and ethnic material into the curriculum in order to reduce racial bias in children'. First, there are those in which multicultural themes and concepts are attached to the standard educational curriculum. Second, there are those approaches that use multicultural materials to provide counter-stereotypical information about groups. Third, those that involve significant changes to the structure and aims of the curriculum to incorporate a more specific focus on issues of diversity and finally, those that encourage children to recognise and confront racism (Bigler, 1999). Today, a plethora of educative programmes exist, although much of the available literature relates to those ongoing in the American education system. Nevertheless, many of the principles remain universally applicable.

However, in their consideration of the role of education, the US-based advocacy group Partners Against Hate (PAH) (see www.partnersagainsthate. org for a number of publications in this area) have suggested that curriculum change alone is not enough to effectively challenge prejudice. As such, they drew upon research in the field to make a number of recommendations of how to maximise the potential for proactively reducing prejudice in children.

First, the organisation points to the importance of *curriculum reform*. Here it is held to be beneficial to restructure school curricula and teaching techniques to include the history, culture, experiences and learning styles of the school in order to promote an inclusive learning experience for all students. The underlying hypothesis here is that a classroom culture of inclusiveness that uses multiple teaching perspectives that are tailored to suit different learning styles will help to ensure that each student has an equal chance of academic success.

Second, improvements in students' interethnic attitudes can be achieved though the creation of *equitable schools and classrooms.* By creating a learning environment that is essentially democratic where each student is respected as a participating citizen, the aggravating issue of inequality that can heighten prejudice can be potentially avoided. PAH suggest that the creation of egalitarian classrooms will provide opportunities for both students and teachers to consider their prejudices, evaluate different perspectives or points of view, acquire information that can challenge the development of stereotypes and also help them to view the undertaking of social action as their responsibility. Furthermore, PAH suggest that schools that avoid the segregation of students on the basis of ability have better interethnic relations amongst their students.

Third is the recognition of the importance of *teacher training and retraining.* PAH stress that extensive and ongoing diversity training for teachers that addresses their own prejudices, enables them to detect and rectify prejudicial attitudes and practices in their classroom and allows them to develop cultural awareness in relation to the groups they will teach is crucial.

The fourth point to be expressed relates to the *desegregation of schools.* Whilst in the UK this has never been official policy the principle remains the same; that students who attend desegregated (or in the UK context, schools with a diverse population) are more likely to experience diverse environments later in life.

Fifth, the educative strategy of *cooperative learning* is advocated. PAH suggest that traditional teaching methods, based on competition and individualisation, are often poor at developing intergroup rapport. Instead, cooperative learning encourages students to work in small groups where they are rewarded for their ability to work interdependently towards a common learning goal. Such an approach, which requires cooperation, the support of authorities, equal status among group members and an interaction that is intimate, individualised, nonstereotypical and interdependent has, according to PAH, consistently shown positive results in terms of improving student achievement, conflict resolution and intergroup relations.

The sixth and seventh approaches are *conflict resolution* and *peer mediation* respectively. Mirroring Sibbitt's suggestion for promoting community cohesion, PAH suggest that conflict resolution programmes can play an important role in enhancing intergroup relations by utilising communication skills and creative thinking to achieve mutually agreed solutions to problems. These programmes can teach students conflict resolution skills that they can employ to overcome any tensions or problems that may exist between themselves and others. Similarly, peer mediation ultimately seeks the same goal of resolving conflicts, teaching students to mediate between conflicting peers, but places less emphasis on prejudice awareness than the conflict resolution method.

In light of these recommendations, PAH list what they describe as a number of promising programmes across America that are based on these guiding principles. Although there is not the space here to examine these, the overriding aims of the programmes are held to be the promotion of understanding, civility and respect, and to help students overcome diversity-related conflicts in imaginative and progressive ways.

In the UK, work with schoolchildren in this field has traditionally been less sophisticated than that described above, often involving short, one-off 'talks' by police school liaison officers or local community groups. In more recent times, however, issues of diversity have become a key aspect of secondary school education. Since 2002, citizenship education has been a compulsory part of the National Curriculum, including statutory programmes of study relating to the changing nature of UK society, which includes the diversity of ideas, beliefs, cultures, identities, traditions, perspectives and values. Schoolchildren are taught about the origins and implications of diversity and the impact of migration and integration on identities, groups and communities, and also study the legal human rights and responsibilities of citizens.

But whilst the idea of preventing hate in children before it develops through educative approaches sounds ideal in principle, it remains a complex and uncertain process. In her review of educative approaches, Bigler (1999) paints a somewhat gloomy picture, and one that still resonates, by stating that such approaches have been relatively ineffective mainly because they have been based upon theoretical and empirical models of attitude formation and change that are far too simplistic and narrow for a concept that is not fully understood. Again, we find that our lack of understanding in relation to prejudice hinders our attempts at influencing its development. She suggests that if educative measures are to be effective, then an ongoing approach that is based upon numerous different theoretical foundations and that combines many of the existing techniques is required across all levels of schooling.

The problem here is that such an approach is simply not available in practice in any coherent or implementable format, and even if it were it would likely be complex and expensive to implement and with no guarantee of any tangible and lasting success. The overriding issue, as Bigler suggests, is that stereotyping is pervasive amongst children and is highly resistant to change. As such, some interventions work some of the time with some children, and others are known to be counterproductive. There is simply no certainty over the outcomes of either existing or speculative educative approaches.

There are also a number of practical limitations to consider too. For example, in a review of diversity education in England, Ajegbo *et al.* (2007) noted concerns relating to the uneven quality and quantity of the education, differing degrees of prioritisation, a lack of confidence and training for some teachers, weak or non-existent links with the community, resulting negative perceptions of English identities amongst some indigenous white pupils, a lack of clarity in learning objectives for classes, a lack of resources and, interestingly for our purposes, the continued presence of racial hierarchies and widespread stereotyping within society generally that hampered the realisation of the 'vision' of diversity education. And of course, a glance back to the bullying literature that we discussed in chapter four adds considerably to the complexity of this issue.

Publicity and the media

Of course, it is not just the formal education system that can provide an educative role. The emergence of anti-hate advocacy groups, and particularly the spreading of their message through the Internet, represents an important development in the fight against hate and bigotry. To this end, Gerstenfeld (2004) suggests that such groups concentrate their efforts on two key issues. First, they seek to educate both the public and law enforcement agencies and therefore raise awareness about the problem of hate and bigotry, and second, they are concerned with the lobbying of authorities to support, promote and take action in the name of their cause. We have already noted the significance of the lobbying activities of advocacy groups in chapter two, but their educative role represents another important function. In the UK too, a number of advocacy organisations exist, both nationally and locally, that perform a similar function to their American counterparts. Readers are advised to see, for example, the websites of the Runnymede Trust, the Joseph Rowntree Foundation, RaceActionNet, Stonewall, the Sophie Lancaster Foundation, and School's Out, to name just a few. In addition to raising awareness of the various issues that they associate themselves with, many of these organisations also make educative resources available for use with children and young people in particular.

Another approach to combating hatred has come in the form of persuasive public awareness campaigns and mass media publicity, both by independent organisations and advocacy groups, and by government and law enforcement agencies. In a society where we are constantly and inescapably bombarded by advertising messages at every turn, such an approach has become popular presumably because of its ability to inform and 'educate' a large audience with relative ease. The question remains, however, as to how effective public awareness campaigns are at reducing prejudice and combating hate more generally.

As with many of the other interventions discussed in this chapter, on the available evidence the answer appears to be that sometimes publicity has an effect, and sometimes it doesn't. In reviewing the limited available literature, Winkel (1997) found that exposing people to material aimed at reducing prejudice caused a reduction in prejudicial attitudes in some people, but conversely an increase in others. In addition, the generalisability of these results is highly questionable and thus we are again unable to draw any firm conclusions about the utility of responding to hate using this method. As Paluck and Green (2009) point out, few studies have gauged the impact of media on large audiences or the impact of large-scale media campaigns in this area.

On the other hand, however, throughout this book I have made reference on occasion to media reports, particularly those relating to the British tabloid press, that have presented a negative picture of intergroup relations, most notably with regard to immigration and asylum, and latterly in relation to disability. In this sense, it would seem reasonable to suggest that such media accounts are damaging to social cohesion and serve to undo the messages of the positive publicity campaigns described above. For me, two prominent examples serve to illustrate these concerns. On 7 March 2005, following an article about an Islamic rap video made to recruit young British Muslims to al'Qaida's cause, the *Daily Star* newspaper announced that 99 per cent of voters in its readers' poll feared that Britain was becoming an Islamic state, although the actual number of votes was not stated (Wickham, 2005). Similarly, on 9 March 2005, *The Sun* newspaper announced on its front page a 'Sun war on Gypsy free-for-all' in which the newspaper launched a campaign against 'illegal gypsy camps across Britain' and invited readers to email their experiences 'of gypsies or travellers being treated as if they are above the law' (Phillips, 2005: 5).

Whilst I do not wish to engage in a discussion about the merits of *The Sun*'s campaign, the *Daily Star*'s poll, or the issues that have led to them, my point is simply that publicity concerning negative aspects about diversity is probably more powerful, more frequent and more persuasive than positive publicity. This is perhaps because it appeals to our natural propensity that we discussed in chapter five to view those that are different to ourselves as inferior and with suspicion, and as a threat to the interests of our own in-group. This is arguably reflected in the terminology used by *The Sun*'s campaign when it described the then government as putting the interests of gypsies ahead of those of 'hard-working people who pay their taxes and obey the law' (2005: 4). Whilst the concerns periodically expressed by the media may or may not be legitimate, the point is that they do little to help the social cohesion of a multicultural and diverse society.

More recently, and in line with some of our earlier discussions, Quarmby (2012) has presented a balanced account of the recent role of the media in relation to portrayals of people with disabilities. On the one hand, she concludes, the media can be a significant force for good in exposing the harms of hate crime, which in turn has put legitimate pressure on the justice system to respond. On the other hand, as we have noted elsewhere, she acknowledges the potential for considerable harm to be done through the perpetuation and creation of negative stereotypes, and it is perhaps for these reasons that the UK government's action plan (discussed above) contains provisions for aspects of the media. Quarmby also makes a final telling point, namely that journalism reflects societal attitudes and, therefore, until these attitudes change, discrimination and prejudice will continue to flourish, as will the crimes that they foster. Once again then, we find ourselves back pondering the nature of prejudice, together with all the seemingly insurmountable barriers that this slippery concept presents.

Assessing strategies for reducing prejudice

Research into 'what works' in addressing prejudice is, perhaps unsurprisingly given what we have already discussed in this book, predominantly rooted within the discipline of psychology where, as Paluck and Green (2009) note, the 'remarkable volume' of literature on prejudice ranks amongst the most impressive in all of social science. In what strikes me as a somewhat monumental undertaking, Paluck and Green (2009) examined interventions aimed at reducing prejudice by reviewing the findings of 958 studies (taking them five years to complete) from across a range of academic disciplines. In doing so, they suggest that whilst the theoretical nuance and methodological sophistication of the prejudice literature are undeniable, what is less clear is the value it holds when assessed in terms of the practical knowledge derived from it.

Of course there isn't the space here to examine Paluck and Green's review in detail, but nevertheless the themes that emerge are of considerable interest, not least given the vast sums of money that are spent each year by policy-makers and others on prejudice reduction initiatives. Their general message is that whilst the literature on prejudice reduction is vast, there is a paucity of research that supports internally valid inferences and externally valid generalisation, meaning that in order to formulate prejudice reduction policies one must extrapolate beyond the available data and use theoretical suppositions to fill the gaps. To illustrate their point, they conclude on the basis of the available evidence that one could argue that diversity workshops (for example) are effective because they break down stereotypes just as easily as one could argue that they aren't effective because they reinforce stereotypes. The evidence for either side is, they suggest, inconclusive, and is illustrative of a situation where we just do not know for certain whether the range of available policies and programmes are effective in general terms, nor under which specific circumstances they work best (Paluck and Green, 2009).

In further exploring this less than convincing situation, Paluck and Green classify the main approaches to prejudice reduction based upon the accumulated evidence (derived from theory, laboratory and field research) for their 'real-world' impact. The best approach to prejudice reduction, they suggest, is *cooperative learning*, where classroom lessons are engineered so that students are obliged to teach and learn from each other. The next most effective approach involves *media, reading and other forms of narrative and normative communication* which, they conclude, hold potential for reducing prejudice through narrative persuasion, social norms (which we considered in chapter six), empathy, perspective taking and extended contact. Other promising approaches included the positive and persuasive *influence of peers*, interventions based on the *contact hypothesis* (advocated by Allport), *value consistency* and *self-worth* interventions (based on self-affirmation theories), and *cross-cultural and intercultural training*. However, despite the promise held by these approaches, Paluck and Green (2009) remain cautious about their generalised impact beyond the field and the laboratory, noting that interventions aimed at changing cognitions or cognitive abilities await comprehensive testing in 'real-world' settings.

That same caution is extended to other such interventions that, they suggest, are also in need of further research and theory. In this regard, they point to the popular but largely untested, unevaluated and theoretically ungrounded approaches of *antibias, multicultural, and moral education and diversity and sensitivity training* often used for practitioners (including law enforcement personnel). Finally, they point out that whilst much work has been done in terms of conflict resolution for professionals, there is little by way of evaluation of *conflict resolution* and reduction for 'ordinary' people living in conflict or post-conflict settings (Paluck and Green, 2009).

In a similar undertaking, Abrams' (2010) review of 'what works' in terms of prejudice reduction strategies from a predominantly British perspective echoes these uncertainties, and in particular highlights the absence of proper evaluatory research into intervention techniques in sustaining such uncertainty. He wryly notes that whilst schools, organisations and government agencies may have plenty of strategies for reducing prejudice and increasing good relations, there is a tendency to assume that they will be effective simply because they have been implemented. In a useful analogy, Stern (2005: 33) points out that:

> if someone ran a pharmaceutical company that said 'I have this pill which will cure disease X. We haven't actually done any long-term studies, but trust us', there would be a legal word to describe such a statement: negligent. Unfortunately, there are ample precedents for costly educational initiatives having no lasting impact.

In short, Abrams suggests that there is some evidence that intergroup contact and school diversity tend to be associated with improved intergroup relations. The evidence for the effectiveness of media campaigns though, as we have already noted, is in short supply but such approaches, he suggests, risk backfiring. Diversity training is also lacking in adequate evaluation and evidence, as are interventions based upon fostering *good relations* within communities, although there is some promise to be found in school-based interventions where prejudice might be influenced in early life. In this respect, Abram notes the promise of *multicultural curricula* and *intergroup contact*, but also the relative uncertainty around *cooperative learning* (note the distinction here with Paluck and Green, above) and *perspective-taking/ empathy*.

On the basis of Paluck and Green's findings, and Abrams' review, it seems that we are left echoing the conclusions that we drew in chapter five, namely that we know quite a lot about prejudice and stereotyping, but very little about how this information can be used to effectively address discriminatory behaviour. Whilst Paluck and Green (2009: 339) are rather gentle in their conclusion that 'the causal effects of many widespread prejudice-reduction interventions ... remain unknown', and Abrams (2010: 88) likewise in stating 'there is strong indicative evidence that a wide range of potential techniques for intervention can be effective under certain conditions. However, there is insufficient evidence and on an insufficient scale to be able to assert what will work best and when', Fiske (2000) has been rather more scathing in her assessment of the situation. In reviewing the best part of a century's research activity in this field, she rightly acknowledges that social psychologists have learned a lot about the complex interplay of motivation and cognition in reactions to out-group members, and should be combining these to produce changes in behaviour. For Fiske, this has not happened enough, and in pointing out that it is behaviour and not thoughts and feelings that exclude, oppress and kill, social psychology, she suggests, needs a 'wake up call ... to get serious about predicting behaviour' (2000: 312). A pessimist, she supposes, would argue that social psychology's neglect of behaviour is a 'disgrace', whilst an optimist would predict a better understanding to be forthcoming in the future, although on the basis of Paluck and Green's research, and that of Abrams, that optimistic wait goes on.

Concluding comments

In this chapter I have presented a brief overview of existing and ongoing efforts to combat hate crime and the prejudice that underpins it. But despite recent advances, the obvious question still remains: *just how effective are these responses to hate?* Unfortunately, as we have implied throughout this chapter, this is a question that it is impossible to answer with any great degree of certainty at the present time. In line with Paluck and Green, and Abrams, Gerstenfeld (2004: 193), speaking primarily of efforts to combat hate crimes in the US, has suggested that:

> There is no shortage of individuals and organisations that wish to combat hate crimes, but there is almost a complete lack of assessment of their efforts. If we knew which endeavours work and which do not, these people could channel their energies and finances in much more useful ways. It will not necessarily be easy to determine what works, but, at this point, any addition to existing knowledge would be of great benefit.

The same can also be said for efforts in the UK and elsewhere. It seems that the best we can suggest is that some techniques work better than others, depending on different circumstances and situations, and the majority of the available evaluatory literature appears to conclude with the message that 'more research and evaluation is required'. The only thing we can say with any certainty is, ironically, that nothing is certain with regard to what works in challenging hate and hate crime. The nature of criminal justice systems around the world ensures that regardless of how effective criminal justice interventions may be (if they exist at all) the majority of hate offenders will never be subjected to them, and even when they are the success of existing interventions, and preventive methods, are uncertain largely because we still do not know very much about prejudice and hatred and how they transform into behaviour. Perhaps then the question should be, are we attempting the impossible by even trying to prevent hate and hate crimes? In the next chapter, we shall address this, and a host of other issues, when we start to ask some awkward questions about hate crime.

9   Questioning the hate crime paradigm

On the evidence presented so far in this book, hate crime is clearly a complex issue. A lack of clarity surrounds aspects such as how to define and conceptualise the problem (chapter one), how it has come to be formally acknowledged, or not, as a contemporary socio-legal issue (chapter two), how much of it exists around the world (chapter three), who should be recognised as victims and what impacts it can have on those who experience it (chapter four), how and why the prejudice that lies within all of us can become the motivation for criminal behaviour (chapters five and six) and how we should respond to it both via the criminal justice system and through other preventive and reformative methods (chapters seven and eight). As such, I have alluded to areas of potential controversy, uncertainty and debate throughout each of the chapters that we have covered so far. In this chapter, however, we shall seek to draw all of these issues together in one place and question, as many people do, whether or not all of these complexities mean that, in reality, our subject is fatally flawed. Before we consider the views proffered by critics of hate crime, however, let us briefly revisit and consolidate the case for viewing hate crime as a distinct category of offending worthy of specific attention in its own right.

Emerging themes and common assumptions

Throughout this book, and in particular from the discussions in chapter four, you will, I am sure, have noticed the presence of a number of themes relating to hate and hate crime, most notably in relation to issues of victimisation. These 'themes' are often used to illustrate that hate crime possesses certain (often unique) characteristics and therefore also to highlight the importance of considering hate crime as a distinct category of criminal offence. Before we begin to question the concept of hate crime, then, let us take a moment or two to briefly consider hate crime's general thematic underpinnings.

Hate crimes are increasing in incidence

We noted in chapter two that social and political concern regarding hate crime in both the US and England and Wales can be traced, at least in part, to concerns about a perceived increase in the number of hate crimes occurring in each jurisdiction (and indeed beyond in the case of concerns relating to racist violence in Europe). Notwithstanding the limitations of statistical estimates of levels of hate crime (see chapters one, three and four), a number of commentators over the past thirty years or so have expressed concerns pertaining to an 'epidemic' of hate crime, particularly in the US and in England and Wales.

Certainly, if one takes the official statistics in England and Wales at face value, the dominant message over that time period is that hate crimes are on the increase. Even when the various statistical limitations are taken into account, victim surveys highlight a significantly greater level of hate crime that is a cause for alarm for many. Furthermore, if we take into account the conceptualisation of hate crime as a process (see chapter four), the problem of the true amount of hate victimisation taking place becomes even more acute.

In addition, in chapter three we noted concerns about increasing levels of violence directed towards Roma and Sinti communities in a number of different countries, and we also discussed the apparent increase in levels of certain types of hate crime held to be a consequence of the global financial crisis, again in a number of countries across Europe. Consequently, then, one of the key themes underpinning the hate crime paradigm is that hate crimes are at an unacceptably high level, are widespread, are increasingly occurring more frequently than in the past (and indeed have the potential to increase significantly further) and that this rising tide needs to be addressed.

Hate crimes are more violent

A second key theme relates to the violent nature of hate crimes. Some of the research discussed in chapter four (and indeed plenty of other research not specifically discussed in that chapter) suggests that hate crimes are generally more likely than comparable non-hate crimes to be interpersonal events, involving physical violence and personal injury to the victim. Again the British Crime Survey (BCS) data discussed in chapter four is useful here in highlighting that hate crimes are generally more likely than non-hate crimes to be targeted at the person rather than at property. Indeed, this finding has long been alluded to by smaller research studies over the years. For example, Goldman (1990), Weisburd and Levin (1994) and Levin and McDevitt (1993), all cited by Carney (2001), were respectively identifying the increased levels of violence in hate crimes and the significantly higher rate of hospitalisation of hate crime victims more than 20 years ago. Indeed, Levin and McDevitt (1993) found that hate crimes are often characterised by extreme brutality. Consequently, the generally more violent nature of hate crime further justifies its consideration as a distinct form of offending.

Hate crimes hurt more

To my mind, the argument that hate crimes 'hurt more' is undoubtedly the single most important issue in justifying the treatment of hate crime as a distinct category of criminal offence. The widely held view that hate crimes have a disproportionately greater impact on victims than comparable crimes without the hate element has long served as one of the central justifications for both the recognition of hate as a distinct form of criminal behaviour and the imposition of harsher penalties for hate offenders. If you recall from our discussion of the emergence of hate crime as a contemporary socio-legal issue (see chapter two), it was in considerable part the findings of early victim surveys that began to shed light on the disproportionate victimisation of some sections of the community, and the impact that this could have on the lives of people who experience this.

Moreover, many of the studies we considered in chapter four have further examined this crucial issue and have implied, either directly or indirectly, that victims of hate crime do indeed suffer disproportionate levels of psychological trauma and heightened perceptions of fear, anxiety, threat and intimidation that can have significant and long-lasting impacts on many aspects of their lives. The findings of the BCS (Smith *et al.*, 2012) that were discussed in chapter four have provided some particularly interesting insights into exactly this issue, where (if you recall) victims of hate crime reported significantly higher and broader levels of emotional impact than victims of non-hate crimes. In doing so, the BCS has added considerable weight to the long purported view that hate crimes 'hurt more' and on that basis deserve specific recognition.

Hate crimes affect the wider community

Beyond the disproportionate impact on the individual victim, many of the research studies we considered in chapter four indicated that hate crime is also a *message* crime. Essentially, the victim is held to be interchangeable because it is some feature over which they have no control that is the target for the offender, rather than the individual traits of the victim themselves. Therefore the perpetrator, through his or her crime against an individual or group, is telling a particular wider community that they are different, unwelcome and that any member of that community could be the next victim.

As such, hate victimisation creates an *in terrorem* effect that extends beyond the individual victim and is projected to all community members creating a sense of group vulnerability and community tension and fear. This view of hate crime was acknowledged some years ago by ACPO (2000: 11–12), who stated that:

> Hate crime victims feel the added trauma of knowing that the perpetrator's motivation is an impersonal, group hatred, relating to some feature that they share with others ... A crime that might normally have

a minor impact becomes, with the hate element, a very intimate and hurtful attack that can undermine the victim's quality of life ... In any close community, the impact of hate crime on quality of life extends to the victim's family, broader circle of friends, acquaintances and the whole community. For every primary victim there are likely to be numerous secondary victims. The perception of the victim is the reality that determines the impact of hate crime on quality of life. This is of paramount importance. Assessing the gravity purely by the physical extent of what has happened can be meaningless.

This assertion is supported by Perry and Alvi (2012), whose research concluded that hate crimes are symbolic acts performed for specific audiences. As such, the awareness of the violence affecting targeted communities instils fear and trepidation, is deemed normative and affects mobility and identity expression, resulting in a profound and negative impact on affected communities, particularly in relation to their perceptions of safety and vulnerability. Furthermore, for Blazak (2011), hate crimes work in exactly the same way as acts of terrorism. That is, as he explains it, targets are randomly selected to make a political, social or religious point and offenders violate the law in the hope of advancing some larger goal and sending a message of fear to the wider community. Addressing this wider impact is therefore an important undertaking.

Hate crimes heighten community tensions and are socially divisive

The *in terrorum* effect, whilst problematic enough in its own right, can lead to other problems in society, as identified by Levin (1999: 18). His research in the US revealed the socially divisive nature of hate crime, noting that they:

> involve a heightening of tension along already fragile intergroup lines, and a heightened risk of civil disorder. Even in the absence of explosive civil strife, the lessening of trust and a change of behaviour among affected groups in a community creates a distinct harm to the public interest.

Whilst this research draws upon the American experience, the race riots that took place in Oldham in England in May 2001 serve as a useful example for a British context in terms of revealing the fragility of intergroup lines, as do some of the hostile reactionary events across England following the murder of Drummer Lee Rigby in Woolwich in May 2013. Levin also points to evidence suggesting that the wider impact of hate crimes increases the risk of further civil disorder through retaliatory attacks along intergroup lines, and also through an increased risk of copycat offending. This was further illustrated in chapter six through McDevitt *et al.*'s (2002) offender typology that identified 'retaliation' and 'defence' as motivating factors for hate crimes, the former of which can lead to further retaliation by the victim's group resulting in a persistent cycle of attack and counter-attack that can involve many innocent victims (McDevitt *et al.*, 2010).

Using 'themes' to justify formal responses to hate crime

Clearly, then, the themes identified above help us to find answers to one simple, but crucial question: *why make 'hate' a crime?* If we think back across the issues discussed thus far in this book, many of which are summarised above, we can see that these themes variously serve as justifications for treating hate crime 'differently', and are clearly woven into the formal responses to hate crime in a number of countries. Consider the importance of these themes to the construction of specific hate crime laws, for example.

The enactment of hate crime laws is, in essence, a statement that such actions will no longer be tolerated and that serious penalties will be applied if such offences are committed. The increased sentences reflect not only the disproportionate harm inflicted upon the victim and the wider community, but also the implication that because an offender is deliberately targeting his or her victim on the basis of an immutable characteristic, then there must logically be a greater degree of intent on the part of that offender. Furthermore, it can be claimed that legislation represents official acknowledgement that the suffering of victims has been recognised and that society takes this type of victimisation seriously, considers it socially unacceptable and is no longer prepared to tolerate it.

Such messages can also be said to contribute to the strengthening of social cohesion because the marginalisation of groups afflicted by the effects of hate crime is officially recognised and countered. Such legislation thereby has the effect of promoting equality across society – something that hate crime necessarily, it seems, seeks to destroy. Simply then, hate crime legislation extends legal protection to traditionally disadvantaged, victimised and marginalised groups, and offers inclusion rather than exclusion.

In addition to the symbolic nature of hate legislation, one of the primary aims of such laws is the intended deterrent effect. The increased penalties for hate offences are meant to act as a strong and effective deterrent to offenders and potential offenders who intentionally target members of minority groups. Furthermore, hate crime laws provide something of an impetus for the police and the wider criminal justice system to take these crimes seriously, to respond appropriately and to be accountable for those actions (Iganski, 1999). In addition to sending a symbolic message to victims and offenders alike, enshrining hate crime in law as a distinct category of offending also sends a clear message to the police and the wider criminal justice system that this type of crime requires serious attention against which their performance will be judged.

So where, then, is the problem? Given the arguments outlined above it may seem rather straightforward, unproblematic and indeed sensible both to recognise, and to legislate against, hate crime as a distinct form of criminal behaviour. Whilst this might be the case in theory, in reality, each of these positions are fraught with moral, conceptual and practical problems and, consequently, hate crime remains a controversial issue. As Miller (2003: 437) explains, for example:

> The intuitions and motivating forces behind such hate crimes legislation seem as obvious and straightforward as they are laudable – at least on the surface. However, there lurk just beneath this placid surface difficulties – conceptual as well as practical – which muddy the waters considerably.

Given these concerns, it is my intention now to spend much of the rest of this chapter playing 'devil's advocate' by examining the critiques of hate crime proffered by those who question its very existence as a distinct category of criminal behaviour.

Questioning the hate crime paradigm

As a concept, as you will probably have gathered by now, hate crime is not without its controversies. Indeed, it is a highly emotive subject for many, for a host of reasons that I shall endeavour to cover here. Some of the most outspoken critics of hate crime include, for example, James Jacobs and Kimberly Potter who, in their thought-provoking book *Hate Crimes: Criminal Law and Identity Politics* (1998), argue the case for abolishing hate crime as a concept, and the laws associated with it, altogether, and Andrew Sullivan (1999), who argues similarly. In essence, Jacobs and Potter, Sullivan and others, challenge the foundations upon which the 'case for hate crime' is made on moral, legal, theoretical, political and practical grounds. Given their apparent extreme stance in this respect, it is important that we examine their key arguments, together with those of others who argue similarly, not least because their critique strikes at the very heart of the key themes identified above.

What is hate?

In chapters one and five we respectively discussed hate crime as a socially constructed political and legal artefact and as a psychological phenomenon. In so doing, we sought to address a fairly straightforward question: in the context of hate crime, *what is hate?* The theories and ideas that we have discussed, however, do not allow for a simple answer, and it is these uncertainties that open the first door to criticism of the subject.

The most obvious thing we have learned is that this simple four-letter word, 'hate', in fact masks a multitude of complexities. This is primarily because, as we have seen, when we talk about *hate* in the context of *hate crime*, what we are really referring to is *prejudice*. Because of this, 'hate' in its contemporary meaning actually refers to a variety of human emotions that are often far removed from real hatred. These other emotions range from prejudice, to bias, or anger, or hostility, through to unfriendliness or a mere aversion to others (Sullivan, 1999), and the definitions of hate crime (and particularly those of an official nature) that we discussed in chapter one for the most part variously refer to all of these emotions. The word *hate* in effect has become a catch-all term for a host of human emotions, behaviours and experiences. Should *hate* then refer to all of these or just some of them? As Sullivan (1999) argues, if hate is to stand for every expression of human prejudice, then the war against hate will be so vast as to be quixotic. A single, simple word, 'hate', in the context of hate crime in truth relates to a multitude of human emotions, beliefs and behaviours that should not and indeed cannot be simply encapsulated in a single word.

Is 'hate' normal?

The fact that 'hate' doesn't really mean 'hate' when we talk about 'hate crime' is problematic for critics. So too is the concept of prejudice, and in particular the notion that having prejudices is a normal part of being human. If, then, when we talk about hate, we actually mean prejudice, then the evidence presented in chapter five poses something of a problem. In chapter five I argued that prejudice is natural to, and definitive of, the human condition. As Sullivan (1999) points out, as human beings we associate, and therefore we disassociate. We have feelings of loyalty and disloyalty, a sense of belonging and unbelonging, and these are entirely natural. Indeed, Sullivan suggests that the existence of prejudices have played a crucial part in the evolutionary history and survival of the human race. Therefore, critics argue that if everyone naturally has prejudices, then whilst we can respond to the *crime* element of hate crime, serious questions should be asked about whether we can and should respond to the *hate*, or more appropriately, the *prejudice* element.

To illustrate the normality of 'hate', Andrew Sullivan (1999: 3) uses two examples that I think will resonate with many of us:

> Of course by hate we mean something graver and darker than this lazy kind of prejudice. But the closer you look at this distinction, the fuzzier it gets. Much of the time we harbour little or no malice toward people of other backgrounds or ethnicities or ways of life. But then a car cuts you off at an intersection and you find yourself noticing immediately that the driver is a woman, or black, or old, or fat, or white, or male. Or you are walking down a city street at night and hear footsteps quickening behind you. You look around and see that it is a white woman and not a black man, and you are instantly relieved. These impulses are so spontaneous they are almost involuntary. But where did they come from?

This raises the question of whether or not 'hate' is a self-conscious activity. If it is then that is one thing, but if, as Sullivan points out, it is primarily an unconscious activity, then the matter becomes considerably murkier. Do humans deliberately and consciously 'hate', or is hate, thus defined, a normal and subconscious product of human differentiation, and how can we know for certain either way? However we look at it, as critics we are faced with the question that if prejudice is normal, then how can we ever hope to stop it being expressed in one form or another?

Have we complicated 'hate'?

For critics, the various definitions of hate crime that have been adopted considerably complicate our understanding of 'hate'. If we think back to Jacobs and Potter's (1998) model that we examined in chapter one, then hate crime would not be difficult to understand if we only applied the term to offenders who truly hate their victim and the group they represent, and where that hate is the sole or predominant cause of that offending behaviour. They are certainly more clear cut and more easily identifiable as 'hate' in lay terms. But, as we have seen, this is not the case for the majority of hate crimes. Indeed, the strength of the offender's prejudice, and the causal relationship between that prejudice and the commission of the offence, do not have to be particularly strong for a crime to become a hate crime. In some cases a causal relationship may not even be evident at all, and therefore the vast majority of what we call 'hate crimes' are not motivated by hate at all.

Hate is also complicated because it manifests and expresses itself in different ways in different people, and indeed serves different purposes for different people, to the extent that no two expressions of hate are ever identical. Yet despite its obvious complexity we still try to label each expression of hate as the same. The significance of understanding and appreciating different types of hate is emphasised by Sullivan (1999). If we think of the hatred felt by the Nazis towards the Jews, the Hutus towards the Tutsis in Rwanda and South Africa's former apartheid regime towards blacks, then for any decent-thinking person these are hates that are wholly unacceptable. But it is reasonable to assume that, as a consequence of their treatment, Jews also feel hatred towards Nazis, Tutsis towards Hutus, and South Africa's blacks towards the apartheid regime. Yet this hate is far more acceptable and easier to understand. What else, Sullivan asks, are the victims of these extreme hates expected to feel towards their haters? So some forms of hate are more acceptable and understandable than others, and some haters are ascribed more blame than others. The problem here, Sullivan suggests, is that if we regulate hate amongst some, then we are forced to regulate it against others, despite the fact that not all hates are equivalent.

In this sense then, hate crime legislation may turn out to be disempowering to minorities, not least because those for whom the law is arguably there to protect may find themselves disproportionately on the receiving end as perpetrators rather than victims. These concerns are echoed by Dixon and Gadd (2006) in their consideration of the impact of provisions for racially aggravated offences in England and Wales (see chapter two). For them, the legislation 'operates only by further criminalizing people who are already seriously disadvantaged in a number of ways ... [and] may be used against disadvantaged people, including individuals from minority ethnic back-grounds' (Dixon and Gadd, 2006: 316–17). In sum, for critics of hate crime, hate is considerably more complicated as a result of formal attempts to simplify it.

Selecting prejudices and equal protection

Because hate has become more complicated (and in effect, watered down to such an extent that it rarely resembles 'hate' at all), any crime might be a hate crime because, as we have seen, everyone has prejudices and everyone is a member of an identifiable group. But if, in response to this, we start to make distinctions between who can and who cannot be a victim of hate crime, then we enter immediately into an immoral and illiberal venture concerning rights to particular and specific protection. As Jacobs and Potter suggest, victims as a whole are a protected group, but the very notion of hate crime, our specific focus on it and our differential response to it means that some victims are now more protected than others. We have already discussed how this has happened (see chapter two), but we should be clear that by intentionally selecting prejudices for official sanction, our response to prejudice is in itself prejudiced and discriminatory (a point to which we shall return, below).

Jacobs and Potter (1998) therefore highlight conflicts over the inclusion of certain prejudices and the exclusion of others, and conflicts over labelling individual hate crimes. We have already noted in chapters one and three the extent of definitional problems and the impact they can have on the 'hate crime problem', and this issue is exaggerated by the lack of uniformity across different jurisdictions in legislative terms (also highlighted in chapter three). What is an offence in one place may not be in another, and where two places outlaw a hate crime, the punishment may in all probability vary greatly between them.

In England and Wales, 'hate' legislation specifically outlaws racially and religiously motivated offending, and contains lesser provisions for homo-phobia, disability and transgender bias, yet makes no mention of other pre-judices. As we noted above, critics argue that what we are effectively saying to society is that the victimisation of these groups is more important than others, and that these victims are somehow more deserving of greater pro-tection under the law. In these circumstances the symbolic message of legis-lation may in fact be a negative one.

The question that arises here is whether or not this undermines the whole point of drawing special attention to hate crime in the first place. We cannot wholly ascribe blame to one group and innocence to others, so if we try to regulate the hate of one group (i.e. the majority), then we are also forced to regulate the hate of others (Sullivan, 1999). The dilemma is that:

> If ... everyone, except the white straight able bodied male, is regarded as a possible victim of hate crime, then we have simply created a two-tier system of justice in which racial profiling is reversed, and white straight men are presumed guilty before being proven innocent, and members of minorities are free to hate them as gleefully as they like. But if we include the white straight male in the litany of potential victims, then we have effectively abolished the notion of a hate crime altogether. For if every crime is possibly a hate crime, then it is simply another name for crime. All we will have done is widened the search for possible bigotry, ratcheted up the sentences for everyone and filled the jails up even further.
>
> (Sullivan, 1999: 14)

On the one hand, identifying what to officially legislate against is problematic and controversial and, rather ironically, is an act of discrimination in itself. On the other hand, if we include all identifiable groups in legislative protections, then hate crime laws will simply be coterminous with generic criminal law, which critics point out is exactly how it should be. As MacNamara (2003) states, every individual's safety and personal property should be afforded the same protections under the law, regardless of the subjective motivation of those who seek to do them harm.

Why treat hate differently?

The criticisms outlined above largely relate to challenges based upon theoretical and conceptual ambiguities concerning the nature of 'hate'. Arguably more direct attacks on hate crime can be found, however, in challenges to the specific themes outlined at the start of this chapter.

Hate crimes are increasing in incidence and in violence

One of the first challenges laid down by critics relates to the themes of increasing incidence and increased violence. For Jacobs and Potter, the alleged hate crime epidemic in America (or anywhere else by analogy) is simply not 'real' – it is a social construction, as we saw in chapter one, and the additional contention that hate crimes are becoming increasingly violent is difficult to assess because of the dubious reliability of relevant statistical data. Indeed, they argue that America is freer of prejudice and hatred now that it has been for the past century and the idea that hate crimes are more

violent now than in the past seems unlikely – a contention seemingly supported by the discussion in chapter two, and by the work of Petrosino (1999,
see chapter six). Rather, for Jacobs and Potter, the 'hate epidemic' is a product of heightened public sensitivity to prejudice, the success of minority
groups in moving 'identity politics' into the realms of criminal justice, the
acceptance of broad legal definitions that encapsulate comparatively meaningless low-level offences for which the strength of the hate element is
debatable and an irresponsible media which exaggerates the latter point.
Ultimately, Jacobs and Potter are of the opinion that there is nothing so
unique to hate crime that means it cannot be adequately responded to by
generic criminal law.

Similarly, MacNamara (2003) echoes the contention that it is impossible
to determine how widespread instances of hate crime really are, and also
questions the notion that they are more prevalent now than in the past,
noting as he does that history suggests that hate motivated crime is in all
reality at an all-time low. Indeed, he questions whether or not hate crimes
constitute an overwhelming problem at all in the US. If we apply his logic to
hate crimes in England and Wales, and in particular to the findings of the
British Crime Survey, then, as we saw in chapter four, hate incidents num-
bered 260,000 out of a total 9,561,000 crime incidents overall. In other
words, if we accept that the BCS represents our 'best guess' in terms of
estimating the total amount of crime in England and Wales, then hate incidents accounted for 2.72 per cent of all the crimes that occurred in 2010/11.
As MacNamara queries in relation to a not entirely dissimilar situation in
New York, 'given the extremely low reported incidence of bias crimes, one
must wonder why the legislators found it imperative to enact special legislation against an almost non-existent problem' (2003: 526). The answer to
this question, he suggests, lies in understanding identity politics where
advocacy groups, politicians and the media all play a part in perpetuating
the misperception that hate crimes are a serious problem.

Hate crimes hurt more and the 'in terrorum' effect

Critics also challenge both the 'greater intent' argument, and the notion that
hate crime has a greater impact upon the victim and the wider community.
With regard to the former, whilst the principle of linking punishment to
motive is viewed as perfectly legitimate, Jacobs and Potter question the idea
that prejudice is more morally reprehensible than other motivations for
crime such as greed, power, spite, jealousy and so on. Simply, they ask, is
the motivation behind hate crime really any worse than the motivation that
propels any other crime? Or, put another way, are hate offenders really more
to blame than offenders who commit similar types of offences when their
motivations might be different but just as reprehensible? In criminal law,
offenders are already punished according to their degree of culpability (for

example, murder is punished more severely than manslaughter, the use of a weapon, so why do we need to make specific provisions for hate crime?

With regard to the 'greater impact' argument, Jacobs and Potter question the extent to which this can be justified. They are highly critical of the research that has underpinned this view, claiming it to be dependent upon dubious empirical assumptions that produce assertions that cannot be substantiated. They also question the 'unique' impact that hate crime has on the wider community, arguing that to suggest that many of the 'low-level' offences spread 'terror' through communities is simply exaggerating the reality of the situation. Indeed, despite the findings of Perry and Alvi's (2012) research into this issue, above, they themselves acknowledge that claims concerning the *in terrorum* effect have largely been unsubstantiated, common-sense assumptions. Furthermore, in noting the limitations of their study, Perry and Alvi highlight the need for more research to be undertaken before this dynamic can be firmly established.

Jacobs and Potter also point out that hate crimes are hardly unique in spreading fear throughout a community. All crimes, they remind us, have the *potential* to spread fear throughout whole communities, and if this is the case, as it undoubtedly is, why is it that hate crime is singled out on this basis? Ultimately, other crimes, and not just hate crimes, have an impact upon innocent third parties, yet these are not specifically legislated against with enhanced penalties in the same way that hate crimes are. Similarly, Andrew Sullivan (1999) argues that all crimes victimise more widely than just the individual victim. In many cases, he suggests, a random murder may invoke more fear and terror in a community than a specifically targeted murder because the whole community, and not just a part of it, may feel threatened. Furthermore, Sullivan suggests, high crime rates of any kind will victimise everyone and spread fear and suspicion and distress far more widely.

Sullivan also argues that claiming that some *groups* are more vulnerable and more intimidated than others is somewhat condescending towards minorities. He suggests that within any community the response to a crime or an incident will invoke many different responses that will vary considerably from fear and panic to mild concern or complete indifference. To suggest that an entire group will be disproportionately affected, he argues, is to make a rather crude and inaccurate generalisation. Finally, not only will there be differences within groups, but there will also be differences between groups, and equating the suffering of one with the suffering of another 'is to set up a contest of vulnerability in which one group vies with another to establish its particular variety of suffering, a contest that can have no dignified solution' (Sullivan, 1999: 14).

Similarly, Jacobs (1993) also questions many of the assumptions made about hate crime victimisation. Jacobs concurs with Sullivan in his contention that all crimes have repercussions beyond the immediate victim, often perpetuated by media accounts of acts of random violence that invariably impact upon people's perceptions of personal safety and their fear of crime. Jacobs also suggests that there is a need for greater empirical verification of both the social and psychological repercussions of hate crimes before we can draw any firm conclusions concerning their true impact. The empirical claim for disproportionately severe impacts on individual victims, he argues, has not been conclusively established and despite recent research suggesting otherwise (see chapter four), many of these studies are based on small samples and their findings cannot be easily generalised nor proved to be conclusive.

Hate crimes heighten community tensions and are socially divisive

Another problem associated with hate crime laws, according to Jacobs and Potter, relates to the negative picture of intergroup relations that such legislation produces, in particular the 'message' that social relations in a country are in such a bad state that an official response is not only required but is essential. Furthermore, publishing crime statistics that they believe do not reflect the reality of the situation simply serve to highlight the poor state of social relations (consider for example the comparative picture of England and Wales compared to the rest of Europe discussed in chapter three).

Andrew Sullivan (1999) builds upon this argument, suggesting that legal attempts to repudiate a past that treated people differently on the basis of some personal or group characteristic may only serve to create a future that permanently does exactly the same. In other words, by responding to a crime that treats groups differently in a way that also treats groups differently, our formal responses to hate crime simply further highlight social divisions along intergroup lines. These divisions, in line with Pound's (1917) contention that the enactment of laws can in some circumstances disrupt rather than repair social relations, may also be the source of resentment towards minority groups where the majority perceive that some groups are in receipt of preferential treatment (Hall, 2009). In such circumstances, levels of prejudice towards minorities may increase rather than decrease.

Legislation and crime statistics therefore have the potential to be socially divisive, rather than encouraging cohesiveness as proponents would claim. In the UK this situation is reflected in an emerging tendency for white people to report their perceived victimisation by non-whites as a hate crime where the motivating factor is often likely to be otherwise (Hall, 2009). This is a situation that has resulted because of what McLaughlin (2002) describes as a determined effort to subvert the meaning of post-Macpherson police policy on racist incidents through the mobilisation of white resentment. In other words, divisions are being highlighted and the strength of social cohesion is being tested by the introduction of new legislation that illuminates group differences, and a perception of preferential treatment for minority groups.

Furthermore, Jacobs also questions the conflict-generating and retaliatory potential of hate crimes, suggesting that whilst interracial hate crimes have the potential to result in intergroup conflict (and in the past have done so), this has rarely resulted from other forms of hate crime such as homophobia, disablism or anti-Semitic attacks. To suggest, therefore, that there will necessarily be a disproportionate probability of intergroup conflict as a consequence of hate crime is also an inaccurate generalisation.

Enhanced penalties, thought crimes, evidential complexities and deterrence

In their critique of hate crime, Jacobs and Potter are particularly questioning of the reasoning behind enhanced penalties for hate offending, and they attack this issue on several fronts. As we have already seen, under such legislation, offences with a 'bias motive' attract higher penalties than those without and, significantly, given that the crime is already illegal under other pre-existing legislation, hate crime laws punish the offender's motivation *in addition* to punishing the offence committed. In this sense, then, hate crime may be viewed as a *'thought crime'* as it is only the offender's motivation that separates it from any other crime.

The question that remains poses something of a legal and moral dilemma; is it right to impose extra sanctions for an offender's prejudice when he or she commits a crime that is already proscribed and therefore punishable by existing criminal law? If the act is likely to be illegal anyway, is it right to additionally punish the offender's thought process behind the commission of that act? And even if we decide that it is right, in the absence of an admission from the offender, how can we accurately judge that thought process? In other words, how can we be sure that an offender is prejudiced and that the offence was motivated or aggravated by that prejudice?

Some of the evidential complications in this regard were noted in chapter seven, and these concerns are shared by MacNamara (2003). In particular, he questions the additional burden that having to prove motive places on prosecutors, the abundance of new evidentiary concerns facing the courts, the inevitable use of plea bargaining, what types of evidence are used to prove motive, the often necessary focus on circumstantial evidence and offender affiliations, the potential admissibility as evidence of the offender's prior statements, writings, reputation and past transgressions and, of course, the constitutionality of such laws. The procedural ramifications and jurisdictional implications are, he suggests, astounding, and may affect a defendant's due process rights to a fair trial. But as MacNamara (2003) points out, no one will contend that bias motivated crime is not repugnant. Rather, he argues, the question is whether or not the government should single out criminal activity that is based on subjective motivation for enhanced punishment.

The 'moral, educational and general deterrent message' contained within hate legislation is also questioned by Jacobs and Potter. They argue that generic criminal law already sends a strong message about which behaviours are right or wrong and therefore the value of specific education or

deterrence in this respect is highly questionable. For example, if an individual is prepared to carry out an offence that already carries a proscribed
punishment, how can we be certain that simply increasing the potential for
punishment will cause the offender to rethink? Jacobs and Potter argue that
at best the deterrent effect will be marginal, and this problem has historically been amplified by the relative ineffectiveness of law enforcement agencies in apprehending, prosecuting and convicting hate crime offenders, and
the imposition of lenient sentences when they do.

MacNamara (2003: 531) concurs, and asks some searching questions;

> All of the enumerated crimes warranting enhanced punishment ... are
> already criminalized in other sections of the penal law. Why, then, is an
> enhanced penalty mandated based on the subjective motivation of the
> perpetrator? Do hate crime laws provide some additional remedy to the
> victim? Do bias crime statutes serve as a deterrent by providing an
> enhanced penalty for acts that are already criminalized? ... It seems
> implausible that someone willing to commit a murder or rape will be
> significantly deterred by the threat of an increased minimum sentence
> based on his or her subjective criteria for the selection of the victim.
> Will the statute serve as a deterrent to lower-level, bias-motivated
> offenses by providing for increased penalties over those already con-
> templated by the existing criminal law? Or will it just increase the pen-
> alty for some comment made on the spur of the moment?

In Britain, Iganski (1999) has also questioned the deterrent effect of hate
legislation. He argues that the logic behind the assumption that legislation
will deter offenders is both contorted and difficult to sustain, and is difficult
to measure empirically. Iganski argues that there is little empirical evidence
to support a correlation between sentence and deterrence and that in any
case the sentence available for a basic offence should be sufficient in itself
without the need for an additional penalty for the hate (in this instance,
racist) element. Furthermore, he rightly points out that what may act as a
deterrent to one person will not necessarily amount to the same thing for
another.

Freedom of expression, belief and opinion

Some of the strongest and most forthright arguments against hate crime,
and in particular against hate crime legislation, emerge from the perception
of hate crime as a 'thought crime'. As we noted above, and discussed in
chapter seven, the requirements of hate crime laws go beyond those of other
criminal laws by straying from concern with issues of *intent* (that a person
meant to commit the offence) to concern with issues of *motive* (why a person
committed the offence). It is this focus on the latter, which is immaterial
in proving other forms of crime, that lead critics to suggest that it is the

offender's thoughts, beliefs, speech, opinions and/or affiliations that are being punished.

This presents a number of potential problems because, as Bleich (2011) points out, freedom of speech, expression and opinion have been corner-stones of the liberal project for centuries, and remain core values in Europe and the US. In his treatise *On Liberty*, for example, the English philosopher John Stuart Mill (1859, 1991: 20) wrote that 'there ought to exist the fullest liberty of professing and discussing, as a matter of ethical conviction, any doctrine, however immoral it may be considered'. Furthermore, Thompson (2012) usefully summarises four often cited arguments in defence of freedom of expression: first, freedom of expression is necessary for the development of self-knowledge, and hence for the achievement of self-realisation. Second, that the right to freedom of expression can be exercised in pursuit of truth. Third, that freedom of expression enables citizens to exercise effective collective control over their governments. And finally, that there is a connection between free speech and specifically democratic gov-ernment. These ideals are of course reflected in the First Amendment to the US Constitution, which states that *'Congress shall make no law respecting an establishment of religion, or prohibiting the free exercise thereof; or abridging the freedom of speech, or of the press; or the right of the people peaceably to assemble, and to petition the Government for a redress of grievances'*.

As such, for critics in the US, hate crime laws infringe upon these con-stitutionally protected rights and, as Blazak (2011) points out, concerns about the vagueness and constitutionality of hate crime laws has kept them in and out of the courts for over two decades. More generally, given the view that hate crimes are in effect 'thought crimes', many critics of hate crime argue forcefully that the associated legislation, with its focus on motive rather than just intent, represents a serious and unacceptable threat to free-dom of speech, expression and belief.

In explaining the concerns of critics, Bleich (2011) notes that there has been a noticeable trend since the 1960s towards penalising racist speech and racist opinion-as-motive. These developments, he suggests, have *slowly* amounted to significant limits on a core liberal value in states where identity and belonging are complicated by racial, ethnic and religious diversity. This 'slow creep' of change, he argues, is important for two reasons. First, he suggests, because it has unfolded slowly over the decades, each individual step has seemed moderate at the time it was enacted, yet the cumulative effect on freedom of expression over time may prove to be increasingly uncomfortable and unpalatable to citizens. Second, he suggests that this problem is compounded by recent developments across Europe where some countries (Britain and France, for example) have expanded various pieces of 'incitement' and other legislation (Holocaust and other genocide denial, for example). These developments, Bleich points out, have opened the door to claimants who want to establish their victimhood as legally unassailable, and consequently, if group after group demands protection for its history, it may, he suggests, prove politically difficult to rebuff successive claims because of the precedents set by earlier decisions.

Can 'hatred' be prevented?

The complexities and controversies outlined in this chapter lead us finally to the crucial question of whether or not hate can ever be prevented. Our understanding of hate is considerably limited by the extent of our knowledge about prejudice as a causal factor in acts of discrimination, which, as we saw in chapters five and eight, is vast but inconclusive. Let's briefly revisit some of the key points. First, we do not know for certain what prejudice is, nor where it comes from, nor how it develops, although it seems that prejudice is entirely natural to the human condition, and is perhaps even definitive of it. As Sullivan (1999) suggests, we are social beings. We have in-groups and out-groups and one can't happen without the other. Humans necessarily differentiate.

Second, there appear to be many kinds of prejudice that vary greatly and have different psychological dynamics underpinning them, and this has important implications for understanding and responding to hate crimes, as we have seen. Third, because prejudices are independent psychological responses it would seem that they can be expressed in a bewildering number of ways, ranging from a mild dislike or a general aversion to others to extreme acts of violence (as illustrated by Allport's 1954 scale), but despite the wide research that has been conducted into prejudice as a psychological phenomenon, we still cannot say with any degree of certainty why it is that prejudice leads to violent behaviour. Critics argue, quite simply, that if we don't know why prejudice results in violence, then we cannot fully know what causes hate crimes to occur. If we do not know what causes hate crimes to occur, how can we respond effectively to them? Fourth, prejudice serves different functions for different people, and whilst these may not always be entirely rational, they usually have their reasons and should not, indeed cannot, be understood or condemned without knowing what these reasons are (Sullivan, 1999). Consequently, these views are (arguably) reflected in the distinct lack of certainty surrounding 'what works' in terms of challenging prejudice and hatred, be it via the criminal justice system or any other form of intervention, and in chapter eight we examined a range of attempts to combat and prevent hate and hate crime, and noted the complexities involved in such a complex (and exasperating) task.

Indeed, the scepticism of critics includes, for example, the educative approaches that we considered in chapter eight, and two particular issues compound the uncertainty about whether or not hate can ever be prevented in this way. First, many of the preventive and educational measures described in chapter eight are based on the assumption that *knowledge* of, and *association* with, the objects of our negative prejudice will somehow prevent that prejudice developing. But this is, for critics, optimistic. Sullivan (1999: 4–5), for example, argues that:

> It is one of the most foolish clichés of our time that prejudice is always rooted in ignorance, and can usually be overcome by familiarity with the objects of our loathing. The racism of many Southern whites under segregation was not appeased by familiarity with Southern blacks; the virulent loathing of Tutsis by many Hutus was not undermined by living next door to them for centuries. Theirs was a hatred that sprang, for whatever reasons, from experience.

To these examples we can also add the persecution of Jews and other minorities in Nazi Germany and wider occupied Europe. In this instance, familiarity failed to prevent the ultimate of hate crimes, namely the killing of over 12 million people in the Holocaust. There is surely no better example to illustrate the old cliché that familiarity can indeed breed contempt. Overcoming ignorance, it would seem, is not necessarily the key to success.

Second, Sibbitt's (1997) research on racist offenders (see chapters five and six) highlighted the influence exerted over youths by both their elders and their peer group in terms of their attitude formation and subsequent behaviour. Sibbitt's findings imply that should such individuals be educated at school in the ways described in chapter eight, then they would likely encounter opposite views at home or with friends. The question then becomes one of who has the greatest influence over the youth, the school or their family and friends? In essence, no matter how positive the message, it has to be both *heard* and *accepted* before any difference can be made, and there are no guarantees of either.

As such, many of the points that Sullivan and other critics make with regard to whether or not attempts to eradicate hate and prevent hate crimes are in fact futile deserve to be taken seriously. Consider these points made by Sullivan (1999: 15–16):

> hate crime law advocates cram an entire world of human motivations into an immutable, tiny box called hate, and hope to have solved a problem. But nothing has been solved, and some harm may even have been done. In an attempt to repudiate a past that treated people differently because of the colour of their skin, or their sex, or religion or sexual orientation, we may merely create a future that permanently treats people differently because of the colour of their skin, or their sex, or religion or sexual orientation. This notion of hate crime, and the concept of hate that lies behind it, takes a psychological mystery and turns it into a facile political artefact. Rather than compounding this error and extending it even further, we should seriously consider repealing the concept altogether.

To put it another way: violence can and should be stopped by the government. In a free society, hate can't and shouldn't be. The boundaries between hate and prejudice and between prejudice and opinion and between opinion and truth are so complicated and blurred that any attempt to construct legal and political firewalls is a doomed and illiberal venture ... in an increasingly diverse culture, it is crazy to expect that hate, in all its variety, can be eradicated. A free country will always mean a hateful country. This may not be fair, or perfect, or admirable, but it is reality, and while we need not endorse it, we should not delude ourselves into thinking that we can prevent it.

For Sullivan, then, our best hope is to achieve toleration of hatred; that is, coexistence despite its presence in society. The answer to hatred, he suggests, is not majority persecution of it, but minority indifference to it. Whilst we can and should create a climate in which hate is disapproved of, he argues, hate is only foiled not when haters are punished, for that may entrench differences, but rather when the hated are immune to the bigot's beliefs. According to Sullivan therefore, there is no solution to the problem of hatred, just transcendence of it. In this sense, hate can never be eradicated, it can merely be overcome.

To summarise, and in making the case for repealing hate crime laws, Jacobs and Potter (1998: 153) conclude that:

Certainly, crime is a problem ... today. But the crime problem is not synonymous with the prejudice problem; indeed, there is very little overlap between the two. With the important exception of crime against women, most crime is intraracial and intragroup. Hard core ideologically driven hate crimes are fortunately rare. Teasing out the bias that exists in a wider range of context-specific crimes that may occur between members of different groups serves no useful purpose. To the contrary, it is likely to be divisive, conflict-generating, and socially and politically counterproductive.

Concluding comments

Given the argument and counterargument across a whole range of very serious and complex issues, the very existence of hate crime as a concept, and in particular as a legislative and policy domain, is telling. Despite the concerns of critics, hate crime laws exist in one form or another in many countries around the world, as we saw in chapter three. It would seem reasonable to suggest then that the case *for* hate crime as a distinct category of offending behaviour, and as a specific legislative concern, outweighs the case *against*.

Whilst the views we have examined in this chapter have been largely theoretical and scholarly in nature, hate crime legislation in both the US and

England and Wales in particular has also been subjected to numerous legal challenges based on a number of different issues. So, if opponents of hate crime laws are by and large correct in their views, then we might reasonably expect challenges to legislation to have been successful in one way or another. The reality, however, is that for the most part they have not, and hate crime laws have survived almost every legal challenge brought against them, with many of them seeking to address the concerns expressed by MacNamara (2003), above.

Nevertheless, whilst the *practical* legal issues may have been largely resolved, many of the *philosophical* questions remain, and the views expressed by critics have rightly sparked important theoretical and moral debates and raised important issues that have to be considered and addressed. The points that underpin the critics' case, as McLaughlin suggests, deserve close attention and serious consideration, and remind us that our subject area is far from straightforward. Indeed, we face many critical issues within our subject area, and it is to these that we now turn.

10 Critical issues in hate crime

The previous chapter served to illustrate the contentious nature of hate crime as a political, legal and scholarly arena. Clearly, there are many commentators for whom the answer is simple – abandon the concept altogether. Of course, this would resolve many of the problems that we have identified in an instant, and having read the debates portrayed in the previous chapter you may well have concluded that to do so is the only sensible course of action. I do not believe, however, that we should abandon the concept, nor give up on our attempts to make life better for those who are the victims or potential victims of expressions of hate. Much has been achieved, and much more can be achieved, but if we are to persist with hate crime as a distinct category of crime, then we face a number of critical issues that still need to be addressed. In this chapter, then, I shall touch upon what I believe to be some of the key issues facing those of us who wish to further the hate crime agenda.

Somewhat ironically, the process of identifying which 'critical issues' to discuss here is somewhat reflective of one of the key criticisms of hate crime itself, namely that selective decisions necessarily have to be made about what to include and what to omit. In many respects I find myself in a 'no-win' situation at the outset of this chapter – by selecting some issues over others I suspect that I will inevitably cause consternation amongst some readers for whom I will have left out issues close to their heart. But, if I try to include all of the seemingly infinite number of issues that might possibly and reasonably be considered 'critical' within our subject area, then they will, for our purposes, cease to be 'critical'. After all, if everything is a priority, then nothing is. With this in mind, I hope you'll forgive and understand my choices in this chapter, and be reassured that I do not limit my personal concerns just to the issues raised here. Necessity (and the prospect of a book that otherwise might not ever end) however, forces prioritisation.

Addressing the concerns of critics

Of course, the process of identifying 'critical issues' within our subject area is largely dependent upon us opting against the total abandonment of the concept. As such, it seems reasonable to me that challenging the views of critics represents a sensible starting point for our discussions in this chapter. After all, if the critics are in fact right, and hate crime is a fatally flawed concept with unacceptable and insurmountable moral and practical implications, then we might as well not bother identifying any of the outstanding issues that might subsequently require our attention. In other words, if abandoning hate crime is the only acceptable course of action, then there really isn't very much left to say. So, what can we say to address and alleviate the concerns of critics? Well, whilst the concerns outlined in the latter part of the previous chapter may seem fairly persuasive, the provocative stance of the various critics has been counter-attacked from a number of quarters, and here we shall *briefly* outline *some* of the key rebuffs that have been made.

Perhaps unsurprisingly, critics' dismissal of the consequences and impacts of hate crime has raised significant concern, particularly in the light of the volume of emerging literature supporting the claims of proponents of legislation (see chapter four). The increasingly consistent message from the research is that hate crimes do indeed 'hurt more'. As such, Iganski (2008: 93) suggests that increased punishments that reflect these greater harms are justifiable:

> The growing body of evidence on the harms inflicted by 'hate crime' ... arguably indicates that the harsher punishment of offences aggravated by hostility on the basis of the victim's 'race', religion, sexual orientation or disability, compared with similar crimes without such aggravation, pursues the liberal principle of proportionate sentencing and provides offenders with their just deserts. In theory it also potentially provides more equitable treatment to offenders by ensuring a greater level of fairness and consistency in sentencing than when penalty enhancement is left to the discretion of the courts.

Critics' concerns surrounding the influence of advocacy groups, identity politics and a distorted media have also been the subject of rebuttal. McLaughlin (2002) suggests, for example, that Jacobs and Potter in particular under-represent the struggle undertaken by minority and advocacy groups in order to have their plight taken seriously by the majority society, and that their definition of advocacy groups as deliberately and inherently antagonistic and divisive is critically flawed. The importance of this 'struggle' for recognition, itself dependent upon the mobilisation of activists, in shaping hate crime policy in the UK is similarly recognised by Mason-Bish (2010), although she acknowledges the ongoing tensions between such groups within the context of this fight for formal recognition. Furthermore, McLaughlin (2002) points out that much of the media coverage of hate crimes has traditionally been significantly less extensive and influential in terms of shaping identity politics than Jacobs and Potter and others claim.

Barbara Perry (2001) also notes the importance of Jacobs and Potter's scepticism. However, she too is critical of their views. Perry takes particular issue with the claim that hate crime laws are socially divisive. Rather, she suggests, it is hate crimes that are, and always have been, socially divisive, and not the legislation. Perry argues that because hate crime is embedded in wider social structures (see chapter six), legislation is not the cause of inter-group hostility. Rather, the enactment of legislation is just one of many ways of responding to the manifestation of long existing antagonisms.

Concerns that hate crime laws unfairly punish the offender's motives in addition to their actions have also been addressed, not just by proponents of hate crime, but also through the decisions of a number of criminal courts, not least the US Supreme Court which, over the years, has arbitrated on a number of debates surrounding the constitutionality of such legislation. In short, the decisions made in a number of contentious cases, most notably in the case of *Wisconsin v. Mitchell* in 1993, have determined that hate crime laws are legitimate because they punish the *conduct* that arises from the motive, and *not* the motive itself.

Although proving the motivation that caused the offence can undoubtedly be problematic, under legislation in England and Wales the problems asso-ciated with proving a *causal* link between the offender's prejudice and the commission of the offence (the two key requirements for transforming a crime into a hate crime under Jacobs and Potter's model – see chapter one), are somewhat mitigated by the legal requirements for demonstrating that an offence was motivated or aggravated by hostility. In this regard, the key issue in the Crime and Disorder Act 1998 concerns the demonstration of hostility by the offender *at the time of committing the offence, or immediately before or after doing so.* As Iganski (2008) explains, here the prosecution need only prove the 'basic' offence, and then the aggravating hostility, thereby bypassing the need to prove that the latter caused the former. As such, the hostility can in fact be completely unconnected with the basic offence where it accom-panies but does not necessarily impel the offender's actions. Of course, as Iganski (2008) further suggests, whilst this allows us to bypass some of the problems surrounding the issues of motivation and 'causal links', we are still left with the situation that such laws do indeed seem to punish an offender's 'bad values'. But, as Iganski (2008) and Kahan (2001) both point out, all criminal law punishes 'bad values', it is just that here, as we noted above, the greater harm caused by these offences is acknowledged in the process.

In concluding that hate crime laws are 'clearly justified', Iganski (2008: 87) also addresses the critics' concerns about whether or not they are *desirable*. In concluding that they are indeed desirable, Iganski refers to the issue of deter-rence, arguing that because of the ubiquity of hate offending, the 'ordinari-ness' of offenders (see chapter six) and the structural context for acts of hate, such legislation provides an important *general* deterrent against offending. In doing so, hate crime laws also serve an important declaratory purpose.

Iganski also refers to the importance of the role of the state in providing an environment where hate can flourish (as we implied in our discussions of political rhetoric in chapter six, and as one might infer from some of the international approaches to hate crime in chapter three). As such, he suggests, the state can therefore play an important role in eroding that environment. Hate crime laws, then, are 'intended to reweave the structural fabric by setting an agenda for appropriate behaviour' (2008: 88), and thereby represent an attempt to repair the damage that hate crime causes to the 'collective conscience' (note the link here to the anomie theories discussed in chapter six).

The concerns of critics in relation to issues of 'preferential treatment' and 'hierarchies of victimisation' have also been the subject of counter-argument. Blazak (2011: 252), for example, is critical of the critics in the US, whom he describes as 'well meaning people who care about the Bill of Rights' but whose views are ultimately flawed, not least in relation to the argument that hate crime laws offer special protection for minority groups over the majority. This erroneous view, he suggests, is based upon a misunderstanding of the language used in law, which, instead of being exclusive, is in fact inclusive. The language of the laws refer to 'hate' motivated by race, religion, disability and so on, not hate motivated by blacks or whites, Christians or Muslims or Jews, or the able-bodied or the disabled. Given that we all possess some or all of these 'protected' characteristics, we are *all* equally protected from crimes motivated by the respective categories of hate, not just some of us. In policy terms in the UK, this very point is recognised by ACPO (2013b) who similarly note the importance of 'inclusivity' which, they state, reflects their core belief that hate crime policy should support a basic human right to be free from crime fuelled by a hostility based upon personal characteristics. As such, the symbolic nature of hate crime laws, Blazak argues, cannot be understated.

Whilst this should alleviate some of the concern regarding 'preferential treatment' *within* categories, we are of course still left with the broader contentious issue of which characteristics to include in any formal response. For scholars such as Iganski (2008) and Mason-Bish (2010), for example, the role of 'identity politics' rightly remains important in this process, although the latter points out that in relation to hate crime policy in the UK, criticisms relating to victim hierarchies and simplistic notions of victimhood have been more about how policy is implemented, rather than about its existence *per se*.

Whilst this issue will inevitably continue to affect hate crime policy-making (in this case in the UK, but inevitably elsewhere too), ACPO (2013b) have taken steps to minimise the extent to which such criticisms can continue to be levelled in this regard. In their guidance to police services, ACPO state that the five strands of monitored hate crime (race, religion, sexual orientation, disability and transgender) are the *minimum* that should be considered and the delineation of these five should not be used as an excuse to ignore other groups affected by hostility-based crime. Indeed, in the consultation process, 21 identifiable groups were considered before the five listed above were selected (ACPO, 2013b) on the basis of their prevalence, their likelihood of being motivated by hatred rather than vulnerability, their impact on community cohesion and their disproportionate impact on the victim (Mason-Bish, 2010). Nevertheless, the 2013 ACPO guidance is clear that agencies and partnerships are free to extend their own policy response to include the hostilities that they believe are either prevalent or are the source of anxiety to local communities.

In legislative terms, concerns about hierarchies of victimisation and 'selective' increases in punishment in England and Wales are also somewhat mitigated by Section 143(1) of the Criminal Justice Act 2003. The provisions here allow the courts to consider the *targeted nature* of the crime, together with a number of other factors that might indicate a greater degree of culpability, when calculating the seriousness of the offence, thereby allowing for the imposition of a greater punishment for hostility on the basis of characteristics not specifically stated within the Act (Sentencing Guidelines Council, 2004).

Finally (for our purposes), the concerns surrounding the fundamental issue of freedom of speech have also been widely addressed. Blazak (2011), for example, challenges the view that hate crime laws unacceptably infringe on people's freedom of speech, expression and belief. He acknowledges that critics worry that hate crime laws are used to punish politically unpopular speech and thought but, as he usefully points out, freedom of speech is not absolute. After all, he notes, one cannot shout 'fire' in a cinema that is not on fire any more than one can claim to have a bomb on a commercial aeroplane, and neither can we libel or slander another person.

Similarly, Norris (2008: 114), in considering whether an incitement to religious hatred law can ever be reconciled with the effective protection of free expression, concludes his thoughtful piece on the tensions that exist between the individual's expressive capacity to disparage and denigrate the views of others, and the right of religious communities to manifest their beliefs, by stating that:

> the symbolic condemnation of extreme intolerance serves to formally enshrine the importance of pluralism to society … hate speech laws thus prevent a situation in which the most forceful and bigoted voices in society suppress a true diversity of opinion. Well tailored restrictions of speech consequently do not overstep the mark when they ensure that expressive contributions are equally valued throughout society.

Indeed, Thompson (2012: 224) rightly states that the need for limitations to be placed on free speech were recognised by arguably their greatest defender, John Stuart Mill (1859: 56) who declared that:

> no one pretends that actions should be as free as opinions. On the contrary, even opinions lose their immunity, when the circumstances in which they are expressed are such as to constitute their expression a positive instigation to some mischievous act.

For Mill, then, it is the particular circumstances in which an opinion is uttered that determine whether or not it should be proscribed (Thompson, 2012). Bleich shares this view, concluding as he does that:

> restrictive laws are the most easily justified if they punish racist expression or racist opinion-as-motive when it inflicts significant harm to individuals or if it incites violence or stirs up extreme hatred, but not when it is merely offensive, even if hurtfully so.
>
> (2011: 932)

As such, Article 10 of the European Convention on Human Rights allows freedom of expression except for in certain limited circumstances where hatred is intended or likely to be stirred up as a result.

Thus far in this section of the chapter we have considered some (but clearly not all) of the arguments made in an attempt to address the very real concerns of critics. Through this process we have strayed a short way into some serious and persistent intellectual debates, but to summarise some of the key messages to have emerged from these discussions I hope you will forgive me for straying into the anecdotal momentarily. Not so long ago I was having a conversation with two close friends (who shall remain nameless here) who both work in different areas of service provision to victims of hate crime. We were discussing over dinner the subject of this chapter thus far, namely why it is that hate crime deserves recognition as a distinct category of crime, and whether or not the critics' view that all this is simply about preferential treatment for some at the expense of others has merit.

The reason I mention this here is because, quite simply, for me their responses encapsulated perfectly and simply the often complex nature of this debate. One explained that, for her, the focus on hate crime was not about preferential treatment, but about the importance of treating people equally rather than treating them the same. The simplicity of the illustrative example she gave belied the complexity of this controversial area:

> 'Assume' she said, 'that I have a room full of people and I offer them all a drink. If I treat them the same they'll all end up with a cup of tea with milk and two sugars. But of course some might not like or want tea. They might want tea without sugar. Or they might want an orange juice. Or water. But if I am treating them equally, then they'll still all end up with a drink, but it'll be a drink that is appropriate to their needs.'

By analogy, the focus on hate crime, then, is about ensuring that there is equity and fairness in protection from victimisation – that is, that basic human rights are protected – but with a recognition that this has to be achieved in different ways, for different people, who have different needs.

The example given by my other friend put a slightly different twist on a similar message:

> 'If' he hypothesised, 'I am in a bar having a drink and I decide to walk home, I should be able to expect that I will get home safely. That should be the case regardless of whether I am a young white male, or a disabled female or an elderly Asian man. But we know that the risks associated with doing so are different for different people often based upon their identifiable characteristics. The focus on hate crime is therefore about "equalising risk" to make sure that the outcome is equal for everyone regardless of their traits. To do that we might just have to invest a little more effort to get some people home safely than we do for others. But in the end, everyone one gets home in one piece.'

In other words, sometimes society simply has to do a little more for some to ensure that everyone has access to the same outcomes.

So where does all this leave us? Well, to my mind, whilst the concerns of critics may not have been put to bed in their entirety, they are not sufficient for us to abandon the concept of hate crime. Rather, they serve as something of a gauntlet thrown down to those of us who wish to further the cause.

Studying hate or hate studies?

Of course, one of the most obvious ways to continue to address the concerns of critics is to increase the knowledge that we possess about the subject area. However, information concerning different aspects of hate crime has hitherto been acquired in rather a disparate manner. For example, you will have undoubtedly noticed from the discussion in chapter four that much of the research into hate crime victimisation has been conducted in silos through the use of discrete categories. The fact that hate crime is socially constructed in the ways that it is (using broad categories, as our discussions in chapter one revealed), is largely because, as a concept, 'diversity' has been similarly constructed. Partly because of our need to simplify and categorise (see chapter five) we label individuals and groups according to certain (usually visually attributable) characteristics which, in terms of hate crime, are commonly *race, religion, sexual orientation, disability* and so on.

Blaine (2008) suggests that there are four perspectives that are useful in helping to understand this conceptualisation of diversity. The first, viewing diversity as a *demographic concern*, illustrates the variety of categories available and the weight we tend to afford some over others. For example, if you have a large group of people, naturally the people within that group will have different characteristics. They will have physical (such as weight and height), psychological (such as confidence or anxiety) and intellectual differences. They will also (most likely) have differences in sex, race, ethnicity, religion, social class, culture, disability and so on. As Blaine points out though, the first three are *individual differences* where everyone differs, and the others are *social differences*, where social grouping and categorising occurs. The social sciences predominantly study diversity using the latter, as do people generally when they identify others (and themselves), because social differences are more available and more informative. Try it for yourself – describe to yourself the next person that you see but that you don't know. How many social categories did you use as opposed to individual differences?

Blaine's second perspective relates to diversity as a *political concern*, which, of course, is particularly interesting for us given the discussions we have had so far in this book. Political conceptualisations of diversity tend to produce categories that relate to historically socially disadvantaged groups and, of course, can be linked to our discussions in chapter two concerning the emergence of hate crime as a contemporary social problem. For Blaine, there are two problems here. One is that by concentrating on historically disadvantaged groups we necessarily restrict the actual diversity of our environment (in other words we focus more on some groups than others – a point not lost on critics of identity politics), and the second is that the political usage of diversity focuses too much attention on *visible* differences to the detriment of those that are not so visually obvious.

The third perspective views diversity as an *ideological concern*, and, Blaine suggests, incorporates perceptions of qualities, or values, that *should* be present in a diverse society, which are subjective and often controversial. One set of values often proffered implies that diversity should be about a society where differences are welcomed and tolerated, resulting, in theory, in a harmonious coming together of different groups, as long as minority groups subscribe to the values of the majority group. A second set of values, often referred to as *multiculturalism*, views diversity as a patchwork quilt, where groups are connected to form a society, but where the values and uniqueness of each group are preserved and differences are more actively maintained. Both have different implications for minority groups, and I suspect you may have heard debates along these lines in politics, the media and/or amongst friends and acquaintances. Such debates, Blaine suggests, conflate both the description and ideology of diversity.

Blaine's final perspective views diversity as a *concern for social justice*. As he rightly states, social justice exists when all groups in a society are afforded the same rights and opportunities and their life outcomes are not unfairly constrained by prejudice and discrimination, and furthermore that the 'successes' of one group are not at the expense of others. However, he continues, as diversity increases in a community, so does the potential for relative disadvantage. As such, given that we know that prejudice and discrimination do indeed disadvantage different groups in different ways and in different places, viewing diversity as a lens through which to address issues of social inequality is important, and as such these efforts are frequently made with, for and on behalf of people within the socially constructed groups that we have already associated with hate crime.

And so, largely as a product of the issues described above, we are left with a number of well-established categories through which to explore the various dynamics of hate crime. Whilst examining hate crime via these discrete categories has, as we have seen, produced valuable information (and in many cases a plethora of recommendations from special interest groups relating to one category or another about what should be done) in relation to the issues impacting upon individuals and communities *within* those categories, there are, however, considerable constraints in employing this approach. For example, some of the resulting dilemmas are illustrated by Hull (2009: 408) in relation to crimes against the elderly in the US:

> as the nation becomes older and more racially and ethnically diverse, issues related to sexual orientation, gender, gender identity, and dis- ability will become more prevalent. It will become increasingly difficult to divine the particular motivation that led to a violent act against the elderly. When a gay, elderly, African American is victimized, will it be clear what motivated the attack? When a white, Jewish, disabled elderly female is robbed, is the offender guilty of a hate crime, guilty of attacking a vulnerable victim, or only guilty of the underlying robbery? These questions will present significant problems for courts in the future in the absence of a uniform approach to prosecuting hate crimes.

Of course, it is not just the courts that may well face challenges in this regard. This issue of *intersectionality*, based upon the rather obvious but seemingly often overlooked fact that we all possess multiple identities, has all sorts of implications for understanding hate and hate crime. For example, a small number of the studies that we examined in chapter four, particularly in relation to LGBT and disability hate crime, have also suggested that the presence of multiple identities interact in complex ways to potentially increase both the risk of being a victim *and* the effects of that victimisation on the individual. The problem here is that the hitherto dominant 'silo' approach described by Blaine (2008) has left a considerable void both in our understanding of these complex interactions across multiple identities *and* in terms of identifying how best to meet the needs of victims who experience these multiple 'hates'. As such, for me, furthering our understanding of intersectionality represents a critical issue, and given the expansive nature of our subject, and the sheer number of possible identity combinations, is likely to remain so for some time.

Similarly, as you will probably have also noticed from the discussion in chapter six, the silo approach to studying hate crime has not been confined just to issues relating to victims and victimisation. Just as we have tended to study victimisation in discrete categories, so too has there been a tendency to study those who offend against those categories in the same way. And so when we talk about 'hate offenders' what we are often really referring to are racists, or homophobes, or xenophobes or whatever. Rarely have we addressed offending behaviour across multiples of the various 'hates'. Moreover, we also noted in chapter six the tendency for explanations of hate motivated behaviour, and theorising in particular, to be firmly located within one discipline or another, and little that has sought to address the theoretical intersections that inevitably exist as a result.

Consequently, whilst studying hate in silos has yielded a range of potential answers from within the different disciplines, these have been somewhat isolated from each other and as such the answers proffered are necessarily incomplete. It is rather like having an elaborate jigsaw puzzle where all of the pieces individually reveal something, but without really knowing how to fit them together to see the bigger picture. Completing the jigsaw puzzle, and perhaps then finding ourselves in a better position find the answers that currently elude us, seems to me to represent another critical issue in our subject area. Fortunately, in recent years there has been some movement in this regard, most notably through calls for (and some signs of progress towards) a discipline of 'hate studies'.

In seeking to justify the need for, and establish, a field of hate studies, Stern (2005) has suggested that such an endeavour could help to address both the 'abundance of questions' and the 'urgent real-world needs' that hate crime clearly presents. As Stern (2005: 41) explains:

> my hope is that the removal of the blinders that afflict each of the disciplines that touch on hate will expand our thinking, not only about what we know but also about what we can do to improve our world, to make it less hateful and dangerous.

He further outlines his hopes and expectations for what *hate studies* might accomplish – to provide better answers to the many questions that we currently face; develop a common vocabulary amongst the various disciplines; encourage an integrated system of knowledge and research; provide a more holistic understanding of the components of hatred; provide testable theories for informed action; spur research on education; debunk myths about certain interventions on which we might be wasting time and money; help define the approaches that work; develop new initiatives; help to quantify the financial cost of hate; encourage governments and others to assess the impact of important decisions of intergroup hate; produce reports incorporating important issues identified by each of the component academic disciplines; guide policy; address hate on campus and spur research and new programmes.

Of course, one might baulk a little at the extent of Stern's hopes and expectations, although he does suggest a number of practical ways for making *hate studies* a reality, based primarily upon multidisciplinary work that might be undertaken within universities. On the other hand, Iganski (2008: 5) suggests that the various disparate fields with an interest in hate crime need not be collectively relabelled as 'hate crime studies', but rather that:

> conceptualising 'hate crime' as a scholarly domain implies a conversation between scholars rooted in different fields of study and different disciplines. This is an analytical conversation distinguished by a focus on the synergies between different forms of oppressive and discriminatory violence, and their intersections where relevant, with respect to the experiences of victims and offenders with a view to informing effective intervention, whether that be the use of criminal law against, or rehabilitation of, offenders, and support and counseling for victims.

Whether we engage in 'hate studies' or in 'analytical conversations', there is a need, as Perry (2010: 31) puts it, for the disciplines to talk to each other 'to enable a richer, more sophisticated understanding of a very complex phenomenon'. Achieving this sophistication is clearly an important task, and there are some forums where this is indeed facilitated. In particular, the *Journal of Hate Studies*, which describes itself as

> an international scholarly journal promoting the sharing of inter-disciplinary ideas and research relating to the study of what hate is, where it comes from, and how to combat it [that] reflects the optimism that as hate is understood, it can be contained and controlled allowing for persons to reach their full human potential without fear of retribution

is perhaps the most obvious of these. In addition, Perry's (2009) five-volume edited collection, which includes contributions from across the various disciplines, similarly contributes to this goal, as too will (I hope) my next project, which is to produce with colleagues a wide-ranging and interdisciplinary edited collection entitled the *International Handbook of Hate Crime* (Hall *et al.*, 2014, forthcoming). The embryonic International Network for Hate Studies represents another new and important scholarly development in this area too. Improving our knowledge base, and the sophistication with which we do so, seems to me to be an important undertaking in furthering our holistic understanding of hate crime.

Bridging the gap between policy and scholarship

Whilst seeking to increase our knowledge and understanding of hate crime and its various complex facets (and to continually improve the sophistication with which we do so) is obviously important, in my view it is not enough. For me, using this knowledge to inform policy and other responses represents a critical undertaking for scholarship. Indeed, the general involvement of academia in the administration of government has been fairly common in the US for some time, and this has been progressively mirrored in recent years in England and Wales, where many policymakers in various hate crime circles both locally and nationally have, for a variety of reasons, become increasingly amenable to the idea of involving 'outsiders' in the policymaking process.

In a recent edited collection examining how we might better bridge the gap between policy and research, I reflected upon my experiences as an academic engaging with the world of policymaking (Hall, 2014). In doing so, I stated my belief that broadly there are two key issues that are crucial in bridging the 'two worlds' of academia (in this case, specifically criminology) and policymaking. First, it is important to ask questions about the *purpose of criminology*, and indeed academia more generally, and second, it is necessary to understand the *different cultures* of academia and policy-making.

In addition to thinking, writing and teaching, I have always taken the view that criminologists should be able to offer something of more immediate and practical value. But whatever our individual beliefs about the purpose of criminology, whether we intend it or not we are probably influencing policy and practice in one way or another (after all, the policymakers of the not too distant future may well be sitting in our classrooms and, logic would dictate, an educated and informed policymaker should be better than one who is neither), and as such, as academics we have a duty to behave responsibly in the things that we do.

Central to this is developing an *understanding and appreciation of the differing working styles and cultures* of academia and policymaking. For me, these cultures differ along a number of different issues. The first concerns the notion of *urgency*. Academic research and writing takes time (often, a lot of time) and this is time that those in the world of policymaking rarely, if ever, have. Research findings that are produced months, or even years, after the research starts may be hugely important in academic circles, but they are often of little use to policymakers who need solutions today, tomorrow or in some cases, yesterday.

The second relates to the issue of *responsibility*. As academics we all have a responsibility, even a duty, to the world of policymaking, but in comparative terms, an academic's level of responsibility is usually pretty low. If we critique a policy, or a response to something, in our writing or teaching, generally that's where our input can end if we choose. Doing something about it, whatever 'it' is, is someone else's problem (usually a practitioner). But with regard to our engagement with policy and practice, either directly or indirectly, it is my belief that as academics our responsibility should increase significantly. Critical thinking is about much more than just being critical and in my view it is incumbent on us all as academics not just to offer criticism, but also to offer up genuine alternatives that address our criticisms. In this sense I share Le Grand's (2005) view that to not do so is intellectual laziness and irresponsible.

The third concerns the *linking of policy with theory and evidence*. The necessary pace and nature of policymaking means that on occasion this is done on the basis of 'common-sense' assumptions rather than on an evaluation of academic theory and evidence, which may simply not be available. Alternatively, such assumptions are made, and then the evidence sought to support them. The issue of the uncertainty surrounding the impact of exposure to hate on the Internet as a causal factor in hate offending serves as a prime contemporary example in this regard (discussed further below). As academics, then, I believe that it is important to furnish policymakers with theory and evidence (both positive and negative) relating to an issue wherever possible, and to seek to fill the gaps where both of these things are either absent or weak. Ultimately, I take the view that theoretically and empirically informed policy is likely, on balance, to be better policy.

A final point, which I have termed *the importance of lunch*, is a metaphor both for relatively short, convenient and to the point engagements between representatives of the 'two worlds', and for the importance of good working relationships, which of course are paramount to the effective, and above all smooth, transfer of knowledge. The reference to 'lunch' is indicative of the often very different realities of the 'two worlds': as an academic I have both knowledge and time (relatively speaking), whilst a policymaker/practitioner often has little of either (and I don't mean for a second to question the intellectual ability of practitioners here, just that they don't necessarily have the particular knowledge that as academics we can impart. If they did we wouldn't need to engage at all). Metaphorically speaking, then, much can be achieved in terms of knowledge transfer over 'lunch' where productive, real-time, 'analytic conversations' can take place, and which can provide a useful *addition* to the often lengthy research, writing and publishing process.

My experiences of working as an academic in and around the 'other world' of policymaking is that the two worlds can indeed usefully combine, but that an understanding of the working practices and cultures on both sides is crucial. Once this is achieved, the possibilities for bridging the gap between them can become considerable, valuable and, ultimately, can begin to impact on the issues that in the end concern us all. Of course this latter point leads us to the most important message of all, namely that as academics what we say and do can and does have real-life implications, whether we are yet to realise it or not. As Le Grand (2005: 322) rightly notes:

> Academics in government do have an important role to play, especially in the assessment of theory and evidence. Academics outside government also have a key role – in the long run, a more important one – in developing the relevant theories and in providing the evidence. But, wherever they are, academics have an obligation to behave responsibly. They have the power to change the world, and that power should not be exercised lightly.

The political prioritisation of hate crime

Meaningful engagement of the type discussed above can, inevitably, only take place if governments, and therefore policymakers, have an interest in furthering the hate crime agenda. In keeping with the theme of policy and politics, then, something that strikes me as particularly important is the extent to which hate crime is regarded as a political priority by governments. As we have seen, the role and political inclinations of the state (and its institutions) can have serious implications for shaping an environment in which hate can potentially flourish. The extent to which a country's political stance serves either to protect or infringe human rights therefore represents an important issue for consideration. In chapter three we noted various concerns relating to the (mis)treatment of different minority groups in a number of countries around the world, and one might reasonably assume that the numbers of recorded hate crimes in any given country are, at least in part, an indication of the importance (or otherwise) with which it is held politically. At the very least, the various calls for improvements to state responses in a number of countries (as noted in chapters three and eight) are an indicator of considerable concern in this regard.

Of course there are different ways in which the politics of a country can shape its policy responses to these issues. This is illustrated by Bleich (2007), for example, who notes that in recent years different countries of the European Union have pursued distinctive paths in their responses to hate crimes. To illustrate this Bleich highlights the primacy of a criminal justice approach in the UK, whilst Germany has devoted resources to civil society groups with the intention of countering right-wing extremism, and France has taken symbolic and educational approaches to the problem (hence, perhaps, the relative absence of hate crimes recorded by the authorities that we saw in chapter three). As Bleich (2007: 160–62) suggests:

> broadly speaking, states have choices to make about how much they use repressive policies aimed at preserving public order versus instructive policies aimed at promoting tolerance and liberal democratic values ... Most commentators agree that much has changed during the past few years, yet most also agree that each state's commitment to eradicating racist violence is not as strong as it could be. Developing nationally effective policies thus depends on learning from other states about the pragmatic steps a country can take. It also depends on responding to domestic actors who articulate concerns about specific problems and suggest possible solutions. Obeying this rule of thumb will go a long way toward limiting the impact of racist violence and toward promoting national cohesion.

Of course, 'commitment', the 'international learning process' and listening and responding to 'articulated concerns' are by no means guaranteed, as reflected in some of the global political stances on these issues that we have discussed previously. In comparative terms, then, in my view the UK is the 'world leader' in terms of responding to hate crimes. This position, as I have argued elsewhere (Hall *et al.*, 2009), is largely a product of the 'legacies of Lawrence', which have been instrumental in generating or accelerating far-reaching and multi-tiered changes to the UK's political and policy responses to hate crime.

The outcomes of this 'paradigm shift' in terms of radically changing the goals of policy and practice, which in many ways is still in progress, can be seen in the range of outcomes that to me set the UK apart from its international counterparts. These include, but are not limited to, *the broad and inclusive definitions of hate crime employed; the focus on appropriate service provision to victims and communities; the True Vision online (and other) third-party reporting system; the volume of incidents reported to the police; the number of diversity strands for which data is collected and published; the scope and strength of legal recognition for diversity issues; the number of cases prosecuted; the level of financial support thus far provided by government, to support the valuable work of NGOs in this area; the previous and current government's Hate Crime Action Plan; the True Vision smartphone app; the engagement with Independent Advisory Groups and other community representatives; the ACPO Hate Crime Policing Manuals; the hate crime 'diagnostic tool' for police and the demand from other countries for knowledge transfer.*

But, whilst the comparative position of the UK should be a source of some satisfaction, it should not become a source of complacency. In recent times, the political commitment of the UK government has attracted some criticism. In 2009, the tenth anniversary of the publication of the Public Inquiry into Stephen Lawrence's murder provided an opportunity to reflect on the extent of progress made in relation to the areas covered by the Inquiry's original recommendations. The consensus of opinion was that 'much had been achieved, but that much still remained to be done' (Hall *et al.*, 2009; EHRC, 2009b; Rollock, 2009; Stone, 2009). However, the period since the tenth anniversary has seen a change of government, and for the first time since the Inquiry was originally published, the 'hate crime' agenda is not under the guardianship of the administration that instigated it. This situation has been the source of some anxiety for many who hold concerns relating to the present government's desire and commitment to further pursuing the agenda set in motion by its predecessor (Muir, 2012), not least in times of considerable financial austerity (the broader impact of which we have already considered in relation to hate crime).

In what are increasingly difficult times globally, sustaining political interest and creating and maintaining an environment in which hate cannot flourish therefore seem to me to be critical issues for the furtherance of the hate crime agenda, not least because, as we have seen throughout this book, much still remains to be done in terms of addressing hate and hate crime internationally. Notwithstanding recent domestic concerns, I would still contend that those of us in the UK are in a *comparatively* privileged position in this regard, although much still remains to be done here too.

However, the question of how to secure the protection of human rights of others elsewhere in the world where combating hate crime has been, and remains, somewhat less of a political priority (perhaps shaped by deep-rooted cultural differences – see chapter six) remains both problematic and unanswered. As Perry (2001: 179) suggests:

> hate-motivated violence can flourish only in an enabling environment … such an environment historically has been conditioned by the activity – or inactivity – of the state … State practices, policy, and rhetoric often have provided the formal framework within which hate crime – as an informal mechanism of control – emerges.

Examples in this regard are not hard to find – Russia's courts have already banned gay pride events for 100 years, nine regions in Russia have outlawed the promotion of 'homosexual propaganda', and in the time between my writing this and you reading it the ban may well have been extended into national law (Grekov, 2013). Elsewhere, we have already noted the popularity of the anti-immigration position of Greece's Golden Dawn party, and Italian political rhetoric concerning the Roma. We might also consider France's 'voluntary repatriation' of Roma in 2010 and the controversial banning of the niqab and burqua in public spaces in 2011 to be influential in shaping an environment conducive to the development of prejudice.

The monumental challenge in this regard, it would seem, is to secure the commitment of states in terms of rhetoric, policy and practice, in the creation of *dis-enabling* environments where the human rights of all are both respected and protected. The issues discussed in chapter three, which only really scratched the surface, are illustrative of the sheer magnitude of this task. On the available evidence, then, international organisations seeking to improve national responses to hate crime undoubtedly have some way to go in this unenviable undertaking.

The far right and extremism

An area of increasing concern with links to both politics and the potential for adversely shaping a 'hate-friendly' environment is that of the far right and other forms of extremism. As Iganski (2008) points out, over the years there has been something of a tradition amongst mainland European and US scholarship of framing analyses of the hate crime problem in terms of organised far-right violence, despite the relatively low number of incidents that can be directly attributed to such groups. Conversely, in Britain, attention has largely been paid to the relative 'failure' of such groups. For example, Sibbitt (1997) has questioned the role and responsibility of organised hate groups and the 'far right' in Britain, arguing that if one examines the number of hate crimes that extremist organisations are *directly* involved in, then in fact such groups play a marginal role with regard to the perpetration of hate offences.

Similarly, Gordon (1994) has suggested that the extent of racist violence in Britain meant that the blame could not be attributed to such groups, and more recently Roxburgh (2002) has noted the importance of maintaining a wariness of neo-Nazi groups such as Blood and Honour/Combat 18 in this country, but suggests that they are 'little more than ideologised hooligans' who are 'tiny in number' (2002: 244 and 245). Thus, the role of such groups in shaping and influencing public opinion and behaviour has been of somewhat greater interest than their direct perpetration of hate offences (although as Gordon, 1994, points out, their collective record of offending speaks for itself), not least because of recent increases in the popularity of many far right political parties across Europe in particular (Renton, 2003; Eatwell, 2000; Zaslove, 2004; Chakraborti and Garland, 2009; Fekete, 2012).

Undoubtedly, however, concerns relating to the far right and other forms of organised hate and extremism are becoming more acute. Writing of the US, Beirich and Potok (2009: 255) have warned of a 'perfect storm' consisting of economic meltdown, high rates of non-white immigration, rapid demographic change and the election of a black president that is fuelling a rise in organised hate groups, particularly those based around race. It is this hate movement and the associated violence and domestic terrorism, they suggest, that now present the most direct challenge for law enforcement. These concerns are reflected in the Southern Poverty Law Center's (SPLC) annual intelligence reports, which document hate groups and other extremists in the US. The SPLC's (2013) records document the current existence of 1,018 known hate groups, including neo-Nazis, Klansmen, white nationalists, neo-Confederates, racist skinheads, black separatists, border vigilantes and others, noting a 69 per cent rise in the number of such groups since 2000. The SPLC also recorded a 755 per cent increase (from 149 in 2008 to 1,274 in 2011) in the number of Patriot groups including armed militia in the first three years of Barak Obama's presidency. Interestingly, in light of our discussions above, the SPLC partially attribute this rise in extremism to 'mainstream media figures and politicians who have used their platforms to legitimize false propaganda about immigrants and other minorities and spread the kind of paranoid conspiracy theories on which militia groups thrive' (SPLC, 2013).

Of course the rise, and indeed diversification, of extremist groups is not confined to the US. In a wide-ranging piece of research examining far-right extremist activities across a number of EU States (including Austria, Bulgaria, Cyprus, the Czech Republic, Denmark, France, Finland, Germany, Hungary, Italy, Netherlands, Poland, Slovakia, Spain, Sweden, the UK, Norway and Switzerland), Fekete (2012: 3) identifies a number of emerging critical issues. The research discusses the *'texture of far right subcultures'* and delineates '*the various stages that the far Right go through as its members make their way from racist ranting and the peddling of hate online, to violence and death on the streets, to the stockpiling of weapons in preparation for race war*'. Having examined more than 100 cases of far right violence occurring across Europe between 2010 and 2012, Fekete suggests that these events should not be viewed as a series of individual acts, but rather as something far more sinister and threatening.

In particular, she points to the development of 'new geographies of hate' with certain areas at significant risk from propaganda and violence associated with fascism. She also highlights Europe's growing counter-jihadi movement and network of 'defence leagues', and the associated dangers posed when anti-democratic tendencies on societal, institutional and state security fronts combine. Fekete (2012) also points to the increasing attraction of extremist political parties offering simplistic messages based upon the ideal breeding grounds of 'ultra-patriotism' and nativism (themselves fuelled by moderate political rhetoric around 'multiculturalism', national identity and 'core values'), whilst also offering scapegoats for anger and disillusion fuelled by economic strain. Just as worrying, she also identifies what she labels a 'shocking lack of professionalism' among key sections of European police and intelligence services in responding to the threats posed. Moreover, she also records incidents that strongly suggest police biases towards, and collusion with, far right groups.

Closer to home, the emergence of 'defence leagues' in the UK has raised a number of interesting issues. Although a number of such groups exist, Garland and Treadwell (2010: 20) suggest that the most prominent, the English Defence League (EDL) and an affiliated group, Casuals United, have recently emerged from the fringes of football hooligan subculture and while sharing some characteristics with established far right parties, mark a different manifestation of the fusing of football hooligan casual culture and extremist politics and pose the most significant threat to community cohesion in Britain's inner cities since the heyday of the National Front in the mid-to-late 1970s.

The 'different manifestation' to which Garland and Treadwell refer relates to the EDL's supposed opposition to the British National Party, Combat 18 and other far right groups, even though, they point out, they do appear to share ideas, street tactics and, indeed, members. Nevertheless, Garland and Treadwell suggest that the EDL's 'relatively thin veneer of respectability' is based upon (at least in theory) its claims to only oppose radical Islam, rather than being racist *per se*. Furthermore, in an attempt to achieve a degree of legitimacy, they note that the EDL have also positioned themselves as pro-Israeli (and therefore not anti-Semitic), pro-gender equality and supportive of gay rights (although Garland and Treadwell question the extent to which the 'rank and file' share these positions).

Thus, the EDL's position is based upon overt hostility towards Muslim communities which, Garland and Treadwell suggest, is borne out of many of the issues that we have already discussed above, and indeed reflect senti-ments that can be traced back hundreds of years. Ultimately, these consist of a strong (but erroneous) sense of injustice that these communities are being unfairly allocated resources at the expense of poor, white, working-class people, and that the interests of Islam have been elevated above those of the 'English' by government. Reflecting the view expressed by Fekete (2012, above), the EDL therefore 'offers the chance for disenfranchised commu-nities to latch onto a cause that seems to embody a sense of national identity and belonging while simultaneously presenting a scapegoat for much of those communities' ills' (Garland and Treadwell, 2010: 32–33). As Treadwell and Garland (2011) suggest in a later case study on the EDL, these feelings of disadvantage and marginalisation prompt resentment and anger, particu-larly in young males who feel their concerns are not being listened to. As such, they suggest, the members of the EDL in their study constructed a specific form of violent masculinity that was socio-structurally generated and individually psychologically justified, resulting in their disenchantment manifesting itself in hostility towards their identified scapegoat. More gen-erally, Lambert and Githens-Mazer (2011) have also documented a 'dra-matic' rise in the number of anti-Muslim demonstrations by the EDL and its sister organisations in recent years, resulting in increased fear and anxiety within Muslim communities.

Although not quite the 'seemingly obligatory chapter on far right perpe-trators of "hate crime"' that Iganski (2008: 15) suggests is to be found in many scholarly texts, this necessarily brief discussion of some of the issues in this area suggests that the apparent global growth and evolution of far right and other avenues of extremism represents a critical issue within our subject area (both in terms of understanding and responding), particularly given that many of the causal and motivating factors identified above show no signs of abating any time soon.

Cyberhate

A further critical issue that has strong (but not exclusive) connections to organised hate groups is that of hate on the Internet, or *cyberhate*. Over the past twenty years or so, interest in, and concern about, the role of the Internet in relation to hate and hate crime has grown exponentially as the Internet has rapidly become *the* most important tool for the distribution of hateful material. Consequently, the Internet has provided a number of 'new' and important avenues for investigation, and as such I should make it absolutely clear that it is not my intention to try to cover all of the issues associated with 'hate on the Internet' here. The complexities of the issues involved means that this aspect of our subject area is clearly deserving (and indeed is the subject) of dedicated volumes. Rather, I will simply (and necessarily) provide an overview of some of the key elements associated with cyberhate that, for me, make it a critical issue.

The Internet as a vehicle for hate

The Internet presents a considerable 'new' set of challenges for those seeking to respond to hate crimes, not least because it provides an efficient, effective, anonymous and often largely unregulated vehicle for the promotion of hateful and prejudiced messages. In particular, concerns exist about the ease with which the Internet allows and facilitates the spread of hateful views, opinions and materials to a potentially unprecedented size of audience. As Meddaugh and Kay (2009) suggest, the technological, geographical and economic advantages of the Internet have proved to be of immense value to hate groups in terms of promoting their messages, recruiting people to their cause, expanding their base to include younger audiences, pursuing individuals who do not fit the stereotypical image of the hate movement and facilitating other activities that promote hate such as online music and video games. They also point out that the Internet has allowed these groups to expose people who would not actively seek out hate material online to their messages through the use of unsolicited emails and misleading weblinks.

In addition, Caiani and Parenti (2009) suggest that the Internet also provides hate groups with the *potential* to generate collective identities through the creation of a virtual 'community', to develop organisational contacts and for easing the process of mobilisation by providing cheap and widespread communication. As such, they too recognise the importance of the Web in allowing such groups to disseminate propaganda, incite violence, raise funds, recruit new followers and reach a mass audience with unprecedented ease whilst simultaneously defying traditional geographical and temporal boundaries. That said, however, they do highlight the contested position of scholars in this area, where it seems there is a lack of consensus about the true function of the Internet in relation to a number of these activities.

Nevertheless, with regard to the communicative messages contained on US hate group websites, an interesting study by McNamee *et al.* (2010) concluded that these centre on four themes – those that seek to educate others, those that encourage participation both within the group and amongst the wider public, those that invoke divine privilege and those that indict external groups and organisations. These four themes can, they suggest, function together to reinforce the group's identity, reduce external threats and recruit new members. Similarly, an interesting examination of the use of new social media by the far right across Europe is provided by Fekete (2012), who discusses examples of the different ways these groups exploit the Internet in countries including Bulgaria, the Czech Republic, Denmark, Finland, France, Germany, Italy, the Netherlands, Poland, Spain, Sweden and Finland.

Furthermore, these issues extend beyond 'traditional' hate-based websites (often run by the groups themselves), which arguably predominantly attract those already of a hateful predisposition, to the use of social networking and interactive blogs and forums where more subtle expressions of hate and prejudice may be aired to a wider, younger and less predisposed audience. For example, a US study examining the content of newspaper online forums relating to American Indians (Steinfeldt *et al.*, 2010: 1) indicated that 'a critical mass of online forum comments represented ignorance about American Indian culture and even disdain toward American Indians by providing misinformation, perpetuating stereotypes, and expressing overtly racist attitudes'.

More recently, the Simon Wiesenthal Center's fourteenth annual Digital Terror and Hate Report (2013) examined approximately 20,000 problematic websites, social networking pages, forums and online games and apps, and raised concerns about a 'subculture of hate' that has formed online. More specifically, Keats *et al.* (2011) make reference to what they suggest is the location for the biggest increase in digital hate – social media sites – which facilitate the appearance of hate on the mainstream Internet. As an illustrative example, they note that Facebook has hosted groups including *Kill a Jew Day, Kick a Ginger Day, Hitting Women, Holocaust is a Holohoax and Join if you Hate Homosexuals*. Of course, other social media – YouTube, Twitter, Google and so on – are not immune from exploitation in similar ways. The increase in the use of the Internet as a vehicle for hate is therefore seemingly undeniable, be it by organised hate groups or those expressing prejudice and hostility in a more casual manner. What is less than certain, however, are the impacts, either direct or indirect, that might occur as a result, and also what might be done to address the issue of hate on the Internet.

The impact of hate on the Internet

Issues relating to both the direct and indirect impacts of hate on the Internet generally fall into two categories: those that affect individuals as perpetrators or potential perpetrators, and those that affect victims and communities. With regard to the former, whilst the Internet can obviously be used by offenders to directly threaten, harass and intimidate their victims, the link between online hate material and the incitement of violence in others is less clear. For example, a literature review conducted by the Institute for Homeland Security Solutions (IHSS, 2009: 2) concluded that:

> the popular media have generally raised alarm about ... online deviance ... resulting in general agreement that the Internet is a powerful instrument for influencing certain behaviors at a minimum or is directly responsible for deviant behaviors altogether. However, within the scientific community, there is less conviction about the extent to which the Internet has served as an important tool for influencing initiation into any of these behaviors.

Indeed, in their guidance to police officers, ACPO (2013b) express similar caution in their claim that Internet hate 'is thought to have a motivating impact on individuals with propensity to hostility or violence through hate crime'. So, whilst common sense might suggest a causal link between exposure to hate on the Internet and subsequent related offending behaviour, the reality is that the theoretical, practical and methodological challenges of firmly establishing such a link are considerable. Indeed, Harris *et al.* (2009) suggest that problems with the reliable collection of data makes it impossible to make viable judgements on which prosecutions could be brought, and that the extent and influence of hate speech on the Internet is overstated.

Consequently, our understanding of the impact this can have on individuals in terms of shaping both their attitudes and behaviour, regardless of whether they are actively 'consuming' the material of hate groups or inadvertently reading derogatory comments posted on a news blog, remains uncertain. It may be, however, that some insight might be drawn from the research into online self-harm and self-injury groups, which has 'illuminated some disturbing correlates to self-injury behaviors among adolescents' (IHSS, 2009: 4). But nevertheless, this remains an area in considerable need of research if the role of the Internet is to be fully understood in terms of its ability to incite others to violence.

With regard to the impact that online hate can have on its targets, the limited information available mirrors the wider research literature that highlights the disproportionate harm that hate crime can have on victims and those close to victims. In considering what these impacts might be, Keats *et al.* (2011) suggest that, although consensus in this area is rare, most commentators agree that the harms of speech that *threatens and incites violence* are sufficiently serious to warrant prohibiting, although the severity will likely vary depending upon the clarity with which violence is encouraged, the specificity with which individuals or groups are identified and obviously whether or not the targets are aware that they are being targeted online. A second area of concern, they suggest, relates to online content that intentionally inflicts *emotional distress*. They recognise that although once again this will be context specific, it is likely to include content that is individually targeted, especially threatening or humiliating, repeated or reliant on especially sensitive or outrageous material. A third area that they identify relates to speech that *harasses* the victim, a fourth that *silences or devalues counter speech*, and a fifth that exacerbates hatred or prejudice by *defaming* an entire group. Moreover, Keats *et al.* (2011) also acknowledge the broader potential for hate on the Internet to imperil digital citizenship. Similarly, Cohen-Almagor (2011: 1–2) suggests that 'hate speech is intended to injure, dehumanize, harass, intimidate, debase, degrade, and victimize the targeted groups, and to foment insensitivity and brutality against them'.

Whilst the general claims made about *why* being targeted online might 'hurt more' seem plausible given the parallels with the existing literature concerning 'offline' victimisation, very little research specifically examines victims' direct experience of cyberhate. Anecdotally, however, the views of those affected do seem to suggest similar outcomes. For example, as part of my submission to the *Inter-Parliamentary Coalition for Combating Anti-Semitism Task Force on Internet Hate* on behalf of the *Cross-Government Hate Crime Independent Advisory Group* in 2011, I presented a range of anecdotal evidence suggesting that direct targets of Internet hate experience significant and ongoing feelings of fear, threat and intimidation, fuelled by the knowledge that their victimisation is encouraged and promoted to a wide audience of potential offenders by individuals 'hiding' in cyberspace. The impact on child victims was also of considerable concern, and again there are perhaps parallels to be drawn with the experiences of victims of cyberbullying, where the impacts are known to affect issues such as self-esteem, levels of confidence, fear and anxiety, loneliness, suicide and general mental and emotional well-being (ADL, 2008; O'Brian and Moules, 2010).

In addition to the direct impact of hate on the Internet, the potential indirect impact that hate material can have is also an area of interest. In particular, concerns exist about the potential provided by the Internet for the general rather than specific incitement of hatred, the promotion of pre-judicial views and negative stereotypes and for the intimidation of certain identifiable communities. Indeed, ACPO (2013a) reflect these latter concerns, stating their belief that 'hate material can damage community cohesion and create fear'. These wider impacts mirror the *in terrorum* effect of hate crimes that we have previously considered, and are of course inextricably, and potentially causally, linked to the direct impacts outlined above, particularly if one applies the common-sense view that exposure to hate on the Internet has the potential to increase the likelihood of physical offending.

Another interesting issue in this regard relates to the ability of individuals to critically assess the information presented to them. For example, Meddaugh and Kay (2009) note that research from the US as far back as 2002 suggested that 94 per cent of college students rely on the Internet for their research (indeed I have often wondered myself what the outcome would be if I set my students coursework and prohibited their use of the Internet, but I digress). They also suggest that whilst many students enjoy the convenience of the Internet, very often they are not equipped with the critical skills necessary to evaluate the legitimacy of the information presented to them. As such, material on the Internet may be able to achieve an undeserved 'legiti-macy' in the minds of many, and thus the uncritical and passive absorption of information that is now much more freely available on the Internet and through social media has the *potential* to shape the perceptions, and pre-judices, of people in ways that would not have been possible before.

Of course, this issue doesn't just apply to students. In applying this general principle, Meddaugh and Kay's (2009) examination of Stormfront's (cred-ited as the first hate website) use of 'reasonable racism' suggests a discourse that appears less virulent than traditional hate speech and therefore more palatable to the naïve reader. It is, they argue, precisely this approach that appears to 'legitimise' their position and therefore may provide comfort to a disaffected but uncritical eye, making this use of softer language (and therefore the website itself) particularly dangerous in terms of spreading hate. Moreover, this point potentially extends beyond overt and subtle forms of specific hate material. Given some of the issues that we have addressed already in chapters six and eight, one might reasonably extend this concern to the ability of people generally to critically appraise the political and other rhetoric that they are exposed to through the Internet and other forms of mass media.

Control, regulation and freedom of expression

When considering how best to respond to hate on the Internet, it is important of course to recognise the immense positive value of the Internet generally, and as we have already debated, to be respectful of people's individual freedoms and rights. Indeed, as ACPO (2013a) point out, whilst there is plenty of material on the Internet that may be offensive, very little of it is actually illegal. Consequently, the control and regulation of hate material on the Internet is complex, not just because of the definitional, practical, legal and indeed global challenges involved, but also because of the moral dilemmas it presents surrounding whether or not *freedom of speech* or *freedom from discrimination* should be prioritised (Brennan, 2009).

This dilemma is further complicated by the extent to which offenders might seek to 'excuse' their actions by using the defence of freedom of speech and expression when such behaviours are often clearly inconsistent with the principles of such rights (as discussed above). Conversely, it is important that any potential legal response to this issue should not be used by any government as a similar excuse to suppress legitimate freedom of expression for views with which it may disagree. Whilst hate on the Internet should be responded to, such responses must still be respectful of the rights of citizens to freely express legitimate views.

So what responses might be usefully employed? Although there is not the space here to do justice to the range of issues deserving of attention in this regard, there is a prevailing view within the literature that legislation is frequently inadequate in this area and that law enforcement responses are also frequently similarly inadequate in such cases. Indeed, ACPO (2013b) recognise the often 'erratic' and 'poor' police response to Internet hate crime in the UK, largely caused by the considerable operational challenges that Internet hate crime poses the agencies of the criminal justice system. These are identified by ACPO as: *establishing the jurisdiction of the crime in terms of the country and force area where the offender posted the material; the anonymous nature of most offending material; the unwillingness of, or legal restraint on, internet industry bodies to disclose user identity; the lack of clear policy guidance; a lack of knowledge amongst many investigating officers and the high workload of force forensic IT specialists.*

Again, a lack of space prevents a full discussion of the wide range of activities currently being undertaken to address the problem of hate on the

Internet, but a useful account of some of the strategies currently being employed around the world is provided by the British Institute of Human Rights on behalf of the Council of Europe (2012b: 5). They suggest that:

> [the] various initiatives undertaken by NGOs in Europe and elsewhere ... can be broadly divided into initiatives designed to monitor hate speech, often in order to remove abusive sites or comments; educational initiatives which aim to address the underlying causes or bring the problem to wider attention; meetings, networks and conferences which allow for exchange of experience and good practice on combating hate speech; work with victims or communities to counter the effects of hate speech; and work with ISPs or governments to influence policy.

So, whilst we have necessarily only scratched the surface of the problem of hate on the Internet here, the inherent complexities and challenges associated with the issue are plentiful enough, in my view, to warrant its inclusion as a critical issue within our subject area.

Concluding comments

Throughout this chapter we have considered a number of issues in the field of hate crime that, in my view, can be regarded as 'critical' for a variety of reasons. Of course, this view is entirely subjective and certainly not exhaustive, and again I offer my apologies if I have failed to cover anything in particular that you consider to be worthy of 'critical' status. Two significant omissions that spring readily to mind are *hate crime in sport* (see Hawkins, 2014 forthcoming, for a wide-ranging consideration of this particular issue) and *hate crime on university and college campuses*. Both of these represent important (and in the case of the former, re-emerging) areas of concern and I hope you will forgive me for omitting them here. As I stated in the introduction to this chapter, however, the line regrettably has to be drawn somewhere.

Usefully though, this brings us conveniently back to the expansive nature of our subject area, and is illustrative of its inherent and perhaps inevitable, complexities, which of course have been the central focus of this book. Having considered a wide range of issues in the preceding pages, it is now time to take stock of what we know, what we think we know, what we do not know and in what direction(s) we ought to be heading. In the following conclusions to this book, then, I shall revisit the seven questions posed in the preface and consider the extent to which we have satisfactorily answered them.

Conclusions

To start to draw this book to a close, let's return to where we started. In the preface I stated that, for me, criminology was about finding answers to seven basic questions – *What* is the problem? *When* is it occurring? *Where* is it occurring? *How much* of it is there? *Who* is involved or affected? *Why* is it occurring? And, crucially, *what should we do* to make the problem better? Throughout the chapters of this book we have addressed each of these and, it is probably fair to say, none of them have been answered to our complete satisfaction. Despite significantly increasing interest in hate crime as a scholarly and policy domain in recent times, and the significant progress that has clearly been made in many areas of that domain, the fact that there remain more questions than definitive answers is telling, and indicative of the relative novelty and undoubted complexity of our subject area. This situation also tells us that if (and at this juncture it is quite a big 'if') we are to eventually provide comprehensive answers to these questions, those of us with an interest in doing so have plenty of work left to do. In this final section, then, I shall briefly revisit each of the seven questions with a view to identifying some of the gaps in knowledge and understanding that we have yet to properly fill.

What is the problem?

Chapter one clearly demonstrated the complexities involved in answering even the most basic of questions – *what is hate crime?* – and as we saw in chapter nine, this leaves the subject somewhat vulnerable to detractors. This lack of conceptual consensus, and the seemingly expansive nature of hate crime can, as Chakraborti (2010) rightly points out, overshadow the efforts of scholarship to be constructive in providing comprehensive and purposeful answers to each of the other six questions.

It is not my intention to revisit debates that we have already covered elsewhere in this book, but answering this question clearly remains a key issue and undoubtedly has considerable implications for our understanding of, and our ability to answer questions relating to, many (if not all) other aspects of our subject area. For example, the expansive nature of hate crime means that beyond the moral questions that we have already explored concerning who to include under the hate crime 'umbrella', the more groups that are ultimately included in our conceptualisation, the more questions there are to be answered about a whole range of factors relating to those groups, and as such our understanding of many aspects of hate crime necessarily remains underdeveloped, and in some cases, substantially incomplete.

Similarly, the 'traditional' categories employed within many definitions of hate crime around the world are rather generic. What, for example, does 'race' mean, both in reality and in popular conceptualisation? And how do they differ? There are numerous different 'races', but a cursory glance at the literature will tell you that 'race' has predominantly been interpreted as black and white, leaving gaps in our knowledge and understanding about other races that are now only slowly beginning to be addressed. The same can be said for 'ethnicity', and for the other broad categories that are used in the construction of hate crime – what do we mean by 'disability', 'sexual orientation', 'transgender', 'faith', or any of the other generic terms employed? The simplicity of the terms used therefore masks a plethora of dynamics that in many instances are yet to be properly understood.

Finding an answer to the question *what is hate crime?* also depends upon the breadth of our interpretation of the subject. Beyond the recognition of certain groups, what else should it entail? Should hate crime refer only to those offences perpetrated by organised extremists? Or should we concentrate instead on the 'ordinary'? Or both? Moreover, should we recognise only crimes, and if so what types, or should we include incidents too? There are pros and cons all round. Concentrating only on the extreme discounts much from the equation. Similarly, focusing only on crimes (be they 'extreme' or 'ordinary') will likely reduce the size of the problem and arguably ease the burden on criminal justice and other resources, but ignoring low-level incidents, where it seems most 'hate' manifests itself, may hinder efforts to address the escalation of offending that Allport theorised (see chapter five). Our interpretation of the question in this regard can, as we saw in chapters three, seven and eight, have some serious implications for understanding and responding to hate crime.

We have also explored the implications of the use of the term 'hate crime' as something of a collective, 'catch all' label. There remains considerable debate amongst both scholars and practitioners about the meaning and value of the label itself, which is perhaps not surprising given our previous discussions about the extent to which 'hate crimes' are in fact motivated by 'hate'. So is *hate crime* the term we should be using? If not, assuming we wish to keep the word 'crime' (itself debatable given the nature of many incidents) what prefix would be preferential – *prejudice, bias, hostility, targeted, difference, human rights, vulnerability* – something else perhaps (see Chakraborti and Garland, 2012, for an interesting consideration of this point)? The recent emergence of the term 'mate crime' to describe hostility towards people with disabilities, reflecting the extent of perpetration by those who are acquainted with their victim (as 'friends', relatives, carers and so on, as opposed to being 'strangers'), is an interesting contemporary example in this regard (see Thomas, 2012, for a useful discussion of this issue). Of course, whilst this differing terminology may be useful in highlighting dynamics specific to one particular form of hate crime, it is unlikely to be reflective of the facets of all, and therefore the prospect of employing multiple terminologies to describe different aspects of hate crime makes the question that we set out to answer even more complicated. Each of the labels available to us will, it seems, bring their own limitations and complications.

It seems to me, then, that the complexities associated with identifying and explaining precisely what the problem is simply serve to illustrate that 'hate crime' means different things to different people (in lay, scholarly, political and practitioner terms), and this relative lack of consensus has important implications for the breadth and depth of our knowledge about other facets of the subject, as we shall additionally see shortly. Moreover, given the importance attached to victims' knowledge and comprehension of what they are experiencing in seeking interventions (see chapter seven), the use of the word 'hate', where it might understandably be interpreted in its strictest, layman's sense, can be misleading and confusing in this process. Nevertheless, I think it is fair to say that the term 'hate crime' has nonetheless achieved relatively widespread recognition in recent years in both scholarly and practitioner circles, both within the UK and abroad, and as such, despite its inherent limitations it is here to stay. How we navigate the associated implications will therefore remain an important issue for everyone interested in hate crime.

When is it occurring?

The discussion in chapters one and two highlighted the point that whilst political, legal and academic interest in hate crime is a relatively contemporary development, the occurrence of events that we would now consider as such has a very long history, indeed across much of the world. As such, we are presented with one of the perennial questions facing historical interpretations of crime – *is the situation worse now than in the past?* Of course answering this question is far from straightforward. Are the events we are referring to comparable? What do we mean by 'the past'? How reliable is the evidence with which we are working? How have past events been interpreted (as Winston Churchill once famously remarked, history is always written by the victors)? Moreover, Sullivan (1999: 10) has argued that 'anyone who contends that America is as inhospitable to minorities and women today as it has been in the past has not read much history'. This rather begs the question that, if indeed the situation is better now than in 'the past', has this occurred because of, or in spite of, efforts to improve it?

Our answers to these questions are necessarily rather speculative, but nevertheless as we discussed in chapter six, our knowledge of history has important implications for our understanding of contemporary hate crime in all sorts of ways. Indeed, if we accept the old adage that history tends to repeat itself, a deeper understanding of history may well be important in predicting, understanding and preventing future occurrences of hate crime. For example, comprehending the historical aetiology of contemporary 'trigger events' (such as the anniversaries of significant events) may provide valuable insights in this regard, as might a greater understanding of how people have historically responded to bouts of particular political rhetoric. Similarly, historical evidence of the effects of previous periods of economic strain on the hate crime problem may yield useful information of somewhat more immediate value to those of us living in the midst of the global economic crisis.

In short, careful and thoughtful analyses of the *when?* question goes far beyond simply reflecting upon what has been. As Godfrey and Lawrence (2005: 1) rightly point out, 'a critical appreciation of the history of crime can inform current understandings of offending, and why historical events ... will continue to affect crime and criminal justice for many years to come'. Indeed, as they additionally point out, we would do well to remember that the past does indeed have a future.

Where is it occurring?

The information discussed in chapter three presented a picture of two extremes. Officially at least, there are plenty of places in the world where hate crime does not occur very often, or indeed does not occur at all. But the reality is that this is simply wrong, and to claim otherwise represents something akin to the 'Emperor's new clothes'. We can refute with some confidence any suggestions that hate crimes don't occur on the basis of the evidence provided by different national and international organisations that suggests a global presence in one form or another, the information derived from various victim surveys, the universal nature of prejudice that implies the potential for hostility wherever human beings are to be found, and (if one wishes to be slightly cynical) on the basis that our expansive conceptualisation of hate crime means that it would be hard for it *not* to occur everywhere.

But of course simply suggesting that hate crime in all probability happens all around the world inevitably masks a number of complexities. Variations in factors such as culture, politics, religion, economics, population demographics and so on, inevitably mean that *what*, and *how much* of what, occurs *where* will in all likelihood vary considerably both between and within different geographical locations. Expanding our knowledge about what is going on in different places is important for furthering our understanding of a number of hate crime's facets, including prevalence, victimisation, perpetration, and for developing and shaping appropriate responses and targeting resources. Clearly the efforts of organisations such as the OSCE, Human Rights Watch, Human Rights First and others are important in this endeavour, particularly where formal denials of a problem may persist.

Within national borders, progress has been made in understanding aspects of issues such as rural hate crime and hate crime in college and university environments. Whilst these are important in helping to fill gaps in knowledge about geographical variations (and are perhaps illustrative of the many variables involved here), we have really only scratched the surface of the much bigger picture of where hate crime is occurring, be it locally, nationally or internationally.

Furthermore, as we saw in the previous chapter, the *where* question has recently moved beyond the traditional constraints of physical geography, most notably in the form of *cyberhate* involving the Internet and social media, but also via other media outlets such as television. These developments have opened something akin to Pandora's box in terms of the inherent complexities of the numerous associated issues. Whilst this is proving to be an area for inquiry that is attracting considerable interest from a number of quarters, in the twenty-first century, it seems, hate knows no man-made boundaries, and with this comes even more avenues for exploration.

How much of a problem is it?

The expansive nature of hate crime, encapsulated in differences in what we mean by hate, by crime and by victims, clearly has profound implications for our attempts to establish its prevalence. As we suggested in chapter one, answering this question is problematic, with some of the very real ramifications highlighted in chapters three and four. Differing interpretations of what *hate crime* is – who can be a victim, who can't be a victim, what sorts of acts are included, which are excluded, the employment of broad or narrow interpretations of 'hate' and so on – mean that establishing any sort of measure, particularly in comparative terms, is difficult enough. But when we add into the mix the methodological complexities involved in undertaking such a task either as an official or an academic exercise, and the fact that hate crimes remain hugely underreported for a whole host of reasons, answering this question with any degree of accuracy arguably enters us into the realms of the impossible.

These uncertainties in providing an answer render this another contentious issue, not just in terms of differences in official statistics, but also in relation to the positions taken on this issue by scholars. In the UK, for example, Chakraborti (2010: 8) refers to the 'inexorably high levels of hate crime' whilst as we saw in chapter nine, writing from the US, MacNamara has described it as 'an almost non-existent problem' (2003: 526) – a conclusion that is not hard to arrive at if one accepts at face value the official statistics presented in chapter three. The extent to which one leans towards Chakraborti's view, or towards that proffered by MacNamara, will have implications not just for one's holistic understanding of hate crime and perceptions that a problem does indeed exist, but perhaps more importantly may significantly affect the extent to which it is considered a political priority and deserving of a response – after all, where is the incentive to invest increasingly scarce resources in a problem that seems not to officially exist (a position that on the evidence of chapter three is very real in many countries)?

Similarly, the claim that 'hate crimes are under-reported' both to the authorities and to a lesser extent to victim surveys (a perfectly sensible claim on the basis of the evidence presented in chapter four and one to which I wholeheartedly subscribe) also masks a myriad of discrete but crucial differences, not least because hate crimes are not uniformly under-reported across victim categories. The findings of the British Crime Survey that we considered in chapter four, for example, usefully illustrate some of the different rates at which under-reporting occurs, reflecting a host of different factors at work in relation to the issues of the knowledge, ability and desire of people to invoke some form of response (as we considered in chapter seven), or indeed in terms of responding to some form of victimisation survey. Furthermore, as the concept expands and more groups become included under the hate crime umbrella (either formally or informally), the more questions concerning prevalence arise – a point that is particularly pertinent given the importance of establishing 'prevalence' in the process of a category achieving formal recognition, as we saw in chapter nine. Consequently, we have a better idea (or at least we think we do) about the extent and nature of racist and homophobic offences where attention has in relative terms been concentrated for longer, than we do about the extent of hate crimes against people with disabilities, or against trans-people, or alternative lifestyles, where both formal and academic interest is far more recent.

Certainly then, establishing anything like a true picture of the extent of hate crime remains a serious challenge, with potentially serious implications for understanding and responding to the problem. It is important, in my view, that the somewhat patchy picture provided by issues such as under-reporting, the absence of uniform reporting and recording practices, the use (and effectiveness) of different research methodologies to survey victims, the extent to which such research is undertaken, the conceptualisation of hate crime as a process and so on, continue to be addressed. Doing so will help strengthen the evidence base upon which we might more convincingly draw others towards Chakraborti's position, and in so doing further the case for the formal prioritisation of, and greater scholarly interest in, hate crime. From here, we will be in a better position to broaden and deepen our knowledge of the subject – a position that is clearly important to achieve if we are to successfully address the problem in terms of developing informed responses, and indeed if we are to keep hate crime in the political spotlight in times of increased competition for the increasingly scarce resources available to tackle seemingly mounting social problems.

Who is involved or affected?

Beyond establishing numerical estimates of prevalence lies the key question of who is involved and/or affected. The simple answer to this question is, broadly, 'victims and communities' and 'perpetrators', as two sides of the same coin. But this simplicity, as will probably be abundantly clear by now, masks a myriad of complexities that once more can be attributed in substantial part to the social construction of hate crime. Let's briefly consider each of these in turn.

As we saw in chapter one, and illustrated in chapter three, who officially 'counts' as a victim of hate crime can differ between jurisdictions, although there is at least some common ground across the different conceptualisations, aided in part by the subscription of many states to the definitions of international organisations such as the OSCE. Nevertheless, as if this didn't complicate matters enough, the debate about who can, should or should not, be a victim of hate crime also extends well into the realms of academia. As we saw in chapter four, beyond the core of formally recognised victim categories, there are many more that could, or indeed perhaps should, be included. Clearly, increasing the number of potential victim groups necessarily increases the avenues for scholarship to explore – the more groups we recognise, the more there is to know about them.

As a consequence of this expansive position, there is plenty of scope for improving both our depth and breadth of knowledge in a number of areas. As Chakraborti (2010) acknowledges, there is not a single aspect of hate crime about which we can say that we know too much, and so there are plenty of gaps left to fill. I have argued elsewhere (Hall, 2012b) that whilst we can genuinely, but rather unhelpfully, make calls for improvements in our knowledge about everything, some key gaps stand out. For me, these gaps in knowledge are most notably found in relation to issues affecting those people and communities included under the broad categories of Gypsy and Traveller, transgender, refugee and asylum seekers, disability, and the impact on white and working-class victims of race hate crime. You may very well have others that immediately spring to mind, and the chances are that you are right, we probably do need to know more about those groups too. There is also a need to further our knowledge beyond broad generalisations of the impact of hate crime within these categories, which of course are not homogeneous. Not all victims of race hate, or homophobic hate, or disablist hate experience their victimisation in the same way, and understanding the subtle and not so subtle differences in this regard is another important avenue for further exploration.

Beyond the need to know more about the factors affecting those within and between discrete victim groups, the issue of *intersectionality* that we discussed in the previous chapter is screaming out for greater understanding. The traditional 'silo' approach to hate crime (viewing and researching it narrowly as 'racism', or 'homophobia' and so on) has undoubtedly served to further our knowledge about, and the interests of, these particular groups, but has by and large failed to properly acknowledge the fact that as human beings we all have multiple identities. If we take, for illustrative purposes, a hypothetical example of a black, disabled, transgender, elderly woman who routinely experiences prejudice-based hostility, what can we as academics, practitioners, students or whatever, claim to know about both the causes and impacts of that victimisation, or indeed any other of the possible combinations of identity? We might glean narrow insights from one branch of research or another, but the holistic picture is missing. For me, then, the various dynamics of multiple identities in relation to the lived experience of hate crime is an issue that we clearly need to know much more about.

Similarly, despite their research in this area, Perry and Alvi (2012) acknowledge that there is more to be done to properly establish and understand the *in terrorum* effect of hate crimes on the wider community. Likewise, in relation to the effects and impacts of hate speech, both on- and offline. Furthermore, whilst recent research (such as the British Crime Survey that we discussed in chapter four) has helped to strengthen the long-held assumption that hate crimes 'hurt more', greater exploration of the manner in which this particular dynamic unfolds in relation to the experience of victimisation within, between and across identities would be beneficial. Indeed, anything that increases our knowledge and understanding in relation to the emerging themes and common assumptions that we identified in chapter nine would be most welcome.

The other side of the equation in terms of answering this question brings us to the complicated issue of perpetrators. Whilst the evidence presented in this book, itself by no means exhaustive of the research in this area, suggests that we have progressed somewhat from Bowling's (1999) 'devilish effigies', there is clearly much more that we need to know about offenders (and their offending behaviour, which we shall consider further when we ask the *'why?'* question, below).

Iganski and Smith's (2011) examination of offender rehabilitation programmes in different parts of the world (that we discussed in chapter eight) identified hate perpetrators predominantly (but obviously not exclusively) as young, male, white, socio-economically marginalised, with a tendency towards violence and aggression, and generalist rather than specialist in their offending. But they rightly acknowledge that data on offenders in different countries is severely limited and inconsistent, and although the not uncommon use of convicted offenders (or those otherwise coming to the attention of the authorities) as a research sample allows for a degree of certainty about their misdemeanours, the activities of the agencies of different criminal justice systems may well play a part in shaping the characteristics of the offender sample. So, whilst the paucity in official data on offenders severely hinders our ability to identify who offenders might be (illustrated perhaps by the difficulties one might have in securing a research sample of offenders in countries where none officially exist, or where only certain motivations are recognised, or by the few numbers actually convicted in countries where prosecutions are relatively more common), searching for answers remains troublesome. As Perry (2010) suggests, we need to be creative in the ways in which we sample offenders if we are to find out more about them.

Beyond trying to identify the basic characteristics of perpetrators, the question of who is involved in this type of offending is also hindered by other gaps in knowledge, many of which were lamented well over a decade ago by Bowling (1999, see chapter six). Whilst *some* progress has been made in respect of issues such as the relationship that offenders have with their victims (see Mason, 2005; Iganski, 2008; Walters and Hoyle, 2012; and in particular the various literature concerning disability hate crime, for example), the social milieux in which prejudice and hostility are fostered (see the various literature discussed in chapters five, six and ten, for example), the extent to which offenders are 'ordinary' or 'extremists' (Iganski, 2008) and the role of gender and masculinities (Blee, 2004; Dobratz and Shanks-Meile, 2004; Treadwell and Garland, 2011, for example), our ability to now refute Bowling's claim that criminologists operate with scant evidence about what is going on in the lives of offenders remains more limited than we would ideally like.

Why is it occurring?

I was tempted to suggest that this represents the $64,000 question. However, given Allport's contention that 'it required years of labor and billions of dollars to gain the secret of the atom. It will take a still greater investment to gain the secrets of man's irrational nature' (1954: xi), to do so would be to significantly undervalue both the question and the answer(s).

In line with Allport's suggestion, whilst we may now be able to say a *little* more about *who* offenders are in terms of identifying some of their basic characteristics, the search for a satisfactory answer to the *why?* question remains elusive. As we saw in chapters five and six, the different branches of the social sciences offer numerous possible explanations, but none that provide us with concrete and holistic answers as to why hate crime occurs.

Our failure to fully explain the causes of hate crime is a collective product of our failure, thus far, to provide comprehensive answers to each of the other questions posed. But perhaps 'failure' is the wrong word to use here. We should not forget that ours is a relatively new area of scholarly interest, and although there is *relatively* little by way of *applied* research on, or *theorising* about, hate crime offenders and the factors that cause such offending to occur, the evidence presented in chapter six in particular suggests a degree of progress in both of these endeavours.

Furthermore, the apparent increasing engagement of the social sciences with the problem of hate crime, both in those branches that you would perhaps expect to have an interest (such as psychology and criminology) and encouragingly those that are arguably less obviously related (such as geography and cultural studies) have produced what Iganski (2008) and Chakraborti (2010) have both described as a 'welcome surge' in scholarly interest in our subject area. This 'welcome surge' is producing a 'welcome flurry' of research and other scholarly activity, bringing with it 'an astounding diversity of methodologies ... to more fully document and comprehend the problem' (Perry, 2010: 19). The trick will be to make sure that this is accessible, available and meaningful for policymakers and practitioners. As such, in my view there are reasons to be optimistic about edging closer to finding the answers to the *why?* question, and indeed answers to the other questions posed here.

What should we do to make the problem better?

Throughout this book, and particularly in chapters seven and eight, we have considered different avenues for responding to, and challenging, hate and hate crime. In doing so, we discussed the many and varied complexities of these undertakings and, notwithstanding pockets of promising work, lamented the resulting absence of any concrete solutions. Once again, our ability to satisfactorily answer this question is fundamentally constrained by our limited ability to provide answers for each of the questions that have gone before. Indeed, as Chakraborti (2010) points out, because of the complexity and ambiguity of hate crime, the deeper we delve to find solutions, the more we are likely to encounter more problems and questions. Nevertheless, he suggests that this quest should act as a unifying theme in scholarship, and indeed it should, because there are many questions that require further investigation if we are to effectively respond to the hate crime problem.

In my view, in addition to finding answers to the questions we have already asked, these include (but certainly aren't limited to): how might we contribute to the creation of an environment where hate cannot flourish? How else might we prevent hate and hate crime? If we can't prevent it, who should be responsible for responding to it? Should legal and criminal justice responses be to the fore? How can we improve these responses? Should we be more or less punitive? Would other non-punitive interventions be preferable? What form should any such alternatives take? How can we be sure that they will have the desired outcomes? How can we avoid unintended or adverse outcomes? Which existing anti-hate strategies, interventions and initiatives work, why do they work and under what conditions? Are they transferable across different 'hates' and different places? Which strategies don't or won't work and why? How can we improve the evidence base upon which to inform existing responses? How can we improve the evidence base upon which to develop new responses? What is the role of education? How can we better support and empower victims and communities? What should the role of government and other 'agents of social change' be? How can we overcome the limitations of viewing hate crime in silos to produce a more holistic response? Is a holistic response even possible or desirable? How might we go about bridging the gap between scholarship, policy and practice so as to provide theoretically and empirically informed responses? Feel free to add to the list as you see fit.

Final thoughts

In grappling with each of these questions, throughout this book we have alluded to what some of the answers might be, and have made suggestions about where some of the other answers might be hiding, but there clearly remain far too many gaps in our knowledge for us to speak with absolute confidence about what works in responding to hate crime. However, despite our inability to fully answer each of the seven questions posed here, and the considerable implications of not being in a position to do so, I wholeheartedly share Barbara Perry's (2010) view that this should not be cause for despair. Rather, as she encouragingly suggests, that there is considerable ground still to cover should serve as an inspiration to those of us working in the field of hate crime, in whatever capacity we are doing so.

That said, having read what I have written here you may well have instead arrived at the conclusion that this subject area is just too complex and that we are deluding ourselves if we think that we will eventually be able to satisfactorily address all of these inherent complexities and provide answers that will yield worthwhile outcomes. As we saw in chapter nine, there are plenty of people who do think in these terms. I too am happy to confess that in moments of exasperation those thoughts have crossed my mind, and who knows, maybe that will ultimately prove to be the case, although it won't be for the want of trying.

However, during these moments I am particularly drawn to Lord Laming's (2003) public inquiry into the failure of statutory agencies in West London to prevent the murder of 8-year-old Victoria Climbié in 2000. In seeking to learn the lessons from Victoria's death for responding to, and preventing, future incidents of this kind, Lord Laming concluded by stating that 'I am convinced that the answer lies in doing relatively straightforward things well' (2003: 13). Whether we are academics, policy/lawmakers, practitioners, students or just simply have an interest in this subject, when we get caught up in the vast complexities of hate crime, maybe there is a lesson in this for us all. Ultimately, though, whatever way we choose to look at it, if we return to the quote from T. S. Eliot at the very start of this book, on the evidence presented throughout these pages we have clearly not reached the end of our exploration. Not by a long way.

References

Abrams, D. (2010) *Processes of Prejudice: Theory, Evidence and Intervention.* Manchester: EHRC.

Ackerman, N. W. and Jahoda, M. (1950) *Anti-Semitism and Emotional Disorder.* New York: Harper.

Ackroyd, P. (2000) *London: A Biography.* London: Vintage

ACPO (1985) *Guiding Principles Concerning Racial Attacks.* London: ACPO.

ACPO (2000) *ACPO Guide to Identifying and Combating Hate Crime.* London: ACPO.

ACPO (2011) *Total of Recorded Hate Crime from Regional Forces in England, Wales and Northern Ireland during the Calendar Year 2010.* London: ACPO.

ACPO (2013a) *True Vision.* http://www.report-it.org.uk/reporting_internet_hate_ crime.

ACPO (2013b) *Hate Crime Manual and Tactical Guidance.* London: ACPO.

Action Aid (2009) *Hate Crimes: The Rise of 'Corrective' Rape in South Africa.* London: Action Aid.

ADL (2008) *Cyberbullying: Understanding and Addressing Online Cruelty.* New York: ADL.

ADL (2011) *Audit of Anti-Semitic Incidents.* Available from http://www.adl.org/ main_Anti_Semitism_Domestic/2010_Audit

ADL (2012a) *Global Anti-Semitism: Selected Incidents around the World in 2012.* Accessed 28 October 2012 from http://www.adl.org/Anti_semitism/anti-semitism_ global_incidents_2012.asp.

ADL (2012b) *ADL Reacts to Release of 2011 FBI Hate Crime Report.* http://blog. adl.org/civil-rights/2011-fbi-hate-crime-report

ADL (2012c) *ADL Welcomes Decline in 2011 FBI Hate Crime Statistics; calls for more progress in training and response.* Accessed 12 December 2012 from http:// www.adl.org/PresRele/HatCr_51/6450_51.htm.

Agnew, R. (1992) Foundation for a general strain theory of crime and delinquency. *Criminology*, 30: 47.

Ajegbo, K., Kiwan, D., and Sharma,S. (2007) *Curriculum Review: Diversity and Citizenship.* London: DfES.

Allport, G. W. (1954) *The Nature of Prejudice.* Massachusetts: Addison-Wesley Publishing Co.

Anti-Violence Project (2007) *National Hate Violence Report.* New York: AVP.

Appleby, R. S. (2012) Religious violence: the strong, the weak, and the pathological. *Practical Matters*, 5: 1–25.

Arnold, T. W. (1935) *The Symbols of Government*. New York: Harcourt Brace and World.

Ashforth, B. E. and Mael, F. (1989) Social identity theory and the organization. *Academy of Management Review*, 14 (1): 20–39.

Association of London Authorities (1993) *Racial Abuse: An Everyday Experience for Some Londoners*. Submission by the Association of London Authorities to the House of Commons Home Affairs Committee Inquiry into Racially-Motivated Attacks and Harassment.

Barnes, A. and Ephross, P. H. (1994, May). The impact of hate violence on victims: Emotional and behavioral responses to attacks. *Social Work*, 39 (3): 247–51.

Baron, R. A. and Byrne, D. (1994) *Social Psychology: Understanding Human Interaction* (7th edition). Massachusetts: Allyn and Bacon.

Barrientos, J., Silva, J., Catalan, S., Gomez, F. and Longueira, J. (2010) Discrimination and victimization: parade for lesbian, gay, bisexual, and transgender (LGBT) pride, in Chile. *J Homosex*. 57 (6): 760–75. doi: 10.1080/00918369.2010.485880.

BBC News (1999) *Liverpool Anger at Straw Jibe*. Retrieved on 11 December 2003 from: http://news.bbc.co.uk/1/hi/uk_politics/324855.stm

Beirich, H. and Potok, M. (2009) USA: hate groups, radical-right violence, on the rise. *Policing*, 3 (3): 255–63. DOI: 10.1093/police/pap020.

Bell, J. (2002) *Policing Hatred: Law Enforcement, Civil Rights and Hate Crime*. New York: New York University Press.

Berger, M. (1952) *Equality by Statute: Legal Controls over Group Discrimination*. New York: Columbia University Press.

Berrenberg, J. L., Finlay, K. A., Stephan, W. G., Stephan, C. (2002) Prejudice toward people with cancer or AIDS: applying the integrated threat model. *Journal of Applied Behavioral Research*, 7: 75–86. doi: 10.1111/j.1751-9861.2002.tb00078.x

Bigler, R. S. (1999) The use of multi-curricula and materials to counter racism in children. *Journal of Social Issues*. 55 (4): 687–705.

Bjorgo, T. (1993) Terrorist Violence against Immigrants and Refugees in Scandinavia: Patterns and Motives. In T. Bjorgo, and R. Witte (eds) *Racist Violence in Europe*. Basingstoke: Macmillan.

Blaine, B. (2008) *Understanding the Psychology of Diversity*. London: Sage.

Blazak, R. (2009) The prison hate machine. *Criminology and Public Policy*, 8 (3): 633–40.

Blazak, R. (2011) Isn't every crime a hate crime? The case for hate crime laws. *Sociology Compass*, 5 (4): 244–55.

Blee, K. (2004) Women and Organized Racism. In A. Ferber (ed) *Home Grown Racism*. New York: Routledge.

Bleich, E (2011) What is Islamophobia and how much is there? Theorizing and measuring an emerging comparative concept. *American Behavioral Scientist*, 55 (12): 1581–1600 doi: 10.1177/0002764211409397.

Bleich, E. (2007) Hate crime policy in Western Europe: responding to racist violence in Britain, Germany and France. *American Behavioral Scientist*, 51 (2): 149–65.

Bleich, E. (2011) The rise of hate speech and hate crime laws in liberal democracies. *Journal of Ethnic and Migration Studies*, 37 (6): 917–34. doi: 10.1080/1369183X.2011.576195.

Bobo, L. (1983) Group Conflict, Prejudice and the Paradox of Contemporary Racial Attitudes. In P. A. Katz and D. A. Taylor (eds) *Eliminating Racism*. New York: Plenum.

Boeckmann, R. J. and Turpin-Petrosino, C. (2002) Understanding the harm of hate crime. *Journal of Social Issues*, 58(2), 207–25.

Bolton, K., Jr. and Feagin, J, R. (2004) *Black in Blue: African-American Police Officers and Racism.* New York: Routledge.

Bowling, B. (1999) *Violent Racism: Victimization, Policing and Social Context.* New York: Oxford University Press.

Bowling, B. and Phillips, C. (2003) *Racism, Crime and Criminal Justice.* Harlow: Longman.

Bradley, R. (1998) *Public Expectations and Perceptions of Policing.* Police Research Series, Paper 96. London: Home Office.

Brennan, F. (2009) Legislating against Internet race hate. *Information and Communications Technology Law*, 19 (2): 123–53. doi: 10.1080/13600830902941076.

Brown, R. (1995) *Prejudice: Its Social Psychology.* Oxford: Blackwell.

Burney, E. and Rose, G. (2002) *Racist Offences: How is the Law Working?* Home Office Research Study 244. London: Home Office.

Byers, B., Crider, B. W. and Biggers, G. K. (1999) Bias crime motivation: a study of hate crime and offender neutralisation techniques used against the Amish. *Journal of Contemporary Criminal Justice*, 15(1): 78–96.

Caiani, M. and Parenti, L (2009) The dark side of the web: Italian right-wing extremist groups and the Internet. *South European Society and Politics*, 14 (3): 273–94. doi: 10.1080/13608740903342491.

Campbell, R. and Stoops, S. (2010) Treating violence against sex workers as a hate crime. *Research for Sex Work*, 12: 9–13.

Carney, K. M. (2001) Rape: the paradigmatic hate crime. *St. John's Law Review*, 75 (2): 315–55.

Cawson, P., Wattam, C., Brooker, S. and Kelly, G. (2000) *Child Maltreatment in the United Kingdom: A Study of the Prevalence of Child Abuse and Neglect.* London: NSPCC.

Cemlyn, S., Greenfields, M., Burnett, S., Matthews, Z. and Whitwell, C. (2009) *Inequalities Experienced by Gypsy and Traveller Communities: A Review.* Manchester: EHRC.

Chahal, K. and Julienne, L. (2000) *"We Can't All Be White!" Racist Victimisation in the UK.* York: York Publishing Services Ltd.

Chakraborti, N. (2010) (ed) *Hate Crime: Concepts, Policy, Future Directions.* Cullompton: Willan Publishing.

Chakraborti, N. and Garland, J. (eds) (2004) *Rural Racism.* Cullompton: Willan Publishing.

Chakraborti, N. and Garland, J. (2009) *Hate Crime: Impact, Causes, and Consequences*, London: Sage.

Chakraborti, N. and Garland, J. (2012) Reconceptualising hate crime victimization through the lens of vulnerability and 'difference', *Theoretical Criminology*, 16 (4): 499–514.

Chan, J. (1997) *Changing Police Culture: Policing in a Multicultural Society.* Cambridge: Cambridge University Press.

Chandler, C. R. and Tsai, Y.-M. (2001). Social factors influencing immigration attitudes: an analysis of data from the General Social Survey. *Social Science Journal*, 38: 177–88.

Chaplin, R., Flatley, J. and Smith, K. (eds) (2011) *Crime in England and Wales 2010/11: Findings from the British Crime Survey and Police Recorded Crime.* Home Office

Statistical Bulletin 10/11. London: Home Office. http://www.homeoffice.gov.uk/publications/science-research-statistics/research- statistics/crime-research/hosb1011/

Cohen, A. K. (1955) *Delinquent Boys: The Culture of the Gang*. New York: Free Press.

Cohen-Almagor, R. (2011) Fighting hate and bigotry on the Internet. *Policy and Internet*, 3: (3) Article 6. doi: 10.2202/1944-2866.1059.

ComRes (2012) *Scope Disability Survey*. Accessed 31 October 2012 from http://www.comres.co.uk/poll/712/scope-disability-survey.htm.

Cooper, C., Selwood, A. and Livingston, G. (2007) The prevalence of elder abuse and neglect: a systematic review. *Age and Ageing*, 37 (2): 151–60. doi: 10.1093/ageing/afm194.

Cotterrell, R. (1992) *The Sociology of Law* (2nd edition). London: Butterworths.

Council of Europe (2012a) *Making Human Tights for Roma a Reality: Promoting Social Integration and Respect for Human Rights*. http://hub.coe.int/web/coe-portal/what-we-do/human-rights/roma-and-travellers

Council of Europe (2012b) *Mapping Study on Projects against Hate Speech Online*. Strasbourg: CoE.

Council to Homeless Persons and PILCH Homeless Persons Clinic (2010) *Submission to the Review of Identity Motivated Hate Crime*. Collingwood: CHP/HPLC.

Craig, K. M. (2002) Examining hate-motivated aggression: a review of the social psychological literature on hate crimes as a distinct form of aggression. *Aggression and Violent Behaviour*, 7: 85–101.

Craig-Henderson, K. and Sloan, L. R. (2003) After the hate: helping psychologists help victims of racist hate crime. *Clinical Psychology: Science and Practice*, 10 (4): 481–90.

Crane, B. and Hall, N. (2009) Talking a different language? Racist incidents and differing perceptions of service provision. In N. Hall, J. Grieve and S.P. Savage (eds) *Policing and the Legacy of Lawrence*. Abingdon: Routledge.

Cronin, S. W., McDevitt, J., Farrell, A, and Nolan, J. J. (2007). Bias-crime reporting: organizational responses to ambiguity, uncertainty, and infrequency in eight police departments. *American Behavioral Scientist*, 51 (2): 213–31.

Crown Prosecution Service (2003) *Guidance on Prosecuting Cases of Racist and Religious Crime*. London: CPS.

Crown Prosecution Service (2012) *Hate Crimes and Crimes against Older People*. London: CPS.

CST (2012) *Antisemitic Incidents Report 2011*. London: CST.

Dick, S. (2008) *Homophobic Hate Crime: The Gay British Crime Survey*. London: Stonewall.

Disability Rights Commission and Capability Scotland (DRCCS) (2004) *Hate Crime against Disabled People in Scotland: A Survey Report*. Edinburgh: DRCCS.

Dixon, L. and Court, D. (2003) Developing good practice with racially motivated offenders. *Probation Journal*, 50 (2): 149–53.

Dixon, B. and Gadd, D. (2006) Getting the message? 'New' Labour and the criminalization of 'hate'. *Criminology and Criminal Justice* 6: 309. doi: 10.1177/1748895806065532.

Dobratz, B. and Shanks-Meile, S. (2004) The White Supremacist Movement: Worldviews on Gender, Feminism, Nature and Change. In A. Ferber (ed) *Home Grown Racism*. New York: Routledge.

Dror, Y. (1959) Law and social change. *Tulane Law Review*, 33: 787–802.

Durkheim, E. (1933, originally 1893) *The Division of Labour in Society*. Glencoe: Free Press.

Eatwell, R. (2000) The rebirth of the 'extreme right' in Western Europe? *Parliamentary Affairs*, 53: 407–25.

ECRI (2012a) *Europe's Governments Urged to Act as Economic Gloom Prompts Rise in Racism.*

ECRI (2012b) *Council of Europe Anti-Racism Commission to prepare report on the Russian Federation.* http://www.coe.int/t/dghl/monitoring/ecri/library/pressreleases/110-09_05_2012_RussianFederation_en.asp

EHRC (2009a) *Inequalities Experienced by Gypsy and Traveller Communities: A Review.* Manchester: EHRC.

EHRC (2009b) *Police and Racism: What Has Been Achieved 10 Years after the Stephen Lawrence Inquiry Report?* http://www.equalityhumanrights.com/uploaded_files/raceinbritain/policeandracism.pdf

EHRC (2011) *Hidden in Plain Sight: Inquiry into Disability Related Harassment.* Retrieved from EHRC website: http://www.equalityhumanrights.com/uploaded_files/disabilityfi/ehrc_hidden_in_plain_sight_3.pdf

EHRC (2012) *Hidden in Plain Sight: Inquiry into Disability-Related Harassment.* London: EHRC.

Ehrlich, E. (1936) *Fundamental Principles of the Sociology of Law.* New York: Arno Press.

Ehrlich, H. J., Larcom, B. E. K. and Purvis, R. D. (1994). *The Traumatic Effects of Ethnoviolence.* Towson, MD: Prejudice Institute, Center for the Applied Study of Ethnoviolence.

Erlich, H. J. (1992) The Ecology of Antigay Violence. In K. T. Berrill and G. M. Herek (eds) *Hate Crimes: Confronting Violence against Lesbians and Gay Men.* London: Sage.

European Commission (2011) *Directive of the European Parliament and of the Council Establishing Minimum Standards on the Rights, Support and Protection of Victims of Crime.* http://eur-lex.europa.eu/LexUriServ/LexUriServ.do?uri=CELEX:52011PC0275:EN:NOT

European Network Against Racism (2012) *After Immigrants, Greek Golden Dawn Targets Homosexuals and People with Disabilities.* http://www.enar-eu.org/Page.asp?docid=30779&langue=EN

European Union (2008) *Framework Decision on Combating Racism and Xenophobia.* http://europa.eu/legislation_summaries/justice_freedom_security/combating_discrimination/l33178_en.htm

Falk, A. and Zweimuller, J. (2005) *Unemployment and Right-Wing Extremist Crime.* IZA Discussion Paper, series no. 1540. Bonn: IZA.

FBI (2011). *Hate Crime Statistics 2010.* Accessed 11 July 2012 from http://www.fbi.gov/about-us/cjis/ucr/hate-crime/2010.

FBI (2012) *Hate Crime Statistics 2011.* Accessed 12 December 2012 from http://www.fbi.gov/about-us/cjis/ucr/hate-crime/2011.

Feder, J. (2012) *The Student Non-Discrimination Act: A Legal Analysis.* Washington, DC: Congressional Research Service.

Fekete, L. (2012) *Pedlars of Hate: The Violent Impact of the European Far Right.* London: Institute of Race Relations.

Felson, M. (2002) *Crime and Everyday Life* (3rd edition). Thousand Oaks, CA: Sage.

Fiske, S. T. (2000) Stereotyping, prejudice, and discrimination at the seam between the centuries: evolution, culture, mind and brain. *European Journal of Social Psychology*, 30: 299–322.

FRA (2013) EU LGBT Survey. European Union Agency for Fundamental Rights. http://fra.europa.eu/en/publication/2013/eu-lgbt-survey-european-union-lesbian-gay-bisexual-and-transgender-survey-results.

Frank, A. (1993). *The Diary of a Young Girl.* New York: Bantam Books. Originally published in Holland in 1947.

Franklin, K. (2002). Good intentions: the enforcement of hate crime penalty-enhancement statutes. *American Behavioral Scientist,* 46 (1): 154–72.

Frost, D. (2008) Islamophobia: examining causal links between the media and 'race hate' from 'below'. *International Journal of Sociology and Social Policy,* 28 (11): 564–78.

Garland, D. (2001) *The Culture of Control: Crime and Social Order in Late Modernity.* Oxford, Clarendon Press.

Garland, J. (2010) 'It's a Mosher just been banged for no reason': assessing targeted violence against Goths and the parameters of hate crime. *International Review of Victimology* 17 (2): 159–77. doi:10.1177/026975801001700202.

Garland, J. and Treadwell, J. (2010) *'No surrender to the Taliban':* football hooliganism, Islamophobia and the rise of the English Defence League. Papers from the British Society of Criminology Conference, 10: 19–35.

Garofalo, J. (1991) Racially Motivated Crime in New York City. In M. J. Lynch and E. B. Patterson (eds) *Race and Criminal Justice.* Albany: Harrow and Heston.

Gaylin, W. (2003) Hatred: the psychological descent into violence. New York: Public Affairs.

Gerstenfeld, P. B. (2004) *Hate Crimes: Causes, Controls and Controversies.* Thousand Oaks, CA: Sage.

Godfrey, B. and Lawrence, P. (2005) *Crime and Justice 1750–1950.* Abingdon: Routledge.

Goldman, D. (1990) Hate Crimes Matter of Turf, Researchers Say. *CHI. TRIB.* June 1 at C29.

Gordon, P. (1983) *White Law: Racism in the Police, Courts and Prisons.* London: Pluto.

Gordon, P. (1994) Racial Harassment and Violence. In E. A. Stanko (ed) *Perspectives on Violence.* London, Howard League.

Gottfredson, M., and Hirschi, T. (1990) *A General Theory of Crime.* Stanford, CA: Stanford University Press.

Grattet, R. (2009) The urban ecology of bias crime: a study of disorganized and defended neighborhoods. *Social Problems,* 5: 132–50.

Green, D. P., Glaser, J. and Rich, A. (1998a) From lynching to gay bashing: The elusive connection between economic conditions and hate crime. *Journal of Personality and Social Psychology,* 74: 82–92.

Green, D. P., Strolovitch, D. Z. and Wong, J. S. (1998b) Defended neighborhoods, integration, and racially motivated crime. *American Journal of Sociology* 104 (2): 372–403.

Green, D. P., McFalls, L. H. and Smith, J. K. (2003) Hate Crime: An Emergent Research Agenda. In Perry, B. (ed) *Hate and Bias Crime: A Reader.* New York: Routledge.

Grekov, I. (2013) *Will 'Promoting Homosexuality' Become a Crime in Russia?* New York: Human Rights First.

Grice, A. (2013) Voters 'brainwashed by Tory welfare myths', shows new poll. *The Independent,* 4 January.

Grimshaw, R. and Jefferson, T. (1987) *Interpreting Policework*. London: Allen and Unwin.

Grossman, J. B. and Grossman, M. H. (eds) (1971) *Law and Change in Modern America*. California: Goodyear.

Haberman, C. (1999) Finding flaws in the logic of bias laws. *New York Times*, 12 March.

Hall, N. (2005) *Hate Crime*. Cullompton, Willan Publishing.

Hall, N. (2009) 'Policing hate crime in London and New York City'. Unpublished PhD thesis: University of Portsmouth.

Hall, N. (2010) Law Enforcement and Hate Crime: Theoretical Perspectives on the Complexities of Policing Hatred. In N. Chakraborti (ed) *Hate Crime: Concepts, Policy, Future Directions*. Cullompton: Willan Publishing.

Hall, N. (2012a) Policing hate crime in London and New York City: reflections on the factors influencing effective law enforcement, service provision and public trust and confidence. *International Review of Victimology*, 18 (1): 73–87. doi: 10.1177/0269758011422477.

Hall, N. (2012b) *Hate Crime in the UK: problems, challenges, policies and practices*. Paper presented to the Hate Crime Symposium, Cardiff University.

Hall, N. (2014) The Adventures of an Accidental Academic in Policy-Land. In N. Chakraborti and J. Garland (eds) *Responding to Hate Crime: The Case for Connecting Policy and Research*. Bristol: Policy Press.

Hall, N. and Hayden, C. (2007) Is 'hate crime' a relevant and useful way of conceptualising some forms of school bullying? *International Journal on Violence and Schools*, 3: 3–24.

Hall, N., Grieve, J. and Savage, S. P. (eds) (2009) *Policing and the Legacy of Lawrence*. Abingdon: Routledge.

Hall, N., Corb, A., Giannasi, P. and Grieve, J. (eds) (2014, forthcoming) *The International Handbook of Hate Crime*. Abingdon: Routledge.

Hamilton, D. L., and Gifford, R. K. (1976) Illusory correlation in interpersonal perception: a cognitive basis of stereotypic judgments. *Journal of Experimental Social Psychology*, 12: 392–407.

Harris, C., Rowbotham, J and Stevenson, K. (2009) Truth, law and hate in the virtual marketplace of ideas: perspectives on the regulation of Internet content. *Information & Communications Technology Law*. 18 (2): 155–84. doi: 10.1080/13600830902814943.

Hasan, M. (2012) Does Ahmadinejad really want to 'wipe Israel off the map'? *New Statesman*. 8 March.

Hawkins, N. (2014 forthcoming) Hate Crime in Sport. In N. Hall, A. Corb, P. Giannasi and J. Grieve (eds) *Routledge International Handbook on Hate Crime*. Abingdon: Routledge.

Heitmeyer, W. (1993) Hostility and Violence Towards Foreigners in Germany. In T. Bjorgo and R. Witte (eds) *Racist Violence in Europe*. London: Macmillan.

Herek, G. M. (2009) Hate crimes and stigma-related experiences among sexual minority adults in the United States: prevalence estimates from a national probability sample. *Journal of Interpersonal Violence*, 24 (1): 54–74. doi: 10.1177/0886260508316477.

Herek, G. M., Cogan, J. C. and Gillis, J. R. (2002) Victim Experiences in Hate Crimes Based on Sexual Orientation. *Journal of Social Issues*, 58 (2): 319–39.

Hibbert, C. (2003) *The Roots of Evil: A Social History of Crime and Punishment*. Stroud: Sutton Publishing Ltd.

HM Government (2012) *Challenge It, Report It, Stop It: The Government's Plan to Tackle Hate Crime.* London: HM Government.

Hogg, M. A. (2006) Social Identity Theory. In P. J. Burke (ed) *Contemporary Social Psychological Theories.* Stanford, CA: Stanford University Press.

Holdaway, S. (1996) *The Racialisation of British Policing.* Basingstoke: Macmillan.

Hollomotz, A. (2012) Disability and the Continuum of Violence. In A. Roulstone and H. Mason-Bish (eds) *Disability, Hate Crime and Violence.* Abingdon: Routledge.

Home Office (2002) *Statistics on Race and the Criminal Justice System: A Home Office Publication under Section 95 of the Criminal Justice Act 1991.* London: Home Office.

Hopkins-Burke, R. and Pollock, E. (2004) A tale of two anomies: some observations on the contribution of (sociological) criminological theory to explaining hate crime motivation. *Internet Journal of Criminology,* 1–54.

Hovland, C. and Sears, R. R. (1940) Minor studies in aggression VI: correlation of lynchings with economic indicators. *Journal of Psychology,* 9: 301–10.

Hull, H. G. (2009) The not-so-golden years: why hate crime legislation is failing a vulnerable aging population. *Mich. St. L. Rev, Summer:* 387–416.

Human Rights First (2008) *Violence against Roma: 2008 Hate Crime Survey.* New York: HRF.

Human Rights First (2010) *Hate Crimes and Human Rights.* New York: HRF.

Human Rights Watch (1997) *Racist Violence in the United Kingdom.* London: Human Rights Watch/Helsinki.

Human Rights Watch (2002) *We Are Not the Enemy: Hate Crimes against Arabs, Muslims, and Those Perceived to Be Arab or Muslim after September 11th.* New York: HRW.

Human Rights Watch (2012) *World Report.* http://www.hrw.org/world-report-2012

Human Rights Watch (2013) *World Report.* http://www.hrw.org/world-report-2013

Hunt, S. (2005) *Religion and Everyday Life.* London: Routledge.

Hunte, J. (1966) *Nigger Hunting in England?* London: West Indian Standing Conference.

Iganski, P. (1999a) Legislating against hate: outlawing racism and anti-semitism in Britain. *Critical Social Policy,* 19(1): 129–41.

Iganski, P. (1999b) Why make hate a crime? *Critical Social Policy,* 19(3): 386–95.

Iganski, P. (2001) Hate crimes hurt more. *American Behavioural Scientist,* 45 (4): 626–38

Iganski, P. (2008) Hate Crime and the City. Bristol: Policy Press.

Iganski, P., Kielinger, V. and Paterson, S. (2005) *Hate Crimes Against London's Jews: An Analysis of Incidents Recorded by the Metropolitan Police Service 2001–2004.* London: Institute for Jewish Policy Research.

Iganski, P. and Smith, D. (2011) *Rehabilitation of hate crime offenders: research report.* Available from http://www.equalityhumanrights.com/scotland/research-in-scotland/the-rehabilitation-of-hate-crime-offenders-an-international-study/

Institute for Homeland Security Solutions (2009) *The Impact of the Internet on Deviant Behavior and Deviant Communities.* http://sites.duke.edu/ihss/files/2011/12/IRW-Literature-Reviews-Deviance-and-the-Internet.pdf

Jacobs, J. (1993) Should hate be a crime? *Public Interest,* 113: 3–14 Fall.

Jacobs, J. B. and Potter, K. (1998) *Hate Crimes: Criminal Law and Identity Politics.* New York: Oxford University Press.

Jarman, (2005) *No Longer a Problem? Sectarian Violence in Northern Ireland.* Belfast: Institute for Conflict Research.

Jenkins, G., Asif, Z. and Bennett, G. (2000) *Listening Is Not Enough: An Analysis of Calls to Elder Abuse Response – Action on Elder Abuse's National Helpline.* London: Action on Elder Abuse.

John, G. (2003). *Race for Justice: A Review of CPS Decision Making for Possible Racial Bias at Each Stage of the Prosecution Process.* London: CPS.

Johnson, M. (2003) *Street Justice: A History of Police Violence in New York City.* Boston: Beacon Press.

Kahan, D. M. (2001) Two liberal fallacies in the hate crimes debate. *Law and Philosophy*, 20: 175–93.

Kahn-Freund, O. (1969) 'Industrial relations and the law: retrospect and prospect', *British Journal of Industrial Relations*, 7: 301–16.

Keats Citron, D. and Norton, H. L. (2011) Intermediaries and hate speech: fostering digital citizenship for our information age. *Boston University Law Review*, 91: 1435.

Kundnani, A, (2001) In a foreign land: the new popular racism. *Race and Class*, 43 (2): 41–60.

Lambert, R. and Githens-Mazer (2011) *Islamophobia and Anti-Muslim Hate Crime: UK Case Sudies 2010.* London: European Muslim Research Centre and University of Exeter.

Laming, H. (2003) *The Victoria Climbié Inquiry.* London: The Stationery Office.

Landau, S. (1981) Juveniles and the police. *British Journal of Criminology*, 21(1): 27–46.

Langton, L. and Planty, M. (2011) *Hate Crime: 2003–2009 – Special Report.* Washington, DC: US Department of Justice.

Le Grand, J. (2006) Academia, policy and politics. *Health Economics, Policy and Law.* 1: 319–22. doi: 10.1017/S1744133106004014.

Lester, A. and Bindman, G. (1972) *Race and Law.* Harmondsworth: Penguin.

Levin, B. (1999) Hate crimes: worse by definition. *Journal of Contemporary Criminal Justice*, 15(1): 6–21.

Levin, B. (2002) From slavery to hate crime laws: the emergence of race and status-based protection in American criminal law. *Journal of Social Issues*, 58(2): 227–45.

Levin, J. and McDevitt, J. (1993) *Hate Crimes: The Rising Tide of Bigotry and Bloodshed.* New York: Plenum Press.

Levin, J. and McDevitt, J. (2002) *Hate Crimes Revisited: America's War on Those Who Are Different.* Colorado: Westview Press.

Levin, J. and Rabrenovic, G. (2009) Hate as Cultural Justification for Violence. In B. Perry (ed) *Hate Crimes* (vol. 1). Westport: Praeger.

Lindsay, T. and Danner, S. (2008) Accepting the unacceptable: the concept of acceptance in work with the perpetrators of hate crime. *European Journal of Social Work*, 11 (1): 43–56. doi: 10.1080/13691450701356655.

Lipsky, M. (1980) *Street-level Bureaucracy.* New York: Russell Sage Foundation.

Lyons, C. J. (2007) Community (dis)organization and racially motivated crime. *American Journal of Sociology*, 113: 815–63.

McDevitt, J., Balboni, J., Garcia, L. and Gu, J. (2001) Consequences for victims: a comparison of bias-and non-bias-motivated assaults. *American Behavioral Scientist*, 45(4): 697–713.

McDevitt, J., Levin, J. and Bennett, S. (2002) Hate crime offenders: an expanded typology. *Journal of Social Issues.* 58 (2): 303–17.

McDevitt, J., Levin, J., Nolan, J. and Bennett, S. (2010) Hate Crime Offenders. In N. Chakraborti (ed) *Hate Crime: Concepts, Policy, Future Directions.* Abingdon: Routledge.

McGhee, D. (2005) *Intolerant Britain? Hate, Citizenship and Difference.* Maidenhead: Open University Press.

McGhee, D. (2010) From hate to 'prevent': community safety and counter-terrorism. In N. Chakraborti (ed) *Hate Crime: Concepts, Policy, Future Directions.* Abingdon: Routledge.

McLaughlin, E. (1999) The search for truth and justice. *Criminal Justice Matters*, 35: 13–15.

McLaughlin, E. (2002) Rocks and hard places: the politics of hate crimes. *Theoretical Criminology*, 6 (4): 493–8.

MacNamara, B. S. (2003) New York's Hate Crime Act of 2000: problematic and redundant legislation aimed at subjective motivation. *Albany Law Review*, 66: 519–45.

McNamee, L. G., Peterson, B. L. and Peña, J. (2010) A call to educate, participate, invoke and indict: understanding the communication of online hate groups, *Communication Monographs*, 77: 2, 257–80. doi: 10.1080/03637751003758227.

Macpherson, W. (1999). *The Stephen Lawrence Inquiry.* Cm 4262. London: The Stationery Office.

Mason, G. (2005) Hate crime and the image of the stranger. *British Journal of Criminology*, 45 (6): 837–59.

Mason, G. (2012) Naming the 'R' word in racial victimisation: violence against Indian students in Australia. *International Review of Victimology*, 18 (1): 39–58.

Mason-Bish, H. (2010) Future Challenges for Hate Crime Policy: Lessons from the Past. In N. Chakraborti (ed.) *Hate Crime: Concepts, Policy, Future Directions.* Cullompton: Willan Publishing.

Matza, D. (1964) *Delinquency and Drift.* New York: John Wiley.

Meddaugh, P. M. and Kay, J. (2009) Hate speech or 'reasonable racism?' The Other in Stormfront. *Journal of Mass Media Ethics*, 24 (4): 251–68.

Mencap (2007) *Bullying Wrecks Lives: The Experiences of Children and Young People with a Learning Disability.* London: Mencap.

Merton, R. K. (1938) Social structure and anomie. *American Sociological Review*, 3 (October): 672–82.

Merton, R. (1949) *Social Theory and Social Structure.* New York: Free Press.

Migration Watch UK (2012) http://www.migrationwatchuk.org.

Mill, J. S. (1859, 1991) *On Liberty and Other Essays.* Oxford: Oxford University Press.

Miller, A. R. (2003) Civil rights and hate crimes legislation: two important asymmetries. *Journal of Social Philosophy*, 34 (3): 437–43.

Mind (2007) *Another Assault.* London: Mencap.

Mirga, A. (2009) The extreme right and Roma and Sinti in Europe: a new phase in the use of hate speech and violence? *Roma Rights Journal*, (1): 5–9.

Moscow Bureau for Human Rights (2010) http://antirasizm.ru

Moscow Protestant Chaplaincy Task Force on Racial Violence (2011) *Quarterly Statistical Reports.* Moscow: MPCTFRV.

Muir, H. (2012) Coalition responds to Doreen Lawrence over race equality. *The Guardian*, 23 December. http://www.guardian.co.uk/uk/2012/dec/23/coalition-respond-doreen-lawrence-equality

National Archives (n.d) *Elizabeth I.* http://www.nationalarchives.gov.uk/pathways/blackhistory/early_times/elizabeth.htm

National Coalition for the Homeless (2012) *Hate Crimes against the Homeless: The Brutality of Violence Unveiled.* Washington, DC: NCH.

Newburn, T. and Rock, P. (2005) *Living in Fear: Violence and Victimization in the Lives of Single Homeless People.* London: Crisis.

Norris, D. (2008) Are laws proscribing incitement to religious hatred compatible with freedom of speech? *UCL Human Rights Review*, 1 (1): 102–17.

O'Brian, N. and Moules, T. (2010) *The Impact of Cyber-bullying on Young People's Mental Health.* London: National Children's Bureau.

Office for National Statistics (2011) *Mid-year population estimates: England and Wales.* Accessed 11 July 2012 from http://www.ons.gov.uk/ons/rel/pop-estimate/population-estimates-for-uk – england-and-wales – scotland-and-northern-ireland/mid-2010-population-estimates/rtf – mid-2010-population-estimates-poster.pdf.

Office for National Statistics (2012) *Census 2011.* http://www.ons.gov.uk/ons/guide-method/census/2011/index.html

OSCE (2011) *Hate Crimes in the OSCE Region: Incidents and Responses.* Annual Report for 2010. Warsaw: OSCE.

OSCE (2012) *Hate Crimes in the OSCE Region: Incidents and Responses.* Annual Report for 2011. Warsaw: OSCE.

Paluck, E. L. and Green, D (2009) Prejudice reduction: what works? A review and assessment of research and practice. *Annual Review of Psychology*, 60: 339–67. doi: 10.1146/annurev.psych.60.110707.163607.

Perry, B. (2001) *In the Name of Hate: Understanding Hate Crimes.* New York: Routledge.

Perry, B. (2003) Anti-Muslim retaliatory violence following the 9/11 terrorist attacks. In B. Perry (ed.) *Hate and Bias Crime: A Reader.* London: Routledge, pp. 183–202.

Perry, B. (2009) The Sociology of Hate: Theoretical Approaches. In B. Perry (ed) *Hate Crimes* (vol. 1). Westport: Praeger.

Perry, B. (2010) The More Things Change … post 9/11 Trends in Hate Crime Scholarship. In N. Chakraborti (ed) *Hate Crime: Concepts, Policy, Future Directions.* Abingdon: Routledge.

Perry, B. and Alvi, S. (2012) We are all vulnerable: the *in terrorem* effects of hate crimes. *International Review of Victimology*, 18: 57–71. doi: 10.1177/0269758011422475

Petrosino, C. (1999) Connecting the past to the future: hate crime in America. *Journal of Contemporary Criminal Justice*, 5 (1): 22–47.

Pettigrew, T. F. (1969) The ultimate attribution error: extending Allport's cognitive analysis of prejudice. *Personality and Social Psychology Bulletin*, 5: 461–76.

Pettigrew, T. F. (1998) Reactions toward the new minorities of Western Europe. *Annu. Rev. Sociol*, 24: 77–103.

Phillips, M. (2005) Stamp on the camps: Sun campaign to stop flood of Gypsies. *The Sun*, March, pp. 4–5.

Poirier, M. R. (2010) *The Multiscalar Geography of Hate Crimes.* Seton Hall Public Law Research Paper No. 1654350.

Pound, R. (1917) The limits of effective legal action. *International Journal of Legal Ethics*, 27: 150–67.

PSNI (2012) *Trends in Hate Motivated Incidents and Crimes Recorded by the Police in Northern Ireland 2004/5 to 2011/12.* Belfast: NI Statistics and Research Agency/PSNI.

Public Law (1990) *Hate Crime Statistics Act of 1990.* 104 Stat. 140. London: HMSO.

Quarmby, K. (2008) *Getting Away with Murder: Disabled People's Experiences of Hate Crime in the UK.* London: Scope.

Quarmby, K. (2012) Media Reporting and Disability Hate Crime. In A. Roulestone and H. Mason-Bish (eds) *Disability, Hate Crime and Violence*. Abingdon: Routledge.

Quinney, R. (1970) *The Social Reality of Crime*. Boston: Little, Brown and Co.

Reiner, R. (1992) *The Politics of the Police* (2nd edition). Hemel Hempstead: Harvester Wheatsheaf.

Reiner, R. (1997) Policing and the Police. In Maguire, M., Morgan, R., and Reiner, R. (eds) *The Oxford Handbook of Criminology* (2nd edition). New York: Oxford University Press.

Renton, D. (2003) Examining the success of the British National Party, 1999–2003. *Race and Class*, 45 (2): 75–85.

Riley-Smith, B. (2012) Disability hate crime: is 'benefit scrounger' abuse to blame? *The Guardian*, 14 August.

Risen, J. L., Gilovich, T., and Dunning, D. (2007) One-shot illusory correlations and stereotype formation. *Personality and Social Psychology Bulletin*, 33 (11): 1492–1502.

Rollock, N. (2009) *The Stephen Lawrence Inquiry 10 Years On: An Analysis of the Literature*. http://www.runnymedetrust.org/uploads/publications/pdfs/Stephen LawrenceInquiryReport-2009.pdf

Roxburgh, A. (2002) *Preachers of Hate: The Rise of the Far Right*. London: Gibson Square Books.

Sandholtz, N., Langton, L. and Planty, M. (2013) *Hate Crime Victimization 2003–2011*. Washington, DC, US Department of Justice Bureau of Justice Statistics.

Scarman, L. (1981) *The Brixton Disorders: 10–12 April 1981: Report of an inquiry: Presented to Parliament by the Secretary of State for the Home Department, November*. London: HMSO.

Sentencing Guidelines Council (2004) *Overarching Principles: Seriousness*. London: Sentencing Guidelines Secretariat.

Sheffield, C. (1995) Hate Violence. In P. Rothenberg (ed) *Race, Class and Gender in the United States*. New York: St. Martin's Press.

Shenk, A. H. (2001) Victim–offender mediation: the road to repairing hate crime injustice. *Ohio State Journal on Dispute Resolution*, 17: 185–217.

Sherif, M. (1966). *In Common Predicament: Social Psychology of Intergroup Conflict and Cooperation*. New York: Houghton Mifflin.

Sherif, M., and Sherif, C. W. (1953). *Groups in Harmony and Tension: An Integration of Studies on Inter-group Relations*. New York: Harper.

Sibbitt, R. (1997) *The Perpetrators of Racial Harassment and Racial Violence*. Home Office Research Study No. 176. London: Home Office.

Skolnick, J. (1966) *Justice Without Trial*. New York: Wiley.

Simon Weisenthal Center (2013) *Digital Terror and Hate Report*. Los Angeles: SWC.

Smith, K., Lader, D., Hoare, J. and Lau, I. (2012) *Hate Crime, Cyber Security and the Experience of Crime among Children: Findings from the 2010/11 British Crime Survey*. London: Home Office.

South African Human Rights Commission (2008) *Report of the Public Hearing on School-based Violence*. Braamfontein, SAHRC.

SOVA Center for Information and Analysis (2012) *Between Manezhnaya and Bolotnaya: Xenophobia and Radical Nationalism in Russia, and Efforts to Counteract Them in 2011*. http://www.sova-center.ru/en/xenophobia/reports-analyses/2012/04/d24088/

Stacey, M., Carbone-Lopez, K. and Rosenfeld, R. (2011) Demographic change and ethnically motivated crime: the impact of immigration on anti-Hispanic hate crime in the United States. *Journal of Contemporary Criminal Justice*, 27 (3): 278–98. doi: 10.1177/1043986211412560.

Stangor, C. (ed.) (2000) *Stereotypes and Prejudice*. Philadelphia: Psychology Press.

Steinfeldt, J. A., Foltz, B. D., Kaladow, J. K., Carlson, T. N., Pagano, L. A., Benton, E. and Steinfeldt, M. C. (2010) Racism in the Electronic Age: Role of Online Forums in Expressing Racial Attitudes about American Indians. *Cultural Diversity and Ethnic Minority Psychology*. 16 (3): 362–71. doi: 10.1037/a0018692.

Stephan, W. G. and Stephan, C. (1996) Predicting prejudice. *International Journal of Intercultural Relations*, 20: 1–12.

Stephan, W. G., Ybarra, O., Martnez, C. M., Schwarzwald, J. and Tur-Kaspa, M. (1998) Prejudice toward immigrants to Spain and Israel: an integrated threat theory analysis. *Journal of Cross-Cultural Psychology*, 29(4): 559–76.

Stern, K. (2005) *Hate Matters: The Need for an Interdisciplinary Field of Hate Studies*. New York: American Jewish Committee.

Stone, R. (2009) *Stephen Lawrence Review – An Independent Commentary to Mark the 10th Anniversary of the Stephen Lawrence Inquiry*. http://www.stoneashdown.org/images/stories/slr_report.pdf

Stonewall (2003) *Profiles of Prejudice*. London: Citizenship 21.

Stonewall (2004) *Understanding Prejudice: Attitudes Towards Minorities*. London: Citizenship 21.

Stonewall (2008) *Homophobic Hate Crime: The Gay British Crime Survey 2008*. London: Stonewall.

Stotzer, R. L. (2009) Violence against transgender people: a review of the United States data. *Aggression and Violent Behaviour*, 14: 170–9.

Streissguth, T. (2003) *Hate Crimes*. New York: Facts on File.

Sullivan, A. (1999) What's so bad about hate? The illogic and illiberalism behind hate crime laws. *New York Times Magazine*, 26 September.

Sutherland, E. H. (1939) *Principles of Criminology* (3rd edition). Philadelphia: J. P. Lippincott.

Sutherland, E. H. (1947) *Principles of Criminology* (4th edition). Philadelphia: J. P. Lippincott.

Sykes G, and Matza D, (1957) Techniques of neutralisation. *American Sociological Review*, 22: 664–70.

Tajfel, H. (1982) Social psychology and intergroup relations. *Annual Review of Psychology*, 33, 1–30.

Tajfel, H. and Turner, J. C. (1979) An Integrative Theory of Intergroup Conflict. In W. G. Austin and S. Worchel (eds) *The Social Psychology of Intergroup Relations*. Monterey: CA: Brooks/Cole, pp. 33–47.

Tajfel, H., and Turner, J. C. (1986) An Integrative Theory of Intergroup Conflict. In S. Worchel and W. Austin (eds) *The Psychology of Intergroup Relations*. Chicago: Nelson Hall.

Tausch, N., Hewstone, M. and Roy, R. (2008) The relationship between contact, status and prejudice: an integrated threat theory analysis of Hindu–Muslim relations in India. *Journal of Community and Applied Social Psychology*, 19 (2): 83–94. doi: 10.1002/casp.984.

Thomas, P. (2012) Hate Crime or Mate Crime? Disablist Hostility, Contempt and Ridicule. In A. Roulstone and H. Mason-Bish (eds) *Disability, Hate Crime and Violence*. Abingdon, Routledge.

Thompson, S. (2012) Freedom of expression and hatred of religion. *Ethnicitie.* 12 (2): 215–32. doi: 10.1177/1468796811431298.

Treadwell, J. and Garland, J. (2011) Masculinity, marginalization and violence: a case study of the English Defence League. *British Journal of Criminology*, 51: 621–34. doi: 10.1093/bjc/azr027.

Trotter, C. (2006) *Working with Involuntary Clients* (2nd edition). London: Sage.

Turner, L., Whittle, S. and Combs, R. (2009) *Transphobic Hate Crime in the European Union*. London: Press for Change.

Tyson, J., Giannasi, P. and Hall, N. (2013) Johnny come lately? The international and domestic policy context of disability hate crime. In R. Shah and P. Gianassi (eds) *Disability Hate Crime*. London: National Children's Bureau.

US Census (2010) *2010 Census Data*. http://www.census.gov/2010census/data/

United States Department of Justice (1997) *Hate Crime Data Collection Guidelines*. Washington, DC: USDOJ.

United States Department of Justice (1999) *Hate Crime Training: Core Curriculum for Patrol Officers, Detectives and Command Officers*. Washington: United States Department of Justice.

Velasco González, K., Verkuyten, M., Weesie, J., and Poppe, E. (2008). Prejudice towards Muslims in the Netherlands: testing integrated threat theory. *British Journal of Social Psychology*, 47(4): 667–8.

Victim Support (2006) *Crime and Prejudice*. London: Victim Support.

Vincent, F., Radford, K., Jarman, N., Martynowicz, A. and Rallings, M.-K. (2009) *Hate Crime against People with Disabilities: A Baseline Study of Experiences in Northern Ireland*. Belfast: Institute for Conflict Research.

Waddington, P. A. J. (1999) *Policing Citizens*. London: UCL Press.

Waller, J. (2002) *Becoming Evil: How Ordinary People Commit Genocide and Mass Killing*. New York: Oxford University Press.

Walters, M. A. (2011) A general theories of hate crime? Strain, doing difference and self control. *Critical Criminology*, (19): 313–30.

Walters, M. A. and Hoyle, C. (2010) Healing Harms and Engendering Tolerance: the Promise of Restorative Justice for Hate Crime. In N. Chakraborti (ed) *Hate Crime: Concepts, Policy, Future Directions*. Cullompton: Willan Publishing.

Walters, M. A. and Hoyle, C. (2012) Exploring the world of everyday hate victimization through community mediation. *International Review of Victimology*, 18: (1) 7–24. doi: 10.1177/0269758011422472.

Weisburd, S.B. and Levin, B. (1994) On the basis of sex: recognising gender-based bias crimes. *Stan. L. & Pol'y Rev*, 5, 21.

Weiss, J. (1993) Ethnoviolence's Impact upon and Response of Victims and the Community. In Kelly, R. (ed) *Bias Crime*. Chicago: Office of International Criminal Justice.

White, R. K. (1977) Misperception in the Arab–Israeli Conflict. *Journal of Social Issues*. 33: 190–221.

Wickham, J. (2005) The most sinister dvd in Britain. *Daily Star*, 7 March, p. 7.

Willis, C. F. (1983) *The Use, Effectiveness and Impact of Police Stop and Search Powers*. Home Office Research And Planning Unit Paper No. 15. London: Home Office.

Winkel, F. W. (1997) Hate crimes and antiracism campaigning: testing the psychological approach of portraying stereotypical information processing. *Issues in Criminological and Legal Psychology*, 29: 14–19.

Wolfe, L. and Copeland, L. (1994) Violence against Women as Bias-Motivated Hate Crime: Defining the Issues in the USA. In Davies, M. (ed) *Women and Violence.* London: Zed Books.

Zaslove, A. (2004) The dark side of European politics: unmasking the radical right. *European Integration,* 26(1): 61–81.

Index

Abrams, D. 95, 161–2
academia and policymaking 194–6
academic definitions 2–4
acceptance of offenders 152
Ackroyd, P. 29–31
ACPO *see* Association of Chief Police
    Officers (ACPO)
Act of Tolerance 1649 20
Action Aid 74
Action on Elder Abuse 75
action plan, UK government 144–5,
    159–60, 198
advocacy groups: anti-hate 56, 132, 136,
    141, 158, 185; English 92; LGBT 49,
    52, 136, 141; US 11, 52, 155, 174;
    women's 26
Afghanistan 53, 70, 108
Africa 53, 70
African Americans 14, 15, 23, 51, 89
age: awareness of social categories 90; of
    offenders 91–2, 102–3, 147; of victims
    59, 61, 62, 71, 72, 75–6
aggressive prejudice 93
Agnew, R. 111
Ahmadinejad, President 107
AIDS 90
Algeria 54
Allport, G.W.: on child prejudice 90;
    contact theory 148, 161; on
    educational programmes 155; five-
    point scale of prejudice 84, 180; on
    prejudice 81–6, 87, 94, 96, 116, 131,
    210, 217
alternative subcultures 76
Alvi, S. *see under* Perry, B.
American Indians 204
Americas 53 *see also* United States
Amish 114–15
anger management 152

Angola 53
anomie 110–11, 114, 187
antibias training 161
Anti-Defamation League (ADL) 28, 52,
    54, 69, 206
anti-Hispanic hate crime 62, 105–6
antilocution 84, 94
anti-Muslim: hate crime 47, 52, 69–70, 145;
    sentiment 90, 101–2, 106, 159, 201–2
anti-Semitism 29–30, 47, 52, 68–9, 108,
    145, 206
Anti-terrorism, Crime and Security Act
    2001 8, 36
Antiviolence Project (AVP) 52, 139
anti-Zionism 108
anxiety: intergroup 89, 90; of victims 60,
    61, 68, 71, 166, 188, 202, 206
Apartheid regime 171
apology in rehabilitation programmes
    152–3
appeal to higher loyalties 115
Appleby, R.S. 107
Argentina 53, 69
Aryans 109
Ashforth, B.E. and Mael, F. 87
Asia 53, 70
Asians in Britain 32
Association of Chief Police Officers
    (ACPO) 167, 187–8, 198, 204, 206,
    207; definition of hate crime 5–12, 17
Association of London Authorities 112
asylum seekers 46, 53, 66–7, 94, 95,
    112, 159
atheism 38
attrition rates 153
Australia 52, 69, 77, 151
Austria 43, 45, 69, 200
authoritarianism and social learning
    theory 90–2